GREATEST GAMES
DERBY COUNTY

GREATEST GAMES
DERBY COUNTY

GARETH DAVIS AND PHIL MATTHEWS

pitch

First published by Pitch Publishing, 2013

Pitch Publishing
A2 Yeoman Gate
Yeoman Way
Durrington
BN13 3QZ
www.pitchpublishing.co.uk

A CIP catalogue record is available for this book from the British Library.

ISBN 978-1-90917-869-4

Typesetting and origination by Pitch Publishing

Printed and bound by CPI Group (UK) Ltd, Croydon, CR0 4YY

Contents

Acknowledgements. 6
Introduction 7
Foreword by Roger Davies 9

1)   Derby County 4 Charlton Athletic 1 10
2)   Derby County 4 Huddersfield Town 3 14
3)   Derby County 3 Chelsea 1. 17
4)   Derby County 5 Bristol City 0 20
5)   Derby County 5 Tottenham Hotspur 0 24
6)   Derby County 4 Manchester United 4 28
7)   Derby County 4 Nottingham Forest 0. 32
8)   Derby County 1 Liverpool 0 36
9)   Derby County 3 Benfica 0 40
10) Derby County 5 Arsenal 0 44
11) Tottenham Hotspur 3 Derby County 5 48
12) Derby County 0 Juventus 0 52
13) Atletico Madrid 2 Derby County 2 56
14) Manchester City 1 Derby County 2 60
15) Derby County 5 Luton Town 0. 64
16) Derby County 4 Real Madrid 1. 68
17) Derby County 3 Leeds United 2 72
18) Derby County 4 Newcastle United 2 76
19) Ipswich Town 2 Derby County 6. .80
20) Derby County 12 Finn Harps 0. 84
21) Derby County 8 Tottenham Hotspur 2 87
22) Derby County 4 Nottingham Forest 1. 91
23) Derby County 3 Watford 2 94
24) Derby County 2 Nottingham Forest 0. 98
25) Derby County 1 Fulham 0 102
26) Derby County 2 Rotherham United 1. 106
27) Derby County 4 Plymouth Argyle 2. 110
28) Newcastle United 0 Derby County 0 114
29) Arsenal 1 Derby County 2. 117
30) Derby County 2 Nottingham Forest 1. 121
31) Derby County 3 Sheffield Wednesday 3 125
32) Derby County 1 Cremonese 3 129
33) Millwall 1 Derby County 3 133
34) Derby County 2 Crystal Palace 1. 137
35) Derby County 3 Leeds United 3 .141
36) Manchester United 2 Derby County 3 145
37) Derby County 3 Arsenal 0 149
38) Liverpool 1 Derby County 2 153
39) Bradford City 4 Derby County 4. 157
40) Derby 3 Reading 0. 161
41) Derby County 4 Nottingham Forest 2. 165
42) Derby County 3 Nottingham Forest 0. 169
43) Derby County 2 Southampton 3 .173
44) Derby County 1 West Bromwich Albion 0 178
45) Derby County 1 Newcastle United 0 183
46) Forest Green Rovers 3 Derby County 4. 186
47) Derby County 1 Manchester United 0 190
48) Nottingham Forest 2 Derby County 3. 195
49) Leeds United 1 Derby County 2 .199
50) Nottingham Forest 1 Derby County 2. 204

Acknowledgements

PULLING together a book like *Derby County Greatest Games* is not a straightforward process and it is far more than a two-man job. Gareth and Phil have consulted so many sources and publications in search of material, and spoken to so many individuals and organisations, that they all deserve credit for the part they have played.

The authors would like to thank Andy Ellis at the Derby County Collection (www. derbycountycollection.org.uk) for his help with sourcing match reports and pictures; the team at Pitch Publishing for allowing this book to happen; Roger Davies for writing the foreword; David Moore for dealing superbly with a late call for information; the Local Studies Library in Derby and its vast archive of old *Derby Telegraph* editions; the staff at the Thomas Leaper in Derby for many fine breakfasts served during planning meetings; and the supporters who have given their feedback on their own favourite matches and memories.

They have also acquired information from the official website of Derby County at www.dcfc.co.uk; the *Derby Telegraph* website at www.derbytelegraph.co.uk; www. soccerbase.com; *Derby County On This Day* (Pitch Publishing); *Derby County Miscellany* (Pitch Publishing); *Derby's Days The Rams' Rivalry With Nottingham Forest* (DB Publishing); *The Derby County Story* (Breedon Books); *Derby County A Complete Record* (Breedon Books); other editions of Pitch's *Greatest Games* series; archives of the *Mirror*; and old editions of *The Ram*, Derby County's match programme and its newspaper predecessor.

Dedication

THE authors would like to dedicate this book to their families, who have supported them through the writing process; to Derby County Football Club for all those great matches to write about; and to the fans who make writing a book like this worthwhile.

Introduction

ASK 50 Derby County supporters to give you their 50 greatest matches and you can almost guarantee that you will not get two identical lists. That is because the Rams have such a rich and storied history that their list of 'great' games does not stop at a mere half-century – it goes well beyond that, just as you would expect for a club that has been in existence since 1884 and was a founder member of the Football League just four years later.

The Rams had their moments in the early days of English football, helped by a squad that included giants of the game at that time such as John Goodall and Steve Bloomer, and their first real triumph arrived in 1946 when they won the first post-war FA Cup Final. There was something of a wilderness period following that success, although there were still some occasions to savour, then the club really took off following the arrival of Brian Clough and Peter Taylor in 1967.

Glory at home and progress in Europe followed and the success continued under Dave Mackay before, in true Derby County style, famine followed feast and by 1984 there very nearly was no club at all.

The renaissance began under Arthur Cox as he returned the Rams to the upper-reaches of the top flight but things soon unravelled, then the Jim Smith era came along and encompassed great names such as Igor Stimac and Stefano Eranio along with a move from the famous old Baseball Ground to the purpose-built Pride Park Stadium.

Life after Smith was tough but George Burley later returned some of the flair to Derby's performances with his shrewd signings and flowing football, then there was promotion to the Premier League in 2007.

What happened in the year immediately after that is best forgotten but even after relegation came the run to the League Cup semi-finals and the arrival of Nigel Clough in January 2009 has also coincided with some fantastic results, not least against Nottingham Forest.

So try picking out just 50 matches from all of the above – it really is not a straightforward task!

We found it tough to reduce our initial list down to just 50 and spent a lot of time debating it before we settled on the final selection, which did not ultimately come until May 2013 when we decided on the last match to include having previously agreed on the other 49.

The important thing for us to say at this stage is that we do not believe this is *the* definitive list of Derby County's greatest matches.

Something like that would be impossible to argue as it is such a subjective discussion point, and we know that not everyone will agree with our choices.

And neither have we organised the matches in order of greatness as, again, trying to do that would be pretty much impossible, so they are listed in date order.

There are some games and occasions that pick themselves but what we have tried to do with the rest is give a variety and include matches that are also significant for having fascinating stories surrounding them and not just being an exciting 90 minutes.

We have gone into the background of each encounter and taken them all in the wider context of seasons and social landscapes too, including plenty of pre-game build-up and post-match reaction comments from those involved.

With our research we have also uncovered some curious and off-beat stories that have formed part of the chapters, ranging from a player being offered the chance to move into boxing to recounting some iconic commentaries.

And we have also added personal memories on occasions too, including Phil becoming a mobile phone ringtone and Gareth passing out at Wembley.

The matches range from eye-catching victories at home and in Europe to ones that were less outstanding in terms of scoreline but vital in terms of the bigger picture; from matches on memorable occasions to those that stood out but were ultimately false dawns.

The matches start with the 1946 FA Cup Final and that is a deliberate choice because while there were some big matches in the early days, the scarcity of information about them is a hindrance and we also want the games in this book to trigger supporters' memories.

There cannot be many fans alive who were at Wembley in 1946, let alone who can remember matches prior to that, so we have focused on a time period that will reach the highest amount of the Rams' faithful.

It has been an enjoyable process to put everything together and we hope that you get just as much from reading this book as we did from writing it.

Gareth Davis and Phil Matthews, July 2013

Foreword

WHEN I joined Derby County in 1971, if someone had told me that I would go on to play in games that would be viewed as some of the greatest in the club's history I would not have believed them.

The club was definitely on the up when I signed for Brian Clough and Peter Taylor and I think everyone knew something special was about to happen – but nobody knew just how special the next few years would go on to be.

Those few years in the 1970s were a wonderful time to be around Derby County Football Club as we achieved some quite remarkable feats.

I knew about Derby's history when I signed and I knew that, apart from the FA Cup in 1946, the club was yet to win a major honour.

Brian and Peter were confident that they could, and would, change that, and they were proven right before Dave Mackay continued their success when he took over as manager.

I feel very privileged to have played my part during that period and it was an honour to line up alongside some genuinely top-class players.

The authors have reliably informed me that of the 50 games featured in this book, I appeared in 11 of them.

I find that an amazing figure to be honest and it is all down to being in the right place at the right time.

On the whole I have great memories of those particular matches and even the European Cup semi-final against Juventus, which didn't end well for me or the club, was still a brilliant occasion to be a part of.

But Derby County's history stretches well before and long after the glory days of the 1970s with some great names having lined up in some great matches.

I have seen the full list of the 50 games that Gareth and Phil have written about and there are many that immediately spring up in my mind the moment I look at the result.

It must have been a very difficult task to select just 50 and I am sure that fans will have their own thoughts on what other matches could have been included.

It is no secret that Derby County as a club has remained close to my heart not only because of my time as a player but my involvement in various capacities in the years since and I have been fortunate enough to have seen many of the other matches that make up this book.

Whenever us former players get together we spend a lot of time reminiscing about some of the great games we played in, and fans will often stop and ask me if I remember a fixture that was a particular favourite of theirs.

That just goes to show what Derby County means to the supporters and I am sure their memories will be triggered when they read through this book and look back at what this great club has achieved over the years.

Roger Davies
July 2013

v Charlton Athletic 4-1

(After extra time)
27 April 1946. Attendance: 98,215
Wembley Stadium. FA Cup Final

DERBY COUNTY:	CHARLTON ATHLETIC:
Woodley	Bartram
Nicholas	Phipps
Howe	Shreeve
Bullions	B Turner
Leuty	Oakes
Musson	Johnson
Harrison	Fell
Carter	Brown
Stamps	A Turner
Doherty	Welsh
Duncan	Duffy

Referee: Eddie Smith

THE story goes that when Derby County moved to the Baseball Ground at the end of the 19th century, a group of travelling gypsies were camping at the site and were so angered by the situation that they placed a curse on the football club.

It was reported that the curse would prevent the Rams from ever winning the FA Cup and even to a non-believer it might have seemed that the occult was triumphing.

Derby were beaten in the 1898 FA Cup Final by Nottingham Forest, the following year's final by Sheffield United, and they went all the way again in 1903 only to be hammered 6-0 by Bury – a scoreline that remains a record for an FA Cup Final.

They were also semi-finalists in 1896, 1897, 1902, 1904, 1909 and 1923, the latter while still a Second Division club when they were beaten 5-2 by West Ham United, missing out on the first final at the newly-built Wembley Stadium as a result.

Derby reached the semi-final again in 1933 but even by the time the Second World War caused an early end to the Football League and FA Cup in the 1939/40 season the Rams had not really threatened to actually break the supposed curse.

There was some football during the war with Derby competing in the Football League North and the Football League War Cup then later the Midland Cup, which they won in 1944/45 along with the Football League North second period championship.

Those league seasons were played for two championships, the first ending at Christmas and the second at the traditional season's end, with two trophies awarded but quite often a different number of games played from one period to the next.

Wartime football also saw players 'guest' for clubs rather than be full signings, such was the informality of arrangements at the time, and this worked in Derby's favour as they were able to field names such as the great England international inside-forward Raich Carter.

When hostilities ended in 1945 preparations were put in place for the return of full-time football and that started with the FA Cup coming back for 1945/46.

It was, however, in a different format as to counter the lack of revenue because of the missing league games, FA Cup ties were to be played over two legs for the first time from the first round up to and including the quarter-finals.

Luton Town were beaten 6-0 by Derby in the first leg of the third round thanks to four goals from Jack Stamps, one from Carter and one from Sammy Crooks, then it was 3-0 in the return with Carter scoring twice and Angus Morrison also netting.

Peter Doherty saw off West Bromwich Albion in the first leg of the fourth round then it was the turn of Carter, Stamps with a penalty and Reg Harrison to earn a 3-1 win in the return.

Round five saw Brighton & Hove Albion vanquished, Doherty scoring twice (one a penalty) with Carter also bagging two in a 4-1 first leg win; then it was 6-0 in the second thanks to Carter's hat-trick, Doherty's pair and Crooks also netting.

Aston Villa were Derby's opponents in the quarter-final and were beaten 4-3 on their own turf with Doherty scoring two, Carter and Crooks also on target, then Carter scored the only goal in the 1-1 second leg draw.

The semi-finals were due to be played as a single match but Derby's 1-1 draw at Hillsborough against Birmingham City, Carter again on the mark, meant a replay was required.

Maine Road was packed with 80,407 fans – still a record for a midweek game between two Football League clubs outside of an FA Cup Final – to see Derby win 4-0 thanks to braces from Doherty and Stamps.

So Derby were back in the FA Cup Final for the first time since that dark day against Bury in 1903 and once again they had a chance to win their first major honour.

Derby had team selection issues to resolve and replaced Jack Parr, who had played in every match in the run, with Jack Howe, who was on a troopship coming home from India when the campaign started, though Howe had featured in the semi-final replay to cover the injured Leon Leuty.

Also seemingly fit was Sammy Crooks. He had missed the semi-final with a knee problem which was apparently cleared up as, on the way back from the FA Amateur Cup Final, Crooks's car suffered a puncture and the outside-right kicked his tyre in frustration.

His knee locked back into place but manager Stuart McMillan took no chances and Crooks missed out with Reg Harrison keeping his place.

Though there very nearly was no FA Cup Final as two days before, the Rams' players were told that their wives and girlfriends would be given only uncovered seats.

The players were not happy and, led by Carter and Doherty, told the board that if there were no covered seats then there would be no match.

They meant it, the board relented, the tickets for covered seats were handed out and it was all go for the first FA Cup Final after the Second World War, a hugely important occasion not just for the teams taking part but for the country as a whole, which was slowly recovering from the ravages of war and getting life back towards even slightly approaching normality.

And in the build-up, McMillan said, 'I have no wish to make a forecast in a match of this description.

'I saw the Charlton team a short time ago. I consider them to be a well-balanced team of experienced and semi-experienced players and I think that Derby County will help to provide a game worthy of the occasion.

'I can only say – may the best team win. Naturally, I hope that team will be Derby County. I am confident that the boys will go all out in their endeavour to bring the Cup to Derby for the first time.'

In their bid to do just that Derby were in command right from the off with Carter and Doherty, a pair whose magic weaved together was unmatched, putting Charlton under plenty of pressure.

At the other end they were rarely in trouble with captain Jack Nicholas leading by example and Leuty really showing his class whenever their opponents attacked.

Derby had the ball in the net in the first half through Stamps but his effort was ruled out for offside while Harrison saw one shot saved well by Sam Bartram.

Welsh and Duffy missed good chances for Charlton early in the second half but it always seemed like Derby's goal would come, which it did with five minutes remaining.

Harrison and Carter were involved in the build-up, Stamps nodded the ball on and Dally Duncan took a shot that deflected off Bert Turner and ended up in the net.

Derby could taste victory but a minute later they were pegged back – by Turner, whose free kick took a wicked deflection off Doherty and beat Woodley.

Extra time would be required but it almost wasn't as Stamps broke through and beat Bartram with his shot, only for the ball to burst just before it went over the line.

But the Rams would take complete control during the extra period and made their first breakthrough on 92 minutes through Doherty, who scrambled in from close range after Bartram could only push out Stamps's shot.

It was 3-1 five minutes later as Stamps added his first of the match, finishing comfortably after being fed by Doherty, and the powerful number nine took his tally to two just after the start of the second period of extra time following another assist from Doherty. And it all meant that Vic Woodley, Jack Nicholas, Jack Howe, Jim Bullions, Leon Leuty, Chick Musson, Reg Harrison, Raich Carter, Jack Stamps, Peter Doherty and Dally Duncan had managed something that nobody connected with Derby County had ever done before.

Winning the FA Cup for the first time marked the biggest triumph so far in the history of a club that had been one of the founding members of the Football League.

It sparked an outpouring of celebration that Derby had never before seen, either as a town or as a football club. In London, supporters flooded to Leicester Square and Piccadilly Circus and packed the West End's drinking houses to mark the occasion.

It was all good-natured with no trouble reported by police and fans then headed to St Pancras Station ready to head home to Derby.

Back in Derby, preparations were already underway for the players to parade their way around the town on the Tuesday after the final, when they were due to return having remained down south for a Football League South match at Southampton.

The players would start their procession on Midland Road before moving along London Road, The Spot, St Peter's Street, Cornmarket, Market Place and Derwent Street before receiving a civic welcome at the town's police headquarters.

And town mayor Alderman T. Johnson said it would be an occasion worthy of the triumph, admitting, 'I am sure that everyone is, like myself, very proud of the men who have brought the Cup to Derby for the first time.'

The mayor had been seated in Wembley's Royal Box alongside the King, Queen and Princess Elizabeth, as she was then, and caused something of a stir by smoking his pipe – only to be told by the cigarette-smoking King that he was clear to carry on.

Reaction quotes from players and management were hard to come by but there was a nice line from *Derby Telegraph* writer Mark Eaton in his match report.

Eaton wrote of the Rams, 'They played like Cup winners and champions rolled into one, and Charlton were a hopelessly outplayed and well-beaten side long before the game reached its dying moments.'

Derby County released a DVD in 2006 called *Kings of Wembley*, marking the 60th anniversary of the great triumph, and it featured lengthy interviews with Harrison and Bullions – then, and at the time of writing, the only two surviving members of that 1946 team.

It is well worth a watch by any Rams fan, not least because it contains rare match highlights from the Wembley occasion including all four goals and more action, including footage of the semi-final against Birmingham.

The DVD also states that captain Nicholas had the infamous curse lifted by a group of gypsies prior to the final, a claim backed up by reports in *The Derby County Story*, a book released in 1998.

The book said that Nicholas had gone from the club's training base in Harpenden to a local gypsy camp, along with a newspaper reporter, where palms were crossed with silver and the curse was lifted.

But an article in the *Derby Telegraph* three days before the final suggested that the curse was no longer active and quoted a gypsy from a camp near to the Harpenden HQ, presumably the same camp that Nicholas and a reporter had visited.

The gypsy had claimed that Derby would win 3-2 and he said, 'A curse only lasts for seven years but in any case, I know that Derby will win. And a gypsy is never wrong.'

He was right about Derby's victory though wrong about the scoreline, not that anyone involved with the Rams would have gone back to complain.

Derby County were FA Cup winners for the first time in their history and were seemingly poised to go on to further glories.

They reached the semi-finals again in 1948, when they were beaten by Manchester United at Hillsborough, and next reached the last four in 1976, when they were beaten by Manchester United at Hillsborough.

That is the Rams' last appearance in the semi-finals of the FA Cup and they have not reached the quarter-finals since 1999 when they lost at Arsenal.

But for that one glorious afternoon in April 1946 they were indeed the Kings of Wembley.

2 v Huddersfield Town 4-3

24 September 1966. Attendance: 15,029
Baseball Ground. Football League Second Division

DERBY COUNTY:	HUDDERSFIELD TOWN:
Matthews	Oldfield
Richardson	Atkins
Daniel	Cattlin
Webster	Meagan
Saxton	Coddington
Waller	Ellam
Hughes	Hellawell
Hector	Dinsdale
Buxton	Leighton
Durban	Quigley
Hodgson	Dobson
Unused sub: Thomas	*Unused sub:* Wallace
Referee: Keith Walker	

THERE are some games that live forever because of the quality of the football, and some that may have had an extraordinary outcome, such as the 12-0 victory over Finn Harps or the day that Roger Davies beat Luton Town on his own with all five goals.

Some games would have huge significance irrespective of the quality of the match; for instance not many people would describe the play-off final win over West Bromwich Albion as a classic.

The game here, though, ticks several boxes at once.

Football fever was rife in the autumn of 1966. England had won the World Cup for the first time, on home soil, and there was a feel-good factor still sweeping the country, everywhere apart possibly from Derby.

Since the club had dropped out of the top flight in the early 1950s they had not mounted a realistic bid to return, and in the latter part of the decade they found themselves playing in the third tier for the first time in their history.

They came back up in 1957 but mid-table mediocrity seemed to be the order of the day after that, with a final place of eighth in the previous campaign the best since the dawning of the 1960s.

Without ambition or big investment from the directors, neither of which seemed forthcoming, it would take an almost accidental catalyst to set the club going in the right direction.

The arrival of 21-year-old Kevin James Hector was that catalyst. With 113 league goals in 176 games for Bradford Park Avenue, Hector was already building a reputation.

As manager Tim Ward had shown a good eye for spotting a player, and however he managed to persuade the directors to part with £40,000, a then club record, it was almost certainly the best piece of business that he did in his time with the Rams.

Goals had been hard to come by in the autumn of 1966 with only nine being scored in the first eight matches, while two players – inside-forwards Eddie Thomas with three and Alan Durban with two – had scored more than half of them.

Durban and Thomas had scored 30 between them the previous season so it was no surprise that they were leading the way again but someone who could be relied upon to find the net regularly was a necessity.

Hector had made a relatively quiet debut on 17 September in a 2-1 away defeat at Crystal Palace so the visit of Huddersfield to the Baseball Ground would be the home fans' first opportunity to see the club's most expensive signing.

Hector and Durban linked up well as inside-forwards immediately and quickly had Huddersfield in a lot of trouble while central striker Ian Buxton had his best game of the season.

In wide areas Gordon Hughes and Billy Hodgson were causing havoc with Hughes setting up one goal for Durban and an even better chance for Buxton. Defensively Derby were not great but they did not really need to be, such was their attacking prowess.

Huddersfield opened the scoring in the fifth minute but from then on they played as if they felt the game had been won and they were pegged back on 25.

Buxton headed the ball on and Hector, who was under pressure from the visitors' Coddington, got there first and with only an apparent half-chance on offer he slipped the ball home for the equaliser and his first goal for his new club.

In fact, such was the impact that Hector made on his debut, reference to his goal was as descriptive as the *Derby Telegraph* match report got beyond the basic facts and figures of the 90 minutes against the Yorkshire club.

What is known is that Durban added the Rams' remaining goals with a hat-trick while the visitors also scored twice but it ended 4-3 to Ward's side.

Durban's treble would undoubtedly have made him the star of most games but there was one name on everyone's lips after this match – Kevin Hector. He had been cheered off the pitch at the end of the match, and many supporters waited for more than half an hour after the final whistle to cheer Hector as he left the ground.

Gerald Mortimer, writing in the *Derby Telegraph*, said, 'I am not one for outrageous forecasts. But I am prepared to stick my neck out and say that Derby County at last have a true star.

'This is the sort of player who will make sports fans leave comfortable chairs and warm firesides in the winter, to stand in the cold on the terraces.

'Not one of the Rams fans could have been dissatisfied with his performance on Saturday.

'There was a buzz of excitement every time he accelerated on to a pass, a gasp every time he burst away from anguished defenders, a roar every time he fired in a shot.

'This 21-year-old is worth seeing – and I'm sure he will score many goals for Derby County given reasonable luck and freedom from injury.'

Hector would finish his debut season at the Baseball Ground as the leading scorer with 16 goals in 30 games but the Rams ended up 17th, and it was decided over the summer that a change in manager was required so Tim Ward was relieved of his duties and a young man named Brian Clough arrived, with Peter Taylor as his assistant.

Many years later, Sammy Crooks, a Rams legend himself and the chief scout who was instrumental in bringing Hector to the Baseball Ground, said, 'Kevin Hector had been recommended to us. Sam Longson, our chairman, asked me if I'd like to go and see him.

Derby County's Greatest Games

'Well, I did. I just paid to go in, you know, because if you go in the boardroom with everybody there, it soon gets around that you're after a player and then you get a gallery of scouts about.

'And I liked what I saw. He was quick and looked born to get goals. His shooting was so accurate. He got several goals when I watched him and he never missed the target.

'And when we got him at Derby, he fulfilled it all.'

Nobody knew it at the time of course, but in September 1966 the career of one of the Rams' greatest ever players had just begun.

3 v Chelsea 3-1

2 October 1968. Attendance: 34,346
Baseball Ground. League Cup Third Round Replay

DERBY COUNTY:	CHELSEA:
Green	Bonetti
Webster	M Hinton
Robson	McCreadie
Durban	Hollins
McFarland	Webb
Mackay	Harris
Walker	Birchenall
Carlin	Tambling
O'Hare	Osgood
Hector	Hutchinson
A Hinton	Houseman
Unused sub: Barker	*Unused sub:* Lloyd
Referee: Vince James	

BRIAN CLOUGH'S arrival in the managerial hot-seat was not by any means an instant success as in the Second Division the club actually finished in 18th place at the end of his first campaign, one position lower than the previous year under Tim Ward.

There was, however, a splendid run in the League Cup that took them as far as their first semi-final in the competition, where they were beaten 4-2 over two legs by Don Revie's Leeds United.

Fans knew that something was starting to happen for their beloved Rams.

The signing of the veteran Dave Mackay from Tottenham Hotspur during the summer of 1968 proved a master stroke and the addition of Willie Carlin to strengthen midfield helped make Derby County a real force.

After the excitement of the previous League Cup campaign supporters were looking for more of the same this time.

In the first round they were given a home tie against Chesterfield, and comfortably beat them 3-0 with Kevin Hector and Alan Hinton netting, allied to an own goal from the visitors' Humphreys.

The next round saw Stockport County come to the Baseball Ground and go home having been almost single-handedly destroyed by Hinton.

The former Nottingham Forest man scored four of the goals, and Hector added the other, in a 5-1 victory against the Hatters.

The results and performances were pleasing but a third round draw away to Chelsea at Stamford Bridge was a different proposition altogether.

The Pensioners, although not the force that they had once been, were still a respectable First Division outfit who finished the 1967/68 season sixth in the top flight having also reached the quarter-finals of the FA Cup.

Derby travelled to the Bridge and held their hosts to a 0-0 draw, which in itself could be considered an excellent result. It set up a replay under the Baseball Ground floodlights and gave the stadium one of its great nights.

For much of the game it looked as if Derby would go out of the competition having fought manfully enough without ever getting the breakthrough that their play deserved.

Chelsea, as you would expect of a side from the top half of the highest division, were strong, hard in the tackle, quick and professional. Unfortunately in the mood they found the Rams in on the night that wasn't enough.

Ironically it was the visitors who took the lead with Alan Birchenall scoring on the breakaway.

But slick inter-passing by the Rams soon left the visiting midfield chasing shadows.

Peter Bonetti in the visitors' goal kept Derby at bay on a number of occasions. It was not hard to see why he kept goal for the England team.

In the opening minutes Hinton raced fully 70 yards, evading two meaty tackles from Chelsea defenders before firing in a cross that Alan Durban got to only to see his shot turned away.

The pitch was wet and Bonetti had to be at his best only a couple of minutes later to turn away a Hinton drive.

So much was coming from Hinton, but on the rare occasions that the Pensioners thought they had worked a shooting opportunity it was denied them.

Birchenall could only look aghast as a chance was taken off him by Roy McFarland who tackled him and was away to set up a move before he knew what had happened.

There are some games when everything that is tried works. This was one of those nights.

Derby's defenders, when under pressure, made all the right decisions. They remained calm and invariably found one of their own men free when they cleared the ball.

Hinton was at the heart of all the dangerous attacks launched by the hosts. One such moment saw John O'Hare provide the winger with a great pass that led to an equally good cross. It was unfortunate that Hector had wandered just offside as he met the ball with his head.

Derby were applying all the pressure without making the breakthrough that their play deserved. Chelsea pulled everybody back, but it was still left to Bonetti to deny Carlin the opening goal. Typically after being on the receiving end of so much it was the visitors who took the lead.

Peter Houseman received the ball out on the Chelsea left, cut inside Ron Webster and then managed to pick out Birchenall who fired in an unstoppable drive from 30 yards that Les Green had no chance of doing anything about.

Undoubtedly disappointed at conceding, Clough's men went back on the offensive and continued to bombard their opponents and David Webb managed to block a piledriver from Hinton.

The home team continued turning the screw with a succession of corners that had Chelsea reeling, but half-time arrived with an unjust scoreline of 1-0 to the visitors.

With the crowd raising the old Baseball Ground roof the team started the second half much as they had played the first by taking the game by the scruff of the neck.

Jim Walker may not have had the skill of Hinton on the opposite wing but he was a hard worker and he was causing the top division side problems. Both Peter Osgood and John Hollins had to resort to fouling in order to stop the Derby man.

Bonetti in the Chelsea goal was showing his ability more and more as the half wore on.

O'Hare had a drive deflected by a defender, Hector had a rocket shot on the turn pushed away, while McFarland started a move by dispossessing his man in his own half before playing a one-two with Carlin and continuing on the overlap.

When Derby pulled level there were only 13 minutes remaining but the quality of the goal matched the quality of the Rams' all-round play up to that point.

Carlin had been a real bundle of energy and caused trouble for the visitors from the word go but they were not expecting his back-heel into the path of Mackay who unleashed a thunderbolt from 30 yards out that was too much for Bonetti.

Walker and O'Hare were both prevented from giving Derby the lead with headed efforts, and Walker then turned hero at the other end of the park when he denied Ian Hutchinson twice in the same move to stop a certain goal.

Hutchinson was, ironically, born in Derby, and with his scoring chance prevented the Rams then went ahead for the first time in the contest.

It was Walker who carved out the opening for the second goal. He burst down the left flank and fired in an inch-perfect cross for Durban to head home virtually without breaking stride.

Three minutes from time the game was safe for the hosts. John Robson played in the perfect centre but O'Hare was unable to make contact, leaving a battle with Bonetti as to who would get there first. Instead it was Hector who reacted quickest and the home side had gone from 1-0 down to 3-1 up in ten minutes.

The scoring may have been over but Clough's men still kept making the chances. Hinton fed Carlin who was clearly held back by Osgood. Tempers flared and both players went into the referee's notebook.

Clough told the *Derby Telegraph*, 'I was delighted for the players. This was easily the best performance since I came to Derby.'

His comments were echoed by chairman Sydney Bradley, who said, 'This was a night I shall remember as long as I live. What a wonderful display by the team and how wonderful our supporters were.'

Assistant boss Peter Taylor later said that it was the night he really felt Derby were on to something and ready to make massive progress.

The next round also gave them a tie away to First Division opposition, Everton, and the Rams once again did a good job to come home from Goodison with a 0-0 draw.

So another floodlit Baseball Ground replay was required and it was another great night as Hector's goal put the home side through to the quarter-finals after a 1-0 win.

In the last eight they avoided the big clubs and hopes were high that they could reach the semis for the second successive season when they came out of the hat at home to Swindon Town.

The Robins were in the Third Division but they followed Derby's lead by getting a 0-0 draw in the away match before winning the replay 1-0 on home soil.

It was no consolation that Swindon went on to win the final by beating Arsenal at Wembley, meaning the Rams had been knocked out by the eventual winners for the second season in a row.

Not that, in the grand scheme of what was to come, it really mattered too much.

4 v Bristol City 5-0

19 April 1969. Attendance: 31,644
Baseball Ground. Football League Second Division

DERBY COUNTY:	BRISTOL CITY:
Green	Watling
Webster	Jacobs
Robson	Briggs
Durban	Wimshirst
McFarland	Connor
Mackay	Parr
McGovern	Skirton
Carlin	Kellard
O'Hare	Bartley
Hector	Garland
Hinton.	Sharpe.
Unused sub: Wignall.	*Unused sub:* Tainton
Referee: Frank Cowen	

DERBY COUNTY might not have been among the favourites for promotion to the First Division in the summer of 1968 having only finished 18th in the Second Division the previous season.

So Brian Clough went out and pulled off one of the biggest transfer shocks of a generation by bringing in Scotland legend Dave Mackay from Tottenham Hotspur.

Clough wanted Mackay to captain the side and use his experience in a role as part of the Rams' defence rather than his more familiar left-half position.

Derby's start to the 1968/69 season was rather inauspicious and they failed to win any of their first five matches, losing two of them.

There was a sense that, despite Mackay's immediate impact, they needed something extra so Clough went into the transfer market again, bringing in midfielder Willie Carlin from Sheffield United.

Carlin went straight in and his arrival, coupled with the return from injury of Alan Durban and the emergence of John Robson as a young full-back of some talent, coincided with a massive turnaround of fortunes.

Derby would only lose three more times all season and by the time they suffered their final defeat, 1-0 at home to Crystal Palace on 5 March, promotion was not so much of a target as a must given their form in the preceding months.

They bounced immediately back with a 3-2 win away to Blackpool, then drew 1-1 at Carlisle United, and from that point on it was the plainest of plain sailing.

Huddersfield Town, Oxford United, Aston Villa, Fulham, Bolton Wanderers, Sheffield United, Millwall and Norwich City were all beaten in an amazing run of eight successive victories.

That period was enough to not only wrap up a return to the top flight but also the Second Division championship as well, meaning that by the time the season-ender at home to Bristol City on 19 April approached the Rams were sure of their fate. And they were also sure of the immediate future with Clough and his assistant, Peter Taylor, agreeing new five-year contracts – the first time any Rams boss had been tied to a deal running for longer than four years.

There had been speculation that the pair might be targets for other clubs but once contract negotiations began, it was a smooth process.

A statement issued by chairman Sydney Bradley read, 'The Board are delighted that this matter has been resolved without the slightest problem.

'The success achieved by Mr Clough and Mr Taylor has exceeded our wildest expectations and we are delighted to be able to show our appreciation in this tangible way.

'We now look forward to a further five years of success.'

Clough described the move as, 'A continuation of the successful partnership between ourselves and Mr Bradley. I am absolutely thrilled.'

For Taylor it was a first contract of any form during his managerial career, and he added, 'Financially the rewards for our work in the last two years have been absolutely staggering and the same applies to the contracts we have been offered.'

Supporters were urged to get to the Baseball Ground early following news that the players' lap of honour, which had been scheduled to take place after the Bristol City game, had in fact been moved to before the kick-off.

Plans for the presentation of the trophy remained unchanged with Mackay still due to get his hands on the silverware following the full-time whistle.

And Derby went into the match boosted by the return of midfielder Durban, back from international duty with Wales.

Durban was immediately handed his number four shirt back so John McGovern reverted to outside-right with seven on his back and Frank Wignall dropped to the bench. His restoration was perfectly timed as he went on to score a magnificent hat-trick – all before half-time.

Durban's first came on 16 minutes. He was involved in the build-up on the left with Alan Hinton, whose centre was headed up in the air by City's Parr and Durban was on hand to nod the ball past visiting goalkeeper Barry Watling as it dropped.

On 31 minutes the second arrived, laid on by Kevin Hector who headed forward a pass from Roy McFarland and Durban powered through before finishing beyond Watling.

Just before half-time came Durban's hat-trick, a poked effort after Carlin stepped over Hinton's cross and left the away defence snoozing.

It could have been McFarland the hat-trick hero in the first period as he twice struck the bar and saw one effort deflected away from danger.

A fourth goal did not arrive until the 64th minute but it was well worth waiting for and it started with Mackay, who had been at his imperious best.

He clipped the ball to Carlin, who had also been on fine form, and moved into the penalty area before back-heeling it into the path of Hinton.

The winger had ran in from behind Carlin and without changing his stride he powered his left-footed drive into the corner of the net.

Hinton later saw Watling save his penalty but Derby were not finished and put the final touches on the scoreline with a fifth two minutes from time as Hector headed home from a corner.

Derby County's Greatest Games

The final whistle was met with an invasion of celebrating fans on to the Baseball Ground pitch as they soaked up the moment and acclaimed their heroes for their achievement in returning to the First Division.

They were in a great position to see the presentation of the Second Division trophy and medals to the players, which took place in the Main Stand.

Mackay formally collected the trophy from Football League chairman Len Shipman – having earlier carried it around during the pre-match parade – while Clough was moved to tears by the reaction of the crowd.

He hugged Taylor while Mackay took a microphone and told the crowd, 'It will be a great pleasure to come back and win the First Division championship.'

Clough, after regaining his composure, took over and joked to the fans, 'Be careful of the pitch – we don't want to spoil our lovely pitch!'

The celebrations continued at the Baseball Ground and then in the town centre as the Derby public came out in force to milk the atmosphere.

That, unfortunately, was the cue for criminals to try and take advantage by flooding the town centre's pubs with forged £5 notes which were said to be 'very good imitations'!

Some of the celebrations got out of hand but overall it was a good-natured night, particularly at the Midland Hotel where Derby were holding their end-of-season celebration dinner and dance.

The event saw a speech from chairman Bradley, as well as what was described as a '45-minute epic' from Clough in which he mentioned almost everyone at the club – apart from himself.

On his captain Mackay, he said, 'If ever there was a man destined to carry a trophy on a lap of honour it is Dave.

'Some people are born with a silver spoon in their mouth but Dave was born with a trophy in his hands.

'He is everything anybody could wish for from a man. He has inspired me this season by his skill and his approach to the game.'

And of Taylor, Clough enthused, 'Peter is more than half the partnership. This is the man who rang me and told me to pick him up at 6am to drive north and sign John Robson; this is the man who gets me on the motorway before dawn; who wants to do everything twice as quickly as everyone else; in fact I sometimes wonder who is the boss.

'This is the man who tells me to go in and blast the lads – then I find him telling them what great players they all are.

'This is the man who smokes all my cigarettes and I hope he is smoking them for the next 45 years.'

Mackay gave a short speech describing 1968/69 as the 'finest season of my career', which was a big statement from a man as decorated as he was. But the season also marked a major personal triumph as Mackay had been named the Football Writers' Association Player of the Year, jointly with Manchester City's Tony Book.

The celebrations did not stop there. On the Monday, thousands of supporters came out to see the players on their tour of the city, a turnout described by police as being bigger than that following the 1946 FA Cup Final victory, and on the Tuesday there was a tour around the county. Then it was time to reflect on the achievements of the 1968/69 season which had seen Derby finish seven points clear at the top ahead of Crystal Palace, quite a feat in the days of two points for a win.

The Bristol City victory was a club record ninth in succession, also giving them a club best of 26 wins in a 42-game season; they conceded just 32 which was another record and the best since Birmingham City were breached just 24 times in 1948; and their points haul of 63 equalled Leeds United's total in 1963 and was one better than Liverpool's haul in 1962.

They did 'lose' one record in 1968/69. Queens Park Rangers were relegated from the First Division having won only four games, less than Derby's five in 1920/21, though the Rams would re-claim that dubious honour in 2007/08.

So the summer of 1969 was a memorable one in Derby as the club prepared for life back in the First Division.

The biggest change at the Baseball Ground came off the field with the construction of the new Ley Stand, running the entire length of the Popular Side.

The stand meant that the ground had a capacity of 41,500 – and it would be full before too long.

v Tottenham Hotspur 5-0

20 September 1969. Attendance: 41,826
Baseball Ground. Football League First Division

DERBY COUNTY:	TOTTENHAM HOTSPUR:
Green	Jennings
Webster	Beal
Robson	Knowles
Durban (Wignall 71)	Mullery
McFarland	England
Mackay	Collins
McGovern	Pearce
Carlin	Greaves
O'Hare	Gilzean
Hector	Pratt
Hinton	Morgan (Want HT)

Referee: Leo Callaghan

DERBY COUNTY were taking the First Division by storm through the autumn of 1969 having carried on the momentum that had seen them charge to promotion the previous season. Still riding high and 11 games unbeaten they set about life in the top flight for the first time since 1953 with relish.

Their start could perhaps be described as modest, with three draws in the first five matches, but the end of August really saw them pick up the pace.

West Bromwich Albion were beaten 2-0 at The Hawthorns, then unbeaten table-toppers Everton were sent away 2-1 and Southampton were beaten 3-0 in Derby.

A fourth successive maximum points haul followed on 13 September when the Rams won 1-0 at Newcastle United thanks to Roy McFarland's goal.

That result in the North-East was enough to take Derby's unbeaten run to 21 league matches spread across two seasons, a club record.

And it set them up nicely for the 20 September visit to the Baseball Ground of Tottenham Hotspur, who had enjoyed a decorated period during the 1960s with trophies and success aplenty, at home and in Europe.

Most of that had been achieved with the legendary Dave Mackay in their side but with Mackay now captaining Derby, the Scot was going to be facing his old club for the first time.

Mackay's career at the Baseball Ground had already seen him continue his successes and he was looking forward to facing Spurs.

Speaking to the *Derby Telegraph*, he said, 'I had some great times with Spurs but I play for Derby County now. Sentiment does not come into it. I shall be the proudest man in England when I lead the lads out.'

But while Mackay played the emotional connections down, manager Brian Clough felt a victory was important for his inspirational skipper and said, 'We must win for David's sake.'

Clough added, 'My information is that Spurs go forward all the time and that is how they have achieved their good start.

'Tomorrow's game promises to be a good spectacle and I know our lads will be giving everything for David's sake.

'He wants to win this match more than anything else.'

Derby would be unchanged for a sixth successive match having won their previous five in all competitions, including a 3-1 victory at Hartlepool United in the League Cup.

That meant goalkeeper Les Green had shaken off a little niggle but Spurs were without Martin Chivers, who had picked up an ankle injury in his side's last match – a 3-2 win at rivals Arsenal, giving them the best away record thus far in the First Division.

And while things were going forward on the field for Derby, off it there were some interesting developments taking place.

It was announced that all season ticket holders – around 20,000 – would be made members of the Rams' Supporters' Association, costing the club around £2,000.

Fans would receive membership cards worth 2s 6d as they entered the Baseball Ground for the Spurs match that would also entitle them to use supporters' club facilities at other stadiums.

Less positively, supporters on the Popular Side terrace were given a warning to watch their language by police.

The message was that the worst offenders would be taken from the ground and sent to court as well as receiving a ban from future matches.

Chief Superintendent H.M. Shelley, head of Derby East Police, agreed that in comparison to other clubs Derby did not have a major problem with their supporters.

But he said, 'I know we cannot empty the Popular Side but we are quite capable of picking out the worst offenders. These people will be taken out of the ground and put in front of magistrates.'

He also announced that supporters would not be allowed inside the ground wearing steel-toed boots because, 'We picked one boy up who actually went to the match with the intention of kicking people simply because someone kicked him at Blackpool.'

There were further issues with the swaying of the crowd on the Popular Side, potentially putting those at the sides and front of the terrace in danger, while supporters were urged to arrive early with a big crowd expected.

It was advised that people moved to the centre of the terraces, where it was usually quieter, to allow more fans into the ground to utilise the space.

And those who did pack in at the Baseball Ground were treated to a quite staggering display from the Rams.

Intent had already been signalled by the time Derby were in front on 15 minutes through Alan Durban.

Mike England tried to pass the ball across his penalty area to a colleague but the ball was loose and in nipped Durban to steal it away before rifling his shot beyond Pat Jennings.

Four minutes later John O'Hare, who enjoyed an outstanding afternoon, collected a throw and turned away from England before rolling the ball through for Kevin Hector to fight off a challenge and emphatically beat Jennings.

Spurs were already up against it but might have got back into the match had it not been for a world-class save from Green.

Jimmy Greaves used immense skill to create a chance for himself just inside the Derby box and let fly with a powerful shot that Green not only kept out, but held on to as he flew away to his left.

That was the cue for Derby to make it three and they broke quickly to earn a right-wing corner that Alan Hinton lifted into the middle where the diminutive Willie Carlin rose above much taller players to head home.

Rams fans had to wait until just after the hour for a fourth goal with Carlin and Durban turning providers to create the chance for O'Hare, who beat Jennings with his shot and finished off a fine move.

Goal number five arrived in the 70th minute. Hector powered down the right and caught the ball up when it looked like it was going out then lifted it back across to give Durban an easy header and his second of the match.

This was the result – and performance – that really saw the First Division sit up and be aware of just how much of a force Derby could be.

They had faced one of the country's top sides and not only beaten them but completely dismantled them with ease.

'MASSACRE AS SPURS ARE TAKEN APART' was the headline above the match report in the *Derby Telegraph*.

It was hard to disagree with that sentiment, especially as Spurs boss Bill Nicholson admitted that his side had been 'humiliated' by Derby.

And Clough felt that the result and performance spoke for themselves, explaining, 'You don't need to say anything after that. I am just very happy for the lads. I was very proud of them.'

But he continued, 'I wouldn't like to pick one [a man of the match] out. The lads will tell you that John O'Hare was and I suppose when you see a centre-half [Spurs' Mike England] stumbling about like a blind man, that's fair enough.

'I think even the real idiots who don't understand football twigged John O'Hare this afternoon.'

And Mackay was also beaming after the match when he said, 'I am happy for the team because everybody played so well.

'Not because it was Spurs we beat but because you can't be anything but happy when you are in a team which plays like that.

'It is the best we have played since I came here.'

It was very much a high point in Derby's progression under Clough and Peter Taylor, not least because the match was played out in front of a Baseball Ground attendance of 41,826.

That was a new record for the stadium which was never bettered during the glory years that followed and it remains the club's highest ever gate for a home fixture, at any of their three home grounds.

The win took the Rams' unbeaten run to 22 matches in the league, and it was stretched to 24 overall four days later with a 3-1 win at home to Hull City in the League Cup, but game 25 proved one too far the following Saturday as they went down 1-0 at Sheffield Wednesday.

Going 22 league fixtures without defeat remains a club record while the total of 20, set in 1995/96 by Jim Smith's team, is the best run contained within a single season.

The defeat at Hillsborough seemed to have a de-stabilising effect on Derby's season as the Rams then struggled for consistency over the coming months.

Before the spring they only won back-to-back matches once, at the start of December, but lost on successive occasions three times.

Perhaps the First Division had found them out after that explosive opening but they came back strongly and lost for the final time on 31 January when they were beaten 1-0 at Manchester United.

The next two matches were drawn, but the following six were won – including victories at Liverpool, Nottingham Forest and Manchester City, and at home to Arsenal.

Momentum continued with a draw at Sunderland followed by a 4-1 home thumping of Leeds United and a 2-0 win at Wolverhampton Wanderers, then a 1-1 draw at Southampton ended the season with Derby finishing fourth.

The team virtually picked itself across 1969/70 with the regular 1–11 being Les Green, Ron Webster, John Robson, Alan Durban, Roy McFarland, Dave Mackay, John McGovern, Willie Carlin, John O'Hare, Kevin Hector and Alan Hinton.

McGovern's 32 games was the lowest total of that unit. Frank Wignall, Tony Rhodes, Peter Daniel, Arthur Stewart and Jim Walker played 24 times between them and Terry Hennessey, the club's first £100,000 signing when arriving from Nottingham Forest in February 1970, added a further 12 appearances.

Most of that group formed the backbone of the side in 1970/71 as Derby dropped to ninth – but key signings like Archie Gemmill and Colin Todd were on the way, as was unprecedented success.

6 v Manchester United 4-4

26 December 1970. Attendance: 34,243
Baseball Ground. Football League First Division

DERBY COUNTY:	MANCHESTER UNITED:
Green	Rimmer
Webster	Fitzpatrick
Daniel	Dunne
Hennessey	Crerand
McFarland	Ure
Mackay	Sadler
Durban	Morgan
Wignall	Best
O'Hare	Charlton
Hector	Kidd
Gemmill	Law
Unused sub: McGovern	*Unused sub:* Gowling
Referee: Harold Williams	

T would not be an exaggeration to say that the Rams' first season back in the top flight under Brian Clough was a resounding success. Adjusting to life at a higher level was easy. The team finished in fourth place and would have qualified to play in Europe but for administrative irregularities.

Partially due to the disappointment of the ban and partially because of the famous 'second season syndrome' where teams seem regularly to struggle second time around at a higher level, 1970/71 never really took off with periods of excitement and quality alternating with mediocrity.

After starting with a loss and then three consecutive wins form nosedived and there were only two victories in the next 14 games, and there was no pattern to either goals scored or conceded.

One week the Rams would bag plenty, and at other times they would concede heavily, while there were also a number of low-scoring bore draws.

There was nothing to suggest what the Boxing Day encounter at the Baseball Ground with Manchester United would bring though.

This was not a vintage United side and they had finished just above mid-table the previous term, less than three years after they won the European Cup.

They were, however, still a flair side, renowned for their attacking prowess.

Their name was still associated with glamour and Rams fans still enjoyed a shiver of excitement when they saw that the visitors' starting line-up featured Bobby Charlton, George Best and Denis Law, United's 'Holy Trinity'.

The Rams took a two-goal lead into the break but ended up with only a point from a game they could and should have won despite the Baseball Ground playing surface being at its most challenging due to heavy rain and snow that had poured down before the kick-off.

The *Derby Telegraph*'s Gerald Mortimer even went as far as to describe the away team as 'for long periods a pathetic husk of a great side', and there was little doubt that on the day the usually reliable Les Green in goal for the home side was responsible for much of what denied the hosts victory.

Ian Ure gave Derby the best possible start when he conceded a free kick just outside the United penalty area for pushing.

Alan Durban's kick was wide of the mark but referee Harold Williams, however, had found himself involved in a discussion with George Best with regards of his awarding the kick, and missed seeing Durban's failed attempt. He insisted that the kick be taken again this time when he was ready.

This time Dave Mackay decided to have a go – and the visitors paid the price.

Jimmy Rimmer had seemingly made a hash of setting up his wall and was only able to watch as the kick flew past him into the back of the net without the aid of a deflection.

The goal spurred Derby on and Mackay was clearly fancying the chance to get his name on the scoresheet again.

Rimmer was having a bad time organising his defensive wall as Mackay was given another free kick opportunity from a similar place a few minutes after the goal.

Once more the defenders failed to do their jobs and it took the keeper's agility to turn the ball away to safety. Brian Kidd then had an attempt to get past Ron Webster on his blind side but the Rams' right-back was too canny for him.

When John O'Hare then found himself in space everyone including the Derby striker hesitated assuming an offside decision. It never came but the moment was lost.

The Rams did not have to wait long to double their lead. Another free kick of unerring accuracy from Mackay was met by Denis Law, who for reasons best known to himself, elected to clear the ball with an extravagant bicycle kick that fell at the feet of McFarland.

Although the centre half's shot was blocked it squirted away to Frank Wignall who made no mistake in beating Rimmer to make it 2-0.

Free kicks by the home team were proving particularly difficult to deal with and Wignall was presented with an opportunity to double his tally when Willie Morgan could do no more than clear another straight to him.

Whether Wignall was surprised to receive the chance or not was hard to say but his first-time volley flew wide of the upright.

In their period of ascendancy the hosts had the chance to post a score that would have been beyond any team to pull back.

United heads dropped visibly after they conceded the second and Mortimer, a long-time watcher of professional football as well as being the Derby County correspondent for many years, described the visitors' first half display in the following words, 'more feeble than anything one has ever seen from this club.'

That United came back in the second half was not a victory for their heart and courage so much as a lesson in how to turn victory nearly into defeat.

The one bright spark for the opposition was the performance of Charlton who was not prepared to be humiliated even if it seemed his team-mates were.

Against that Green in the Derby goal had a night that he would never forget and for all the wrong reasons.

Law brought the visitors back into the game in the early stages of the second half by playing a ball from the centre of the park out wide to Morgan on the right before racing into the box to head the ball past Green, who had come off his line and found himself stranded out of position.

The equaliser wasn't long in coming and arrived thanks to a Charlton corner from the Rams' left.

Green again failed to deal with it, this time fumbling the ball to the feet of Best who had a fairly simple tap-in despite the attempts of Webster on the line to clear it.

If pulling level from a seemingly lost position was not bad enough the Red Devils then almost immediately went ahead.

Again it was a Charlton corner, this time from the Derby right, and alarm bells were starting to ring.

Both Mackay and McFarland failed to deal with the cross and let it go over their heads. Law must have thought that it was his birthday as, totally unmarked, he was provided with the opportunity to dive full length and head the ball past the exposed Green, whose only consolation was that he could take none of the blame for this goal.

It was Gemmill who brought Derby back into the match, the willingness of his running and his direct dribbling style causing huge problems to the visitors.

He was virtually unstoppable as he burrowed his way into the United area. His initial shot was blocked but he managed to wrestle it back off the opposition and this time he kept hold of it until Hector had worked his way into a scoring position. The King left Rimmer sprawling on the ground as the ball hit the back of the net.

Three minutes later the Rams were back in the lead and again Gemmill was at the heart of it. Terry Hennessey started the move with a ball passed out to Hector who was lurking on the flank. Hector took the ball forward before finding Gemmill with a pass of slide rule accuracy.

The Scottish midfielder's shot went in off the post with Ure unable to do anything about it.

The scoring was still not over, and this time Green was both hero and villain. The Derby keeper did well to push a goalbound shot from Best out for a corner, but then undid his good work from the ensuing dead-ball kick.

Once more it was delivered by Charlton and Green seemed culpable as he failed to cut out a cross that he should have done better with. As a result Brian Kidd rose to head the ball home.

The scoring was over, but Clough's men had emerged with a solitary point from a game that they should have run away with.

It would be wrong to ignore the state of the pitch when apportioning blame. In the days before the beautiful playing surfaces that we are so used to now rain and snow had wreaked much havoc, especially in both goalmouths.

There was little doubt, however, in the minds of Clough and Peter Taylor where the problems lay, and that was with goalkeeper Green.

He was dropped for the next match and never regained his place between the sticks for Derby, having made 129 appearances after signing from Rochdale, having earlier played for Clough and Taylor in their time in charge of Hartlepools United.

Colin Boulton had been chomping at the bit with the reserves for his chance, after his earlier taste of first-team football in the 1960s, and once given it refused to let it go.

Boulton kept goal for every minute of every game in both Derby's title wins, and in doing so became the only player to have completed those most memorable of ever-present campaigns.

There were a number of players of international pedigree in the first championship side, and even more the second time that they won it. Boulton, for all his consistency, incredibly was not one of them.

Boulton's return to the team was for a 2-1 FA Cup third round win away to Chester City on 2 January, and the Rams made it through to round five before bowing out 1-0 away to Everton.

His league recall saw the Rams go down 2-1 at home to Wolverhampton Wanderers the following week before a run of five successive victories was followed by five games without a win.

Boulton kept clean sheets in the final two matches of the season, 0-0 away to Coventry City and 2-0 at home to West Bromwich Albion, which left the Rams ninth in the table and pondering how they would make the next step in the following season.

And the 4-4 scoreline is so rare that Derby did not encounter another one for almost 30 years.

7 v Nottingham Forest 4-0

19 February 1972. Attendance: 31,801
Baseball Ground. Football League First Division

DERBY COUNTY:	NOTTINGHAM FOREST:
Boulton	Barron
Webster	Gemmell
Robson	Winfield
Durban	Chapman
McFarland	Hindley
Todd	Cottam
McGovern	Lyons
Gemmill	O'Neill
O'Hare	Cormack
Hector	Richardson
Hinton	Moore
Unused sub: Hennessey	*Unused sub:* McIntosh
Referee: Bob Matthewson	

THERE are not many clubs capable of winning English football's top division these days but back in the 1970s it was a vastly different competition and far more open. This is illustrated by the fact that, in the six seasons leading up to 1971/72, the country had seen six different champions – Liverpool, Manchester United, Manchester City, Leeds United, Everton and Arsenal.

Something notable about that group is that they were all big-city clubs but with the football landscape as it was then, smaller clubs from provincial towns were able to fight their way into the mix with a combination of good management and clever signings.

By the time February 1972 rolled around, Brian Clough's Derby – in only their third season back in the First Division following promotion in 1969 – were right in with a shout of becoming champions for the first time in the club's history.

Despite being one of the founder members of the Football League in 1888, major honours had so far not come Derby's way with only the FA Cup in 1946 to show for their efforts over the previous 82 years.

But with Clough in charge and working his magic, Derby were in the hunt. Although they had lost 2-0 at Arsenal in their last match prior to the visit of struggling Nottingham Forest to the Baseball Ground they had, for most of the season, been collecting the wins on a regular basis to keep themselves up with the challengers.

On the other side of the coin, Forest's direction appeared to be downwards. They were coming to Derby on the back of four successive defeats and were right in the thick of the battle to avoid relegation.

A curiously Reds-led editorial in the *Derby Telegraph* a couple of days before the match asked a simple question, 'ARE FOREST ON THE WAY TO OBSCURITY?'

In the piece it was reported that Forest, five years previously, had reached the FA Cup semi-final and finished second in the First Division, their highest spot to that point, while Derby were 'lurching towards' finishing 17th in the Second Division. The Reds' record in the transfer market was questioned after key players Terry Hennessey and Frank Wignall had moved to Derby while Rams target Henry Newton had instead signed for Everton with Forest's directors refusing to do any further business with their counterparts from the Baseball Ground.

The article spoke of Forest's weaknesses in defence and struggles to score goals, and added, 'Some of the players seem to have become resigned to the fact that they will be relegated.' Football wasn't the only landscape different back then to the modern day as the country was almost crippled by a strike by miners that was causing massive problems from Land's End to John O'Groats.

As a result, power restrictions had been imposed by the Government on many industries, meaning that even football matches were hit as they could not be played in midweek because that would have meant using floodlights.

Clough, who made no secret of his Socialist stance, sympathised with the miners and announced his intention to picket with them on the day following this match.

And he also revealed that, as a 'personal gift', he had given them 100 tickets for the FA Cup tie at home to Arsenal the following week.

He said, 'I think the miners are a deserving cause. They are entitled to special treatment because of the job they do. I see them as a group of people I can help person-ally. It would be the same whoever they were.

'A lot of people are suffering because of this strike, including me, including everyone who reads this, but I am sure that nobody is suffering more than the miners themselves.

'They are short of money and they might well find that they have no jobs to go back to. I do not think I will hinder a fair settlement to the dispute by doing this. Nothing and nobody can do that, not even the Prime Minister.'

As for the match, Derby were in control of it from start to finish with John McGovern on top form in midfield while Archie Gemmill and Alan Durban were also at their best.

Their display meant that Alan Hinton had the freedom to do his thing from the left and be the biggest thorn in the side of a Forest team that, with more than two months of the season still remaining, looked certain to be relegated.

Derby's first goal came on 34 minutes from Hinton after the Rams had been on top of their visitors pretty much from the first whistle.

Kevin Hector, normally a scorer himself, turned provider with an excellent through pass that left Hinton clear against his old club and he made no mistake with a delicate chip past goalkeeper Jim Barron.

Given their dominance it was a surprise that Derby had taken so long to go in front but it only took them four minutes to double their lead.

Forest's defence was split again thanks to McGovern's work and despite pressure from two visiting defenders, there would be no denying John O'Hare as his strength and composure were enough for him to find the back of the net.

Only four minutes had passed of the second half before two became three and O'Hare was at the heart of things once more when he was fouled on the edge of the Forest box.

Hinton's free kick was superb, crashing its way past Barron to give the Rams' number 11 his second of a game he was clearly enjoying.

He might have had a hat-trick after good work from O'Hare and Hector but the Rams' fourth goal of the afternoon was not long in coming.

Derby County's Greatest Games

A loose clearance struck Hector and was picked up by 'The King' so he charged forward with Hinton supporting him but, choosing to use the winger as a decoy, Hector carried on going and planted his low shot firmly in the corner.

Derby struck the woodwork through Hinton and Hector as they went in search of a fifth and Colin Boulton went largely untroubled until the last few minutes when he was called upon to make a save from a Martin O'Neill shot.

The headline on the *Derby Telegraph* report of the game was one that any Rams fan would have enjoyed, 'FEEBLE FOREST ROUTED'.

And the result was also a significant step for the Rams as it meant they had put an end to their recent cycle of winning at the City Ground and then losing to their rivals at the Baseball Ground, as had been happening over the last few seasons.

The newspaper continued, 'It was all too easy.' It was metaphorical music to the ears of Derby fans.

The strikes mentioned earlier on meant that media coverage of this week was somewhat limited and Clough was strangely quiet in the days after the match.

The next time we heard from him publicly was as Derby were preparing for that FA Cup match at home to Arsenal which would be attended by the striking miners.

The next edition of *The Ram*, Derby's official publication, was focused on the visit of the Gunners. *The Ram*, a newspaper rather than a match programme but released only for home games, was ahead of its time and gave readers a very different insight into the club.

But rather than talking about Arsenal, Clough was instead voicing his opinion on the chances of Derby – looked upon by now as serious title candidates – actually challenging for the major honours.

The result had left them third in the table with games in hand over Everton and Liverpool, who occupied the top two places, but Clough was not sure what the future held.

He said, 'I have no more miracles in my locker. What the Rams have achieved so far in recent seasons is nothing short of miraculous, but we have now reached a turning point.

'The age of the quarter-million-pound transfer has now arrived; it will probably happen before the end of the season … and Derby County simply cannot compete as things stand.

'We just haven't the money. Whenever a top player looks like coming available, we are often linked with him, together with Arsenal, Manchester United, Leeds United and the rest, as possible bidders.

'This is very flattering – but not realistic. We cannot find that kind of money in our present situation, and even if we could, we then could not pay the appropriate wages.'

Arsenal's Peter Storey was highlighted as an example as he was believed to be available but the England defender's wage demands would have been well out of Derby's range.

Clough continued, 'Peter Taylor and myself will continue to scour the country in the search for players to improve the team, but we can no longer pull signings such as Roy McFarland, John O'Hare and Alan Hinton out of the hat.

'Things have now reached the stage where even Colin Todd, at £170,000, was cheap at the price. We deserve credit for seeing this at the time but everyone else has woken up to the fact, and we will be outbid next time.

'Unfair in a way of course, but money talks. Until, or rather unless, we begin to attract several thousand more spectators – and what more can we do to bring them in – we will have to make do as we are.'

Clough got his wish on increased attendances when a season's high of 39,622 packed in for the FA Cup tie the following week, although Arsenal eventually triumphed at the third attempt, then more than 38,000 saw the Easter home games against Leeds United and Newcastle United while the season-ender against Liverpool saw 39,159 crammed in.

That £250,000 transfer before the end of the season did not materialise although the British record was pushed to £225,000 in August 1972 – by Clough, who signed Leicester City defender David Nish for Derby.

What happened on the field after the Forest victory is documented in the next chapter and the Rams would not do the double over their greatest rivals for another 40 years when they managed it in 2011/12, with a Clough once again in the manager's chair.

v Liverpool 1-0

1 May 1972. Attendance: 39,420
Baseball Ground. Football League First Division

DERBY COUNTY:	LIVERPOOL:
Boulton	Clemence
Powell	Lawler
Robson	Lindsay
Durban	Smith
McFarland	Lloyd
Todd	Hughes
McGovern	Keegan
Gemmill	Hall
O'Hare	Heighway (McLaughlin 72)
Hector	Toshack
Hinton	Callaghan
Unused sub: Hennessey	
Referee: Clive Thomas	

AFTER that February victory over Nottingham Forest, the Rams were neatly positioned among the chasing pack at the top of the First Division table. Beating their rivals was certainly something of a spark for Brian Clough's side as it was the first in a run of five successive wins in a period of seven maximums and a draw from eight matches that took Derby through to the start of April.

By the time April arrived they were serious title contenders and the last match in that sequence was one that struck a potentially crucial blow in the championship race as Leeds United, runners-up the previous season, were beaten 2-0 at the Baseball Ground with John O'Hare on target and a Norman Hunter own goal wrapping things up.

Clough always savoured any success against Don Revie's side but privately he must have known that it was a result which gave the Rams a great chance of going on to win their first ever Football League championship.

There was a growing feeling the longer 1971/72 went on that Derby might just be ready to upset the apple-cart and finish top of the pile ahead of the likes of Leeds, Liverpool and Arsenal. Not since Ipswich Town a decade previously had a 'smaller' club won the title, in their first season after promotion from the Second Division, but outside of Derby the belief was that one of the more fancied city clubs would triumph.

Derby was, at the time, a small provincial town but inside its boundaries the feeling was that the Rams were more than capable of coming out on top.

But then things started to get a little nervy and on Easter Monday, just 48 hours after the Leeds success, the Baseball Ground was breached for the only time all season as Newcastle United left with a 1-0 victory.

That was followed by a 0-0 draw at West Bromwich Albion though the Rams quickly steadied the ship with a 4-0 win at Sheffield United and a 3-0 cruise at home to Huddersfield Town.

The penultimate game of the season saw a 2-0 defeat at Manchester City, who went top although that was their last match of the campaign.

Derby still had one to play while Leeds and Liverpool both had two to play in a rather fragmented end to the season that would never happen in the modern era.

The Rams' final game saw them host Liverpool on the first Monday in May and they knew that a win would lift them from third to the summit on 58 points.

Though they would then have to wait for another week with Liverpool and Leeds not scheduled to finish their matches until the following Monday because of the upcoming FA Cup Final between Leeds and Arsenal.

A point would be enough to secure a place in the following season's UEFA Cup, the competition Derby missed out on in 1970 because of off-field matters, but only two points would be enough to keep them in the title hunt.

And they could not have approached the Liverpool meeting in a more positive mood following news the Saturday before that Clough and Peter Taylor, who were midway through their current contracts, had agreed new deals to stay at the Baseball Ground for the next five years, warding off apparent interest from Coventry City.

The *Derby Telegraph* reported that the deal made them 'almost certainly the highest paid managers in the country'.

And while Clough was pleased to have everything in place he was mainly focused on the immediate task in hand, adding, 'I am delighted that this has all been settled. My main concern at the moment, however, is the game against Liverpool on Monday.'

Chairman Sam Longson also used the announcement to reveal development plans for the Baseball Ground that included seating to be installed at the Normanton End similar to what had been done at the Osmaston End the previous summer, and an ultimate ambition to turn the venue into a 40,000 all-seater.

On the pitch, Clough's only team selection issue was whether to re-shuffle his defence and bring in Terry Hennessey to cover the injured Ron Webster or throw in 16-year-old Steve Powell at right-back for only his second Football League start.

Clough said, 'The chances are that Steve will play. If so, it will be something special for him, but I do not consider age in these things, only ability and temperament.

'I don't expect Liverpool to come for a draw. I expect them to play their normal game and see no reason why this should not be a very memorable match.'

Powell was told the news of his inclusion before going for an afternoon nap ahead of the match but his performance was anything but sleepy as he starred in the number two shirt and looked like a player who had a decade of experience rather than just a couple of games.

Right from the start it was evident that he was more than vindicating Clough's decision to throw him in at the deepest of ends as he kept Ian Callaghan at bay with consummate ease.

And there was one particularly memorable moment in the second half of a tight match when he flicked the ball calmly up over the head of Emlyn Hughes, making the England international look rather foolish.

But the game's most outstanding point came in the 62nd minute as Derby scored the goal that would put them top of the table. Kevin Hector took a throw on the right and found Archie Gemmill, who worked his way across the box looking for space.

He rolled the ball to Alan Durban but the Welshman dummied and John McGovern, timing his run to perfection, drove his shot past Ray Clemence from the edge of the box.

An already raucous Baseball Ground atmosphere went up a notch as the Rams' title hopes were re-ignited.

The goal came after Liverpool's one big chance when John Toshack just watched an inviting Kevin Keegan centre rather than apply the finishing touch, and the visitors later saw substitute McLaughlin's shot turned away by Colin Boulton.

But an equaliser never came with Roy McFarland and supporters' Player of the Year Colin Todd magnificent at the heart of the home defence, flanked by the equally outstanding Powell.

Given the elongated nature of the championship race, the immediate post-match focus was on the performance of Powell against some of the country's leading players.

'Taylor raves over Powell the great' read the headline in the *Derby Telegraph* above the story that saw the Rams' assistant boss describing the teenager's work as, 'Undoubtedly the most amazing display any of us are likely to see again from a 16-year-old.'

He added, 'It would have been brilliant whatever the circumstances. Bear in mind the crowd, the importance of the game and the opposition, then consider the way Steve played and it makes you wonder if you were dreaming.

'When Steve is playing for England in a few years' time we will all look back and recall his game against Liverpool. And the great thing is, one can say this about him and know that it won't make a scrap of difference to him.'

Powell had to come back down to earth quickly as he remained in Derby to continue his A Level studies while the rest of the players headed out to Majorca for a short holiday with Taylor.

They were due to be away for the whole week, taking in the following Monday's events when they would be finding out whether they had become champions or not.

It would remain a three-pronged fight for the top as, while Derby were beating Liverpool, Leeds kept their hopes alive with a 2-0 win at home to Chelsea.

Their last match was at Wolverhampton Wanderers while Liverpool headed to Arsenal, who Leeds went on to beat 1-0 in the FA Cup Final 48 hours before the final showdowns.

Taylor continued, 'We will arrange to be telephoned at our hotel after Leeds and Liverpool play next Monday. Brian is going to the Scilly Islands for a few days tomorrow, so I suppose he will pick up the result on television.

'There is nothing more we can do now, so there's no point in getting worked up.'

As the night approached, attentions turned towards the 1972/73 season and Derby's plans to strengthen their squad with the challenge of European football – either in the UEFA Cup or European Cup – on the horizon.

The Rams were reported to be willing to spend £500,000 to get the two men they wanted, believed to be a defender and a forward, with a host of names being linked.

They had been interested in Birmingham City's young forward Trevor Francis, though the Blues' promotion to the First Division made that one unlikely, while George Best was mentioned in the press but was not a target as Taylor said they were not looking for an 'erratic genius' such as him or Rodney Marsh, who they had previously approached Queens Park Rangers for.

Then the crucial Monday arrived and the equation was simple – a point or more for Leeds at Molineux would be enough to deny Derby the title, as would Liverpool winning at Highbury. Those two events combined would have seen Derby drop to third.

In the end both results went in the Rams' favour as Leeds were beaten 2-1 by Wolves and Liverpool could only manage a 0-0 draw at Arsenal, meaning both teams finished on 57 points with Derby ahead of them on 58.

'RAMS CHAMPIONS!' was the simple and effective headline on the front page of the following day's *Derby Telegraph* as it proudly exclaimed that Derby County, founder members of the Football League in 1888, had landed the ultimate prize for the first time having been runners-up three times.

Liverpool boss Bill Shankly conceded that Derby had been worthy champions as he felt they had been the best team his players had faced during 1971/72.

And Clough, speaking while still on his holiday, said, 'You cannot imagine a better place to be when you're top of the league. I'm just about to take my wife and the bairns to see the flowers and the gardens.

'Of course I was surprised last night when I found that we were at the top. But I had never abandoned hope. Hell no! Our league is not so bad that two away games are foregone conclusions.

'But people should remember that titles are not won overnight. We thought that we had a good side last year and all our training and pre-season tour was geared towards finishing at the top this year.

'We have won because everyone has worked hard for eight and nine months. Talented players have won the league for us. It is obviously more of a feat for Derby to finish top than one of the big city clubs.

'But we have not set a pattern. The city clubs will continue to run the game and will become stronger every year. The only way in which we can match them is on the field.

'Over the last five years we have bought well and bought courageously. We spent £175,000 on Colin Todd which was a fortune at the time, and everyone said that we were crackers. Other clubs cannot come and do it because there are no more Toddys available.

'We have to continue to try and keep up and we have to be in on every transfer deal which breaks. The moment we are not, we shall know we cannot cope.

'When Peter and I came to Derby we were full of muck and birdseed. We dreamed of winning championships and now we have woken up to find that we are champions.

'I want a framed picture of that league table and the team which won it.'

News of Derby's triumph sparked wild celebrations across the town and a few days later the players were able to join in as they received the iconic trophy at the Baseball Ground before embarking on a parade as the Derby public welcomed their heroes, who had also won the Texaco Cup and the Central League championship.

The Rams did not manage to strengthen their squad as planned over the summer and had to wait until the early weeks of the season when they signed David Nish from Leicester City for a British record fee of £225,000.

But Derby County were the champions of England for the first time and about to represent the country in the European Cup – a statement that still sounds as great today as it did in 1972.

9 v Benfica 3-0
25 October 1972. Attendance: 38,100
Baseball Ground. European Cup Second Round First Leg

DERBY COUNTY:	BENFICA:
Boulton	Jose Henriques
Robson	Malta Da Silva
Daniel	Humberto
Hennessey	Messias
McFarland	Adolfo
Todd	Jalma Graca
McGovern	None
Gemmill	Toni
O'Hare	Baptista (Jordao 55)
Hector	Eusebio
Hinton	Simoes

Referee: Bertil Wilhelm Lööw (Sweden)

THE Rams could have been old hands on the European stage by the start of the 1972/73 season but for administrative irregularities that saw them barred from UEFA competitions after finishing fourth and in a qualifying place at the end of 1969/70. The early 1970s were, however, the club's great days and they would not be denied the chance forever.

And in missing out on the UEFA Cup for 1970/71 their success in winning the First Division in 1972 meant that their first footballing venture onto the continent would be in the European Cup, the premier competition.

Their first ever European opponents were FK Zeljeznicar Sarajevo from Yugoslavia, not a name familiar to most Derby fans.

Brian Clough's men did not find them particularly challenging and emerged with a comfortable 2-0 win at the Baseball Ground in the first leg, Roy McFarland having the honour of scoring the club's first goal in Europe and Archie Gemmill adding the second.

Alan Hinton and John O'Hare earned them a 2-1 win in the away leg in front of 60,000 supporters and they eased their way through to the second round, which was also the last 16 in the days when the competition was far more exclusive and open to just the national champions.

Defending champions Ajax could have been opponents, as could Bayern Munich, or perhaps the greatest name of them all – Real Madrid, who had dominated the European Cup's early days.

Instead the opponents were Benfica, still one of the biggest matches that could have come out of the hat. Benfica were known by neutrals worldwide and their exploits in Europe were legendary.

They won the European Cup in 1961 and 1962, and were runners-up in 1963, 1965 and 1968, the latter defeat seeing Manchester United become the first English club to win the competition.

And leading the line was the famous Eusebio. He had been one of the stars of the 1966 World Cup finals in England, and although nearing the end of his career with Benfica at this stage had scored 40 goals for them in the previous season.

They had the pedigree and the experience, they were used to the big occasion, the big names, the huge arenas. What they had never experienced before, however, was the mud heap known as the Baseball Ground pitch. It was something that they would never forget.

It is certainly true that with the heavier rains of winter the grass would be worn away, leaving only the cloying clay to play on.

The weather around the time of this game had not been particularly bad and the playing surface should have been fine. When the Benfica squad went to the ground for a look round they found it very muddy.

To say that they were shocked would be an understatement with what must have been an extremely localised shower. They may have been less surprised had they been able to listen in on a conversation between Clough and the local fire department suggesting that they might like to test their fire engine hoses on the pitch.

Those who saw the Benfica players trying to negotiate the pitch in their suits say that the game was already lost for many of them as soon as they saw the mud oozing over their loafers.

Many so-called experts had decided that this match was to be a classic one-sided affair. One-sided it most definitely was – but not in the manner predicted by the pundits, as the visitors were washed away by wave upon wave of flowing Derby football.

Whatever style of football the Portuguese giants were used to it was clearly not this. They were pretty much dead in the water before they had even had time to draw breath.

Benfica had every reason to be confident as they came into this match on the back of a seven-game unbeaten run with 30 goals scored.

The Rams made their intentions known right from the off, so much so that the television commentator David Coleman was forced to break off from revealing his command of statistics to state, 'And Derby showing straight away that they intend to attack hard.'

There was nearly a goal from the first move of the game. John Robson, breaking from the back, carried the ball forward before playing it on to O'Hare.

O'Hare had an almost telepathic understanding with Kevin Hector, and after battling his way to a suitable position passed it to Hector who was only denied by some solid defending in the visitors' box.

Robson was in the team as the Rams' 'European' full-back as he was out of the First Division side owing to the British record signing of Leicester City's David Nish in August. Nish was not, however, eligible to play in the European Cup, so Robson was back in for the continental nights.

Even clearing the ball to the halfway line provided little respite for Benfica as McFarland and Terry Hennessey combined to drive the ball back into the danger areas.

This time Hinton picked up the ball in far more space than he should have been allowed, and from fully 25 yards out unleashed a blistering volley that if not actually close enough to the goal to cause the visiting goalkeeper any real problems would certainly have given him much food for thought.

His goal kick was deep into Rams territory, but even with McFarland beaten there was the ever reliable Colin Todd behind him to sweep up and clear the ball to safety.

The truth is that the supposedly superior side were penned in their own half unable to break free. Even when they won a free kick for offside the visitors were so panicked that they played the ball straight to John McGovern.

The petulance shown by the visiting defenders emphasised their frustration when contesting something as petty as a thrown-in.

The nearest that Colin Boulton came to being called into action during the opening stages was fielding back-headers from his own defenders.

Home attacks were being mounted from all angles; down the right, through the middle and on one very dangerous occasion down the left.

Hector combined with Gemmill who was unstoppable down the left, and linking up with Hector he won a corner.

The dead-ball kick was simplicity itself. Hector and Hinton stood together and Hector rolled the ball a few feet in front of him allowing Hinton to pick it up and fire it across the face of goal to McFarland who rose above everybody else to head home.

It was the first corner of the game, and with it came the first goal.

When Peter Daniel, playing in the left back slot, set Gemmill running down the flank again panic once more ensued in the heart of the visitors' defence. The Scot won a throw-in deep in enemy territory and found McGovern. McGovern linked with O'Hare and when the ball reached Hector in the area Benfica were relieved to put it out for a corner.

Their relief was only temporary however as Hinton trotted over to take another of his lethal dead-ball kicks.

Again it was from the left, but this time it was played right across the face of goal to McFarland who headed the ball out to Hector.

Hector was running away from goal but lifted the ball back sublimely over the visiting stopper and into the far corner to really send the Baseball Ground into overdrive.

Hector then found that he was causing many problems merely standing in front of the visiting keeper when he went to kick the ball clear.

Commentating for the BBC, Coleman made the point that the Benfica keeper did not get much practice in his art at home as his team were so dominant and all-powerful.

Whatever the reason there is little doubt that his kicking was finding a white shirt nearly every time.

One notable clearance was picked up by Robson and forwarded to McGovern. Even when he lost it the follow-up clearance was picked off by Daniel and passed to Gemmill who was in a more central position this time. When Gemmill looked for an outlet he found McFarland storming down the left wing.

The captain's cross was cleared as far as Daniel who played it long to Hector. The ball fell loose as Hector challenged in the air for it and in came McGovern to fire home the third from 12 yards out.

The Derby midfielder should not have been favourite for the ball with three Benfica players around it, and though the player nicknamed 'Border' was not the fastest around the park he was definitely fast of thought.

With 35 minutes gone the Rams were 3-0 up against one of the giants of the European game.

Interestingly there is footage of the game available, but it always ends with the scoring of that third goal and realistically the game was over at that stage.

Hector had a chance to make it four later on but opted to shoot from a narrow angle with better-placed team-mates screaming for the ball in front of goal.

Boulton did have a couple of meaningful saves to make late on in the game but it was too little too late.

Gerald Mortimer, writing in the *Derby Telegraph*, said of the night, 'People came to see Eusebio. They stayed to marvel at the power of Alan Hinton.

'Hinton did not score but his shooting was explosive and, utterly in character, he laid on two of the goals.

'They saw, too, Colin Todd dispute Peter Taylor's claim that Roy McFarland is the best player in the world. Todd was everything at the back – quick, intelligent, savage in the tackle.

'Not that McFarland was much behind him. He is as powerful and his skill in tight situations marks him out as a master player.

'This was a superb team performance.'

Even the Portuguese press were magnanimous, with a writer in football paper *Bola* saying, 'It is a long time since I saw Benfica so outplayed. I've never seen Benfica made to look so bad.'

No one was kidding themselves that it was game over with a second leg to come in Portugal, but if the home win had been all about the power and precision of Derby's attacking play the away leg would be all about the quality of their defending.

The Rams went to the Estadio da Luiz – the Stadium of Light – and knew that they would have to be tight at the back, which they were.

Boulton knew that he would have to deal with everything that came his way, which he did, and with not being required to score a goal all they had to do was shut Benfica out, or at the very least lose by no more than two clear goals.

In the end they turned in a disciplined performance that saw them pick up the 0-0 draw they needed and earn their place in the quarter-finals, which would take place the following spring.

All of a sudden they were getting towards the business end of the European Cup and in the draw they avoided the big guns like Madrid, Munich and Ajax, and ended up with a tie against Czechoslovakian side Spartak Trnava, with the first leg away from home.

And their win over Benfica saw them do something to the Portuguese giants that no other club had done – prevent them from scoring in a two-legged European tie.

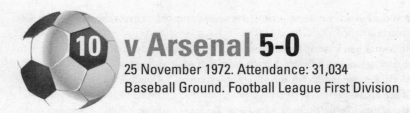

10 v Arsenal 5-0

25 November 1972. Attendance: 31,034
Baseball Ground. Football League First Division

DERBY COUNTY:	ARSENAL:
Boulton	Wilson
Webster	Rice
Nish	McNab
Hennessey	Storey
McFarland	McLintock
Todd	Simpson
McGovern	Marinello (Armstrong 58)
Gemmill	Ball
Davies	Radford
Hector	George
Hinton	Kelly
Unused sub: Durban	
Referee: Arthur Jones	

IT must seem hard to Rams fans of the modern era – say since the 1980s – who have been used to long spells of anonymity in the middle reaches of what is now known as the Championship and the occasional flirtation with life in the top flight, but in their peak years Derby County have not only run with the best but have frequently come out on top.

At one stage the Rams' biggest rivals were Liverpool and Arsenal rather than the team in red from 17 miles down the road.

Derby and Arsenal met five teams in the 1971/72 season, the home and away encounters in the First Division and a marathon FA Cup fifth round match.

The first tie, played at the Baseball Ground ended in a 2-2 draw, with the hosts' goals coming courtesy of Alan Durban and a penalty from Alan Hinton.

Despite extra time being played in the replay at Highbury neither team could break the deadlock. In those days penalty shoot-outs were not an option and the tie went to a third game. This time on neutral ground at Filbert Street, Leicester.

A bad back-pass by John McGovern led to the only goal of the game and dreams of FA Cup glory were over for another season.

It is fair to say that ultimately the Derby camp were not too bothered as it cleared everyone's minds for what proved to be a successful run at the top division title.

For top teams losing to a close rival is something that is not dwelt on but can be used as a spur to success at the next meeting.

If Brian Clough and Peter Taylor chose to wind their players up with reminders of the hurt they felt in the Cup it worked spectacularly.

After the excitement of winning the title the 1972/73 season had got off to a quiet start. It took three games to register the first win, and a further three to gain the second.

By the time that the Gunners came to visit the home side had only won seven out of their 19 games.

However, a 2-2 draw in the previous home game against Crystal Palace followed by the first away victory of the term at Upton Park against West Ham United suggested that perhaps a corner had been turned.

Kevin Hector had scored twice in that success at West Ham while the goals in the draw with Palace came from Hinton and teenager Steve Powell, his first senior effort just months after his staggering appearance as a 16-year-old against Liverpool in the match that ultimately clinched the title.

Those two results, and particularly the performances, indicated that perhaps Derby might be getting back towards something like their best form.

They had been wildly inconsistent as they started life as First Division champions for the first time and, starting with their 2 September home win over Liverpool, they went on five successive sequences of a victory followed by a defeat.

It was a curious bunch of results for any club, especially the defending champions, so there was an element of trepidation as they prepared to welcome Arsenal to the Baseball Ground. Arsenal were not in bad form as they looked to regain the championship that they had won in 1971 and travelled north while sitting second in the table.

They had won four of their last six matches, including the previous two – 1-0 at home to Everton and 3-1 away to Wolverhampton Wanderers.

It was sure to be a big day at the Baseball Ground, especially for young striker Roger Davies – when joining from Worcester City the previous year he had become the record signing out of non-league football – who was going to be called in to make his home debut, having only previously appeared in a 4-0 defeat at Manchester City at the start of November.

It was evident right from the first whistle that this would be Derby's day as they got into their opponents with verve and vigour, then used the ball with intelligence and class when they had it.

Charlie George missed a couple of good chances for the visitors but they were minor aberrations in the Rams' performance and once they opened the scoring on 21 minutes, the only subject up for debate was how many goals they would rack up.

John McGovern had already gone close twice and he was successful at the third attempt. Bob Wilson failed to hold a centre from Archie Gemmill and Hector played the ball back in, where McGovern was waiting to apply the finishing touch and get things going for his side.

A penalty appeal for a foul on Terry Hennessey was rejected, and a Roy McFarland goal was ruled out as referee Arthur Jones was not ready for the taking of a free kick, but this only served to inspire the Rams as they completely blew their opponents out of the water before half-time.

Goal number two arrived on 37 minutes from the right boot of Hinton, who had cut inside from the left and got past Pat Rice with ease before hitting a ferocious shot into the far corner beyond Wilson.

Three minutes later Hinton took a short corner to Ron Webster, picked the ball back up and delivered a perfect centre for McFarland to head home.

And on 42 minutes the scoreline read 4-0 with Hinton once again providing an inviting cross and Hector getting himself on the end of it.

Arsenal simply did not know what had hit them and when the whistle blew for half-time, the Baseball Ground rose as one to applaud and acknowledge what had been a truly stunning opening 45 minutes by the home side.

Not that Clough's men were finished there and only two minutes into the second half they extended their lead to five.

Less than two minutes after the restart, Arsenal once again showed that they had not been taking too much notice of the cause of their problems as they gave Derby yet another free kick in a dangerous wide area.

Hinton took it and delivered the ball into the centre with his usual aplomb and this time it was Davies who rose highest to head it in and open his Rams account.

Davies had given Arsenal plenty of problems throughout the first half with his ball control and clever use of possession, though it was a major surprise that – given how rampant Derby were – his goal was the last of the afternoon.

Clough's men gave a controlled display after that and were rarely threatened themselves, and on the rare occasions Arsenal did break forward they found a defence in no mood to give anything away with Webster looking particularly up for the challenge.

'This was a supreme exposition of quality by Derby County, eleven players who, in this form, cannot be denied,' read the match report in the *Derby Telegraph*.

There was talk among the pundits present that Arsenal goalkeeper Wilson was to blame for his side's heaviest defeat of the season on his first match back after seven months out injured.

They had not trailed 4-0 at half-time in a game for 20 years and it was said that Wilson was culpable for three of the goals.

Wilson offered up a stern 'no comment' when approached by the press after emerging from the Arsenal dressing room following 45 minutes of strong words from manager Bertie Mee to the entire squad.

Mee had banned all of his players from speaking after the match but there were no such problems in the Derby camp.

It was left, however, to assistant manager Taylor to deliver the verdict and he leapt to the defence of Wilson – to a degree.

He said, 'I would only fault him for two of the goals, the first by McGovern and the second by Alan Hinton.

'The others were from dead-ball situations and Wilson had to come off his line. You couldn't blame him.'

The resounding victory was just what Derby needed after their autumn difficulties and it did indeed appear as if they were starting to find their feet.

After beating Arsenal they went to Wolverhampton Wanderers and came back with a 2-1 success thanks to goals from Hector and Hennessey, then Coventry City were beaten 2-0 at the Baseball Ground with Gemmill and Hinton netting.

A 1-1 draw at home to Newcastle United extended the unbeaten run to six games but after a 4-0 defeat at Stoke City in the next match the inconsistency returned again.

From that pre-Christmas defeat at Stoke the Rams did not win back-to-back matches again until the last game in March – 1-0 at Arsenal thanks to Powell's goal – and the first in April, 2-0 at Coventry with O'Hare and Hector doing the damage.

By that time they were well out of the title race but they did at least finish on a very positive note with three successive home wins to end the season in seventh, 14 points behind eventual champions Liverpool, with Arsenal in second.

Davies continued to make progress in his first run of regular professional football and he finished with a haul of seven goals from 19 starts and one substitute appearance, when he had climbed off the bench to net in a defeat at Sheffield United.

He scored three times in the final two matches, one in the 3-0 defeat of Ipswich Town (Hector adding two), and two as Wolves were beaten by the same scoreline with McFarland also joining him on the scoresheet.

But coming in seventh was a disappointing end to the season for a side that had held high hopes of mounting a championship challenge once again.

11 v Tottenham Hotspur 5-3

7 February 1973. Attendance: 52,736
White Hart Lane. FA Cup Fourth Round Replay

DERBY COUNTY:	TOTTENHAM HOTSPUR:
Boulton	Jennings
Webster	Evans
Nish	Knowles
Hennessey (Durban HT)	Pratt
McFarland	England
Todd	Beal
McGovern	Gilzean
Gemmill	Perryman
Davies	Chivers
Hector	Peters
O'Hare	Coates (Pearse 90)

Referee: Don Biddle

FOR a club with as lengthy a history as Derby County, and certainly a history so dominated by periods of time in the top two divisions, great days or nights in the FA Cup have been few and far between.

The Rams were frequent visitors to the semi-final and final stages of the competition in their early years but had only once won the trophy, and were embarrassingly on the receiving end of the biggest defeat in the final – 6-0 against Bury in 1902/03.

However, even in a book celebrating 50 great Rams games, the one that we are about to discuss is one of the few that actually made an independent list of all-time great matches when the BBC compiled a list of classic FA Cup ties.

As has been detailed elsewhere in the book the 1972/73 season had been a strange one, with highs, lows, and an awful amount of mediocrity thrown into the mix.

There were a number of reasons for this. It had been a supreme effort by a small squad the previous year to win the title, and this time round they were there to be shot at by other sides that believed they had worked them out.

There was also the small matter of the European Cup. Before the current Champions League, continued involvement in the competition depended on winning two-legged ties, adding extra pressure to the teams involved.

In the FA Cup, Derby had found their way through the third round thanks to a 1-0 win at Peterborough United with Roger Davies scoring the only goal, while Tottenham Hotspur won 6-0 at non-league Margate.

In the First Division Derby had earlier beaten Spurs 2-1 at the Baseball Ground with Kevin Hector scoring and Alan Hinton adding a penalty so when the two teams were drawn together at the same venue in the fourth round, there were high hopes of a similar outcome.

Instead they fought out a 1-1 draw with Davies, making his way in professional football having signed from non-league Worcester City in 1971, scoring again.

That meant a replay was required and the feeling among supporters was that the opportunity to progress had been lost with the draw at home and momentum was now with the Londoners.

Those monitoring proceedings from afar would probably see the scoreline as the game drew towards its close and feel that their feelings were right.

Not only was this ultimately a great display by Derby but a game considered by many neutrals as one of the greatest comebacks of all time.

Brian Clough's men dominated from the first whistle but gained no rewards for their efforts. They had shots blocked, hit the woodwork, and according to the *Derby Telegraph*, 'generally given Spurs a lesson'.

Cyril Knowles initiated the move that would give the hosts an undeserved lead, bursting out of defence after helping to break up yet another Derby attack.

He carried the ball down the left flank and picked out the run of Martin Chivers through the middle.

The visitors' defence was caught flat-footed and the Tottenham forward did not need to break his stride in order to lash the ball past a helpless Colin Boulton in the Derby goal and open the scoring.

Scorer turned provider as half-time approached. Chivers, who was renowned for his long throws, hurled the ball from the dead-ball line, level with the left edge of the opposition penalty area as the Rams faced up.

He picked out the head of Alan Gilzean whose initial effort at goal beat everybody but hit the crossbar and bounced back to him.

Given a second chance, and with Boulton out of the way having hurled himself at the initial shot, he put the home side two goals up.

It was scant justice for all the Rams' efforts, but there remained a belief in the dressing room that if they kept at it their reward would come.

Archie Gemmill played the ball out to his left and when it was returned into the box it fell to Hector who somehow managed to volley the ball from a tight position into the net and give a feeling that all was not lost.

Unfortunately the comeback was halted before it even had a chance to pick up momentum and it was an incident full of controversy.

Knowles delivered a free kick almost from the corner spot and the ball struck the hand of John McGovern.

It looked for all the world like accidental contact but the referee still pointed to the penalty spot.

Centre-half Mike England was the designated penalty taker, and the confidence of his spot-kick showed why as he rammed it into the net.

Time was running out and all Derby's efforts seemed likely to be in vain.

Back came the Rams, though, and a Hector corner fell to Gemmill outside the box.

Roy McFarland and John O'Hare tried to get in on the action but the ball squirmed away to where Davies was lurking outside the area. His strike fizzed past any number of bodies and the dream was suddenly alive again.

Davies then proceeded to double his tally with arguably the goal of the night.

Ron Webster took a throw from a point level with the edge of the penalty box and found O'Hare.

He played the ball short to Davies who, from a tight angle, and with his back to goal, turned and in one movement volleyed the ball past the keeper and into the net.

Seemingly from the dead the Rams had pulled it back to all square.

It wasn't too late to save the game, but it was too late for some supporters who, convinced that all was lost, had headed back to the station for the miserable journey back north with their FA Cup dreams once again in tatters.

It was with mixed emotions that those who had given up on their team learnt that the team had not given up on victory.

Not only did those who stayed to the end see a stunning comeback, they saw young Davies come of age as he took the experienced England apart time and again.

Davies completed his hat-trick in extra time and his third goal was set up by a Hector corner from the Derby right.

McFarland was lurking on the near post alongside Spurs keeper Pat Jennings, but was only acting as a decoy. The ball was played long to Davies, who despite having already scored twice, was left totally unmarked to head the ball into the net, giving him three goals on the night and five in seven games.

The fifth and final goal was a classic piece of end-to-end simplicity. Boulton kicked the ball from his hands down the park. Davies, standing on the halfway line, headed it into the path of Hector. All the energy that Spurs had put into the game was starting to tell on them in extra time, and a clear lack of concentration left the home defence standing square and flat-footed.

Hector ran into the box with four defenders trailing in his wake and though Jennings tried to make himself look big he could do nothing to prevent the goal.

As the final goal hit the back of the net Barry Davies, commentating for the BBC, said, '5-3 to Derby and surely one of the greatest comebacks of all time in the FA Cup.'

Facing the victors was a game against Queens Park Rangers, and Rangers captain Terry Venables was at the White Hart Lane replay to run his eye over his opponents.

The man who later took charge of the England team admitted that he would have preferred to meet Spurs, which was understandable.

He had played successfully for the team from White Hart Lane before moving to Loftus Road. Local derbies are always special as well, but he admitted, 'Let's face it there was only one team in it. It's going to be very tough for us. Derby are fantastic.'

He was undoubtedly right as Derby proceeded to destroy QPR at the Baseball Ground in the fifth round.

It was the same pair who had done all the damage in the replay, but this time it was Hector who got the hat-trick while Davies picked up one in the 4-2 success.

Leeds United were drawn at the Baseball Ground in the sixth round, but there was to be no fairytale end to the cup run as the Rams stumbled out of the competition with a 1-0 defeat.

It was the year that Leeds reached the final only to lose to Sunderland, who became the first team from the Second Division to win the FA Cup since 1931 thanks to Ian Porterfield's goal and Jim Montgomery's wonder-save.

The night has gone down in legend and often comes up in conversations about the Rams' greatest results, particularly when people are talking to Davies, who has remained involved with Derby County in various capacities since his playing days came to an end.

And in a 1998 book, *The Derby County Story*, Davies reflected, 'Everybody says, "Do you remember the Tottenham game?"

'Obviously you never forget a night like that. I was still young and it was still early days for me in the first team.

'We played them on the Saturday and we drew 1-1, and I hadn't had a particularly good game. They'd scored and we got a free kick. Toddy mis-hit it and it came to me. I just toe-poked it first time and it went in and we tied 1-1.

'Monday morning comes, and we're training and Cloughie was talking about Wednesday night and he said, "People like you, you'll be one of the first names on the sheet for Wednesday, for the replay", giving you confidence, building you up.

'I can still hear him saying it, "You'll be the first or second name on the sheet for Wednesday."

'So we went down there and I think it was a good game all round. We got behind. We got back in it at 2-1, and they got a penalty for 3-1.

'We were still on equal terms. We were playing well and in with a shout. And one went in for me, then another one, and your confidence starts getting higher.

'Then another one went in and Kevin finished it off at 5-3. A tremendous night. People never forget that. They always remind me of it. And you know, they can never take things like that away from you.'

v Juventus 0-0

(Juventus won 3-1 on aggregate)
25 April 1973. Attendance: 38,450
Baseball Ground. European Cup Semi-Final Second Leg

DERBY COUNTY:	JUVENTUS:
Boulton	Zoff
Webster	Spinosi
Nish	Marchetti
O'Hare	Furino
Daniel (Sims 71)	Morini
Todd	Salvadore
McGovern	Causio
Powell (Durban HT)	Cuccureddu (Longobucco 67)
Davies	Anastasi
Hector	Capello
Hinton	Altafini

Referee: Francisco Soerio Marques Lobo (Portugal)

DERBY COUNTY in the semi-finals of the European Cup. Even now at the time of writing, 40 years on, it just doesn't seem real. But back in the 1970s the Rams were one of English football's top names and in 1972/73 they were on the hunt for the Holy Grail, the crowning glory that would have surely been rated as their greatest success of all.

They had made Europe sit up and take notice when eliminating Portuguese giants Benfica in the second round and that earned them a place in the quarter-final.

There they came past Czechoslovakian side Spartak Trnava with a 2-1 aggregate win, having lost the first leg away from home before returning to the Baseball Ground and going through thanks to goals either side of half-time from Kevin Hector.

The King had been the main man on one of the Baseball Ground's finest nights and now Derby were two steps away from becoming Kings of Europe, a remarkable feat for any club let alone one from a small provincial town in its first season in the European Cup.

The line-up for the last four saw the Rams in the pot with Italian side Juventus, six-times European champions Real Madrid and Dutch giants Ajax, who had won the competition in 1971 and 1972 and were gunning for a hat-trick.

A 'dream' final for the neutrals would have been Madrid against Ajax but the two sides were paired together in the draw, meaning the two perceived lesser lights – Juventus had not yet transferred their domestic success into the European game – would face off with the first leg in Italy. And that first leg at the Stadio Delle Alpi could warrant an entire book on its own, such was the level of controversy and intrigue that surrounded it.

The straightforward facts of the matter are that Juventus won the game 3-1. They were in front on 27 minutes through Jose Altafini, only for Hector to quickly equalise and become the first player from an English club to score on Italian soil in the European Cup.

A goal from Franco Causio midway through the second half put Juventus in front once again and Altafini's second of the game with seven minutes left gave them a real advantage going into the second leg.

Another indisputable fact was that Roy McFarland and Archie Gemmill were both booked in the first leg by the West German referee Gerhard Schulenberg, suspending them for the return at the Baseball Ground.

It was the night of the famous 'cheating bastards' quote from manager Brian Clough when he spoke post-match to the press.

By the time the second leg came around two weeks later Clough had calmed down somewhat and had turned his attentions to how he could guide Derby through to the European Cup Final.

He was given a boost with Alan Hinton, Roger Davies and Ron Webster all declaring themselves fit to play.

His only team selection choice was one from Tony Parry, Alan Durban or Steve Powell to start in the middle of midfield.

Clough knew that his side faced a tough task if they were to get through but he was drawing on the inspiration of previous rounds on home turf when Derby had beaten Zeljeznicar Sarajevo 2-0, Benfica 3-0 and Spartak Trnava 2-0. Another 2-0 success would be enough for overall victory thanks to the away goals rule.

Clough said, 'We have to repeat one of those previous scores. But really we have to do better because Juventus are the finest team that we have faced in the competition so far.

'We are also facing a bigger deficit than we did against Spartak although the same margin will put us through.

'It is a situation which suits the Italians but I honestly and sincerely believe that Derby County can reach the final.'

And his assistant Peter Taylor added, 'The players are prepared to sell their souls for the club.

'After last Saturday's game against West Ham [a 1-1 draw at the Baseball Ground], which was thoroughly frustrating for players and spectators, a complete outsider, a German in fact, told me that, considering we faced a European Cup semi-final four days later, the effort of the players was magnificent.

'He said that he had not seen anything like this on the continent. We must give our players credit for that.'

The Baseball Ground atmosphere was absolutely electric for a match that, even as recently as five years previously, Rams fans must have thought they would never see.

And that made for an explosive opening from the players with Webster forcing Dino Zoff into a scrambling save and Portuguese referee Francisco Soerio Marques Lobo rejecting a strong penalty appeal – all inside the first couple of minutes.

John O'Hare and Hinton forced Zoff into further good saves as the half progressed with the Rams in the ascendency and Juventus having to defend strongly.

That was the style Italian clubs were famed for however and while they were under plenty of pressure they were not looking too troubled.

Davies was, however, causing them plenty of problems, and he might have done better than shooting over when he collected a fine pass from Colin Todd.

Knowing the danger Davies was causing, the Italians stepped up their physical treatment of the man who had been signed from non-league side Worcester City in 1971.

They were particularly strong-arm in the second period and eventually, after plenty of rough treatment from Morini, Davies snapped and headbutted the defender.

He had been provoked continually but referee Lobo was correct in sending off Davies, which meant the Rams had to play out almost half an hour with only ten men.

The dismissal came at the end of a period which arguably ended Derby's hopes of reaching the final.

Six minutes previously, after several earlier unsuccessful appeals, they had been awarded a penalty after Spinosi's foul on Hector, the Italians' 25th such offence in a tetchy performance.

At that stage they were starting to look rattled and if the penalty had found the back of the net it would have made for an exciting finale to the night.

As it was, Hinton – in his first senior game for a month – stepped up and, despite normally being so deadly from the spot, fired his effort wide.

With Hinton's penalty and Davies's departure went Derby's drive and verve that had served them so well up to that point.

There was no shortage of effort, and they continued to push forward, but by then they were not likely to break through.

It was only in the later stages that Juventus seriously pushed forward themselves, content that they were going to progress through to the final.

Colin Boulton produced fine saves from Anastasi and Longobucco to at least ensure that the Rams were going out having not lost on the night.

Indeed, they had the curious statistic of exiting the European Cup at the semi-final stage having not conceded a goal in any of their four home fixtures in the competition.

Surprisingly given his usually outspoken nature, Clough had very little to say in the days immediately after the second leg.

His main target was Davies, about whom he blasted, 'Davies will be fined a week's wages. He was disgraceful. There is no excuse for being sent off in the way he was.'

Davies's indiscretion cost him a fine of £100 and also earned him a suspension for the Rams' next three European matches, although as the 1972/73 season drew to a close they were not likely to be back in Europe next time around.

Their hopes of retaining the championship they won in 1972 had evaporated and they were also well off the pace for qualification for the UEFA Cup.

They eventually finished ninth, a disappointing outcome given the almost unbridled success of the Clough and Taylor era.

Derby did return to European competition for the 1974/75 campaign, and the two seasons after that, but they never again got close to winning a tournament.

Juventus's reward for getting through was a first European Cup Final though they were beaten 1-0 by Ajax to give the Dutch side a third successive victory in the competition.

But the controversy that surrounded both legs of the Juventus tie never went away and there were rumours that Portuguese referee Lobo, who had taken charge of the second leg, had been approached with a bribe to sway the match in favour of the Italians though an official inquiry found nothing. The situation surrounding the first leg, however, was far less clear-cut as it later emerged that referee Schulenberg had accepted 'gifts' from the Turin club prior to the match.

And an interview with Taylor, later printed in a 1998 book, *The Derby County Story*, saw the assistant shed more light on the events of 1973.

He said, 'At Juventus it was a sad day for football and it was certainly a black day for Derby because we were the innocent parties and we played a side that cheated. There's no question, although it's never been proved. That ref was bought, hook, line and sinker.

'John Charles [the former Leeds and Juventus great], who we took along with us, told us prior to going out that their sub had been into the referee's room twice.

'They were both German. Haller was the player on the subs' bench for Juventus, and the referee was German. And that wasn't on, for a start. So I was already suspicious.

'By half-time we were playing so well that there was no way we could have lost that match. Then I saw Haller go to the ref. I had no choice but to follow him because there was intrigue going on and I let them know.

'Then all hell was let loose and I never got to the dressing room. They knew I'd rumbled them. I couldn't do anything about it and by the time it was all over, the sides were then going out for the second half.

'It was all the result of me sensing the situation and them knowing I had. The consequences were frightening really.'

But back to Davies, who – if his football career turned sour following his dismissal – found himself with an alternative career path.

The *Derby Telegraph* reported that Loughborough boxing manager and trainer Buddy Thomas, the former RAF light-heavyweight champion, was open to the idea of Davies quitting football and getting into the fight game.

Thomas, a member of the Midlands Area Boxing Board of Control and also landlord of the Loughborough Hotel, said, 'I saw this lad on television last night and I liked his style. He has got a good left hook although, of course, he won't be able to use his head in the ring.

'This is no gimmick. Davies is a big fellow. He is fit and I think that with a few weeks' training he could be very useful. He has a lot of promise.

'I know Davies must be well paid at Derby but I can guarantee him more money in boxing than he will ever earn in football – he could get £2,000 a fight.'

v Atletico Madrid 2-2

(AET, 4-4 on aggregate, Derby won 7-6 on penalties)
6 November 1974. Attendance: 35,000. Estadio Vicente
Calderon. UEFA Cup Second Round Second Leg

DERBY COUNTY:	ATLETICO MADRID:
Boulton	Reina
Webster	Capon
Nish	Diaz
Rioch	Adelardo (Marcelino HT)
Daniel	Benegas
Powell	Eusebio
Newton	Alberto (Salcedo 61)
Gemmill	Luis
Davies	Garate
Hector	Irureta
Lee	Ayala

Referee: Ferdinand Biwersi (Germany)

DERBY COUNTY were in the UEFA Cup at the second attempt. They had first qualified for European football's second tier competition after finishing fourth in the 1969/70 First Division but were banned from taking part because of off-field financial issues.

So the 1974/75 tournament was the Rams' second crack at conquering Europe and they earned their place by finishing third in the First Division at the end of 1973/74.

Only one of their playing squad, summer signing Francis Lee, had tasted success in Europe before, having won the European Cup Winners' Cup with Manchester City in 1970.

Manager Dave Mackay had won the same competition as a player with Tottenham Hotspur in 1963 and he had also played in the UEFA Cup with Spurs and Scottish club Heart of Midlothian, where he had started his playing career. Mackay had only been in the Rams' hot-seat for less than a year having taken over in October 1973 and had done well to stop the wheels coming completely off, let alone win a place in the UEFA Cup.

Three other English clubs – Wolverhampton Wanderers, Stoke City and Ipswich Town – joined Derby in the competition though the Rams were the only team to get past the first round.

Ipswich were vanquished by FC Twente, Stoke by their fellow Dutch side Ajax, and Wolves went out to Portuguese giants Porto.

Derby's opponents at the first hurdle were Servette FC of Switzerland and their passage through to the next round was comfortable.

Kevin Hector scored twice in a 4-1 victory at the Baseball Ground in the first leg, with Peter Daniel and Lee adding the other goals, then Lee and Hector netted again for a 2-1 success away from home.

This was an era where the big clubs regularly played in the UEFA Cup if they were not champions of their country so Derby could have faced Inter Milan or Ajax, or they could have had another crack at Juventus – a match that would have undoubtedly been spicy.

In the end they drew Atletico Madrid, the 'second' team of Spain's capital though certainly a formidable opponent.

By that time Atletico had won La Liga seven times, the Copa del Rey on four occasions, been runners-up in the 1973/74 European Cup and won the European Cup Winners' Cup in 1961/62.

The first leg at the Baseball Ground had ended in a 2-2 draw with the Rams twice coming from behind.

Ruben Ayala put Atletico in front on 13 minutes, David Nish levelled it two minutes later, a penalty from future Spanish national team coach Luis Aragones put his side back in front on 77 only for Bruce Rioch's spot-kick on 85 to make it 2-2.

With away goals counting double Derby could certainly be deemed to be up against it when they travelled to Madrid for the second leg.

They were without Colin Todd, who had missed the previous Saturday's 1-0 win at Leeds United with injury, so Mackay named the same starting line-up that had been successful at Elland Road.

That meant Roger Davies was able to play in Europe for the first time having served his three-match ban for being sent off in the second leg of the 1972/73 European Cup semi-final against Juventus.

In the build-up to the match Mackay dismissed speculation that he had put in a bid of £350,000 for Leicester City's England international goalkeeper Peter Shilton.

It was an interesting one as the previous week, prior to travelling to Leeds, Mackay had been ready to drop goalkeeper Colin Boulton because of poor form – only to be convinced otherwise and fully rewarded at Elland Road.

And Mackay also dismissed any notion that Atletico may have felt that they had almost done enough by getting the draw at the Baseball Ground.

He said, 'If that is the case we must have a good chance. It is essential that we stop them from scoring, particularly in the first half, and if we can put one in the game is wide open.

'We shall miss Toddy of course. But at Leeds Steve Powell was exactly the man for the job. They attacked so much that pace was not required and Steve was able to use his strength in the air.

'I have no doubts that he can do as good a job against Atletico but they break quickly and this is where Todd's speed would have been invaluable.

'However we have survived so far without Roy McFarland [injured since May after damaging an Achilles tendon while on international duty with England] and we can get through this one without Todd.

'We would obviously have been happier coming here with a lead but the tie is still in an intriguing state.'

A 1-1 draw in the second leg would have sent Atletico through on away goals while a higher scoring draw than 2-2 would have put Derby through in the same way.

The only way the Rams could have faced a first ever competitive penalty shoot-out would have been by drawing 2-2 at the Estadio Vicente Calderon.

Mackay's hopes of Derby keeping things tight and scoring early on were dashed with just five minutes on the clock as they fell behind, both on the night and on aggregate.

A free kick was chipped in from near the goal line by Adelardo and Luis was left in far too much space to head past Boulton.

Lee and Rioch missed great chances to level for the Rams before half-time and there was a sense that you don't get too many opportunities in a game such as this one, especially when Atletico roared back and Alberto hit the Derby bar and then fired a shot narrowly over.

The Spaniards started the second half quickly too but within nine minutes the tie was all square once again.

Hector's centre was headed down by Davies and in ran Rioch to put the ball beyond Miguel Reina.

That stunned the home crowd and they were completely silenced on 63 as Derby went ahead for the first time.

Lee was under pressure and found Archie Gemmill, on his 200th appearance for the Rams, and the Scot's cross was perfect for Hector to control and finish off with style.

All of a sudden Derby were in command but they knew that one goal from the home side would send the match to extra time.

Newton saw a shot glance a post and that was the escape Atletico needed as they levelled things up once more with 15 minutes left.

Newton was harshly penalised for handball and up stepped Luis to curl home the free kick.

By now it was anyone's game and both sides pushed for the winning goal on a night of flowing football that went from end to end.

But neither could find a breakthrough before the 90-minute mark so extra time came along, and went with no further additions to the scoreline, meaning that first competitive penalty shoot-out for the Rams had arrived.

Rioch and Hector scored for Derby, Luis and Ayala for Atletico, then Reina turned Davies's kick on to the post and Salcedo put the home side in the driving seat after three penalties each.

Nish netted but the pendulum swung once more when Capon fired his effort over the bar and after Lee and Irureta both scored, it was 4-4 after five shots each and sudden-death was required.

Gemmill, Newton and Powell all did the necessary for Derby, as did Benegas and Garate for Atletico, but their eighth kick, the 16th of the shoot-out, was the crucial one.

Up stepped Eusebio – not the Portuguese great who had been in the Benfica side beaten by Derby in the 1972/73 European Cup – but Boulton was equal to the challenge and turned his effort on to the post.

A night of the highest drama had finished in the most exciting way imaginable and Derby's players, each one a hero, celebrated the most thrilling of victories.

The late, late finish in Madrid meant that readers of the *Derby Telegraph* had to wait until the Friday edition to find out what Mackay had to say about his team's thrilling triumph.

Mackay's delight was clear to everyone and he was also turning his attentions towards the following Saturday's home First Division game against Queens Park Rangers.

'They [the players] had a good night out on Wednesday, and I would have expected that as a player,' he said.

'This has been the best week since I came to Derby. We beat Leeds and then eliminated Atletico.

'Now we have to come down from the clouds and get a result tomorrow. With three home matches out of the next four, we have a great chance of being up among the leaders.

'It was a great night on Wednesday and we have to reproduce it tomorrow. I am happy that there is still a place for Steve Powell, who had a fine match, and after Madrid I am again forced to wonder why Archie Gemmill is not in the Scotland squad.

'Nothing in the match was more fantastic than the way he sprinted 90 yards to stop an Atletico forward getting in a shot.'

The draw for the third round pitted Derby with Yugoslavian side Velez Mostar, with the first leg to the played at the Baseball Ground on 27 November.

Mackay admitted he would have preferred to have had the second leg at home and said he didn't want to travel to Yugoslavia without a victory, although he pointed to the elimination of Atletico as firm evidence that ties are not lost if the first leg at home is not won.

Back in the First Division, Derby did get the win against QPR – 5-2 with Hector netting a hat-trick and the others coming from Lee and Rioch – then they went down 3-1 at Arsenal before beating Ipswich 2-0 at the Baseball Ground.

That set them up nicely for the first leg against Mostar but they fell behind on two minutes, before Alan Hinton levelled on 74 and a double from Jeff Bourne appeared to have put them in command.

Away from home in the second leg it was a different story and the Rams were three down before Hector levelled the tie on 58 minutes, only for a penalty four minutes from time to send Mostar through to the quarter-finals.

They were beaten by FC Twente, who went on to lose the final 5-1 over two legs to Borussia Moenchengladbach.

It was a disappointing way to go out for Derby but they were back in the European Cup as English champions the following season and had another go at the UEFA Cup in 1976/77 when they only lasted for two rounds before bowing out.

14 v Manchester City 2-1

28 December 1974. Attendance: 40,188
Maine Road. Football League First Division

DERBY COUNTY:	MANCHESTER CITY:
Boulton	Corrigan
Webster	Hammond
Nish	Donachie
Rioch	Bell
Daniel	Doyle
Todd	Oakes
Newton	Horswill
Gemmill	Royle
Davies	Marsh
Bourne	Hartford
Lee	Tueart
Unused sub: Hinton	*Unused sub:* Henson
Referee: John Gow	

PERHAPS Dave Mackay saw echoes of his own arrival when he signed Francis Lee for Derby County in the summer of 1974. Mackay had taken over and steadied the ship following the turmoil surrounding the departure of Brian Clough and Peter Taylor in October 1973.

He guided the Rams to third in the First Division but they were never really title contenders and needed an extra edge if they were to regain the championship they had first won in 1972.

Step forward Lee, who at the age of 30 had already scored more than 200 goals in the Football League for Bolton Wanderers and Manchester City and had won 27 England caps too.

With City he had won the First Division in 1967/68, the FA Cup in 1969 and League Cup in 1970, plus the Charity Shield in 1968 and 1972 along with the 1969/70 European Cup Winners' Cup.

It was a big signing for Derby, of that there was no doubt, and Lee scored the Rams' first goal of the 1974/75 season in a 1-1 draw at home to Coventry City.

He complemented the striking options provided by Roger Davies and Kevin Hector not just with his goals but his all-round performances and his experience in the game.

Lee was in good form during the first half of the campaign and up to Christmas he had scored nine goals in the First Division, one in the League Cup and two in the UEFA Cup. But as his first return to Manchester City in a Derby shirt approached he had been struggling for goals and had not netted since a 5-2 win at home to Queens Park Rangers on 9 November.

The 28 December encounter was already shaping up to be a big one in Derby's season with more than half of the First Division's teams all within striking distance of the top of the table.

And Mackay's men knew they needed to spark themselves into life again as, after that victory over QPR, they had then lost three of their next five and only ended that run with a 2-1 win at home to Birmingham City on Boxing Day.

Mackay felt that beating of the Blues was vital and he told the *Derby Telegraph*, 'Yesterday's victory over Birmingham put us back in business.

'It was getting to the stage where, if we lost one more game, we would have been out of the running.

'I still think someone will make it up to 56 points and if it is going to be us, it makes it a very hard target.

'We were very tense when we lost at Luton but I hope we will go into the game tomorrow in a more relaxed frame of mind.

'We beat an impressive side yesterday. Birmingham were very sharp and one or two of them, particularly Howard Kendall, played extremely well.

'We were much more composed in defence than we have been recently and Peter Daniel did a tremendous job against Ken Burns.'

Mackay named the same side to face Manchester City as had beaten Birmingham so that meant a 501st appearance in a Derby shirt for dependable defender Ron Webster.

Webster was only 18 when he made his Rams debut in an away game at Bury in March 1962 under Harry Storer and after really establishing himself in Tim Ward's 1964/65 team Webster had been a fixture in the number two shirt.

His milestone appearance against Birmingham meant he had become only the fourth Derby player to reach 500 games, along with Geoff Barrowcliffe and Jack Parry – who Webster had played alongside – and Steve Bloomer.

City went into the game defending an unbeaten home record so far in 1974/75 and piled on the early pressure but could not find a breakthrough as Derby stood firm.

And it was the visitors who opened the scoring on 21 minutes through Henry Newton, whose display to that point had been purely focused on defending from midfield. Bruce Rioch's centre was cleared out and won by Newton and the ball fell to Lee, who was under pressure so laid it back to his colleague.

Newton let fly from outside the box with a superb shot that flew into the top corner for his first goal of the season.

City battled hard to get back into the match but they were struggling to create many real clear-cut chances with Peter Daniel and Colin Todd outstanding in the centre of Derby's defence.

When they did get a sighter they were met by Colin Boulton's fine saves from Marsh, Doyle and Tueart, though the goalkeeper almost caused problems for himself with a clearance from his hands that caught in the swirling wind, went almost straight upwards and landed close to goal.

City's eventual equaliser in the 63rd minute was well crafted and one of the rare times they managed to get in behind Derby.

Hartford started the move from outside the box, Marsh rolled the ball through and Colin Bell ran in to finish off the chance and drive his shot past Boulton.

That might have been the catalyst for the home side to push on and win the match but instead they found themselves behind again two minutes later.

David Nish was involved as he pushed down the left and fed the ball to Lee, who had his back to goal and was on the corner of the penalty area with two City defenders behind him.

So he did the only thing that seemed on and turned away from his markers, came inside a bit on to his right foot and smashed his shot well beyond the dive of Joe Corrigan.

It was just as well that the game was being screened on that night's edition of *Match of the Day* because the goal was worthy of endless repeats, helped especially by Barry Davies's iconic commentary:

'Lee, interesting ... VERY interesting! Oh! Look at his face! Just look at his face!'

Corrigan had been a virtual spectator for the second period but could only look on as he was beaten by a stunner from his former Maine Road colleague.

City looked to their big performers like Marsh and Tueart but they failed to fire the home side to a recovery, despite them enjoying plenty of the ball.

Newton and Archie Gemmill were excellent in helping out their defenders with Davies and Bourne also tracking back when required.

It was a result that left Derby three points away from the First Division's leading two teams, Ipswich Town and Middlesbrough, but with only five points separating 13 teams as 1975 approached it was anyone's guess as to what the next few months held.

Although it was Lee who took the headlines for his goal, Mackay was just as pleased with his side's defensive effort when he gave his post-match analysis.

He said, 'Our defence was tremendous. We will go out to play any team, but if we have to defend then we'll do it. The tackling and covering was great and we marked really tightly.

'City were allowed very few other chances.'

And Lee, still with fond emotions for his old club, said, 'I don't play for City any more and have to do my best for Derby. But if we don't win the title, I hope City do.

'They put us under a lot of pressure. When City equalised I expected even more pressure, but we were lucky enough to break away and score again.'

As well as the result, Mackay had plenty of other issues to deal with, not least speculation that defender Roy McFarland would not be playing at all during 1974/75.

McFarland, the captain of the 1972 title-winning side, had picked up a serious Achilles tendon injury while playing for England at the end of the previous season and had not lined up for the Rams' first team since.

He had appeared for the 'A' team at the end of November but had not trained for the ten days prior to the victory over Manchester City because of what had been termed by Mackay as a 'setback'.

The manager added, 'Of course we are disappointed by the delay. He was going so well that he was a certainty to be back by Christmas. But, in guarding the left ankle, he strained the right.

'It is such a tiny thing. There is one spot, almost a pin prick, where his ankle is sore. Roy will be consulting a specialist and if he comes up with the right answer, we could have Roy back for two months of this season.

'At this stage, it is simply not possible to rule him out for a specific period.'

And Mackay was also dealing with transfer talk linking him with a move for Southampton striker Peter Osgood, who he had targeted with a proposed exchange deal with Roger Davies earlier in 1974 before eventually landing Lee.

Osgood was available again but Mackay said that if he was after a new striker he would be looking for a younger man, adding, 'We have Francis Lee and Kevin Hector both around 30 and if we got Osgood, we would find them all growing old together.'

Derby did not add a new striker, preferring instead to rely on Lee, Hector and Davies, with support from Jeff Bourne as required, and when Lee was out of the team towards the end of the season Alan Hinton was able to return and help guide the club towards the finish line in a remarkably tight First Division.

Lee finished 1974/75 with 12 goals in his 34 First Division games, along with one each in the FA Cup and League Cup plus those two in the UEFA Cup for a total of 15 in his first term at the Baseball Ground – earning himself a second championship medal in the process.

McFarland did eventually return to the side but only for the final four games of the season, initially taking over from David Nish at left-back for one match before taking back his more familiar number five shirt from Daniel in the last three encounters.

Daniel had stood in for McFarland admirably since the start of the campaign and, such was his form, he claimed the Jack Stamps Trophy after being voted as the supporters' Player of the Year.

Webster played his 535th and final game for the Rams in a 1-1 draw at Chelsea on 10 September 1977, setting a record that was eventually overhauled by Hector on his way to 589.

15 v Luton Town 5-0

29 March 1975. Attendance: 24,619
Baseball Ground. Football League First Division

DERBY COUNTY:	LUTON TOWN:
Boulton	Barber
Thomas	John Ryan
Nish	Buckley
Rioch	Anderson
Daniel	Faulkner
Todd	P Futcher
Powell	Jim Ryan
Gemmill	Husband (Seasman 72)
Davies	R Futcher
Hector	West
Hinton	Aston
Unused sub: Bourne	
Referee: Ray Tinkler	

AFTER the whirlwind excitement of the Brian Clough era had subsided, and the dust storm caused by the arrival of Dave Mackay as manager had settled the Rams reverted to winning ways.

And there were changes to the playing style to go along with the managerial alterations.

While Clough was insistent on a solid spine to the team and a strong and defensively sound back four, Mackay was more cavalier in his approach. He took the view that his teams had to entertain and he didn't mind if they conceded three provided his side scored four.

It was a great policy, and easy to administer with the likes of Kevin Hector, Roger Davies and Alan Hinton already on board.

With new signings Bruce Rioch and Francis Lee, plus the emergence of Jeff Bourne from the reserves, goals seemed in plentiful supply.

This was shown by the fact that the Rams had only failed to score in seven of their first 34 First Division matches in 1974/75 prior to the visit of Luton Town to the Baseball Ground on 29 March.

Their first four games in March had seen eight goals with Rioch, Davies and Peter Daniel netting in a 3-1 win at home to Tottenham Hotspur, Daniel and Hinton securing the points at Chelsea, Hector on target in a 2-1 defeat at home to Stoke City and a 2-0 win at Newcastle United coming courtesy of goals from Rioch and David Nish.

Davies had scored six goals before the Luton game, a modest return for a striker but with the whole team chipping in regularly there was no real pressure on any one man to lead the scoring charts.

And his afternoon against Luton turned into one of those occasions that lives in the memory forever.

Sportsmen and women refer to it as 'being in the zone' when absolutely everything they do or try comes off.

For Davies that would mean achieving something not managed by a Derby County player for 40 years

Luton had been promoted at the end of the previous season and as is so often the case they struggled to compete at the higher level.

Although they were relegated at the end of their one season in the top flight it wasn't all doom and gloom for them and they enjoyed a few good days, one of which came on 21 December when they beat the Rams 1-0 at Kenilworth Road.

But if they thought that beating Derby once made any difference to the return match they were very much mistaken.

John Faulkner was the luckless defender whose job it was to mark Davies on this occasion. The centre-half did not know which way to turn for the best. It is difficult to know if he was at his strongest in the air or on the ground as the Derby striker consistently had the beating of him in both departments.

It is fair to say that even with Paul Futcher alongside Faulkner and the two full-backs, Davies seemed like an unstoppable force of nature.

As with so many Rams goals of this period much credit has to go to Hinton and his corner was met by the head of Davies to put Derby a goal up after nine minutes.

As a tall man you would expect Davies to be reasonably good in the air. The fact seemed to escape the visitors however, who did not appear to have done their homework.

They were undone again four minutes later. This time it was a cross from Rod Thomas that did the damage.

Thomas was an attacking right-back and having gone on one of his gallops down the flank he played the ball into the box.

It was probably not the cross that he intended to deliver, in fact the *Derby Telegraph* said that he 'gave it too much air'. Only Thomas will know the truth, but there is no doubt what the effect was.

Panic once more prevailed in the Hatters' defence. Davies met the ball with his head, John Ryan made a despairing attempt to prevent it going over the line and Derby were 2-0 up with less than a quarter of an hour played.

Davies had not been a regular in Mackay's team but had been working on his game while out of the side and had shown the benefits of all the extra work that he had put in when recalled to play against Tottenham four games previously.

He scored on his return, but failed to find the back of the net in the next three games. Even so, the Luton scouts did not appear to have done their job as far as their report on the Rams striker was concerned.

They should probably have also spent some time checking out the attacking threat of Thomas as he set up both the second and the third goals.

If there was any suggestion of a mistake in the way he provided Davies the first time there was nothing wrong with the second.

Once more Thomas took the ball away from defence and played a devastating forward pass for the rampant striker to run on to.

By this stage of the game poor Faulkner not only did not know what time of day it was, but was undoubtedly struggling without the aid of a calendar to even make a reasonable stab at which month he was in.

Added to this Luton goalkeeper Keith Barber was doing his best impression of a rabbit caught in the headlights of an approaching car.

The first two goals had been headers, but this time Davies showed his versatility by firing home a cross-shot.

There were no more goals before half-time, but that isn't to say that there were no more attempts by the home side.

There were, and twice more it was Davies who had the ball in the back of the net.

The first time it was Archie Gemmill who provided the opportunity. The wee Scotsman nodded the ball towards Davies who dived low to make contact. Referee Ray Tinkler denied him glory though by ruling it out for offside.

Hinton created a further opportunity before the break but Davies was adjudged to have handled before firing home.

It was a shame because the pass from Hinton was described as 'exquisite'.

Still, a hat-trick in under 45 minutes was no mean feat and in the state Luton were in who could know what the second half would bring.

The crowd had a sense that there was something special about this game. Most of them would have seen hat-tricks scored – both for and against Derby County – but the simple fact that there had been three goals by one man and could have been five made for excited chatter on the terraces during the interval.

As is so often the way with a game totally dominated by one side for an entire half the second period was a bit of an anti-climax.

Luton contributed little by way of attacking threat, but managed to undo any pride that a scoreless second half may give them when a poor back-header from John Aston fell to the one person it shouldn't have done.

There were probably many places that the ball could have landed but at the feet of the man who on that particular day was the most dangerous striker on the planet was the worst possible one. It was now 4-0 to the home side and there were still 12 minutes of regulation time to be played.

Could Davies make it five in the time remaining left to him? Almost as if it was scripted especially for him the answer was yes.

With 86 minutes on the clock Hinton fired in another inch-perfect pass which Faulkner again totally misjudged.

There was only ever going to be one place where it was going to land, and sure enough Davies turned the ball home to make him the first player since Hughie Gallacher to score five in a Derby shirt.

In the remaining minutes Kevin Hector tried to set up his strike partner for a sixth, but for once Barber in the visitors' goal was more than a match for the Rams and pulled off a superlative save.

Luton nearly had a goal of their own but Colin Boulton was equal to the attempted header from Aston.

So Davies ended the match with five goals but that could so easily have been eight.

On a day of personal triumph it was only fitting that he was congratulated by players from both teams on the referee's final whistle.

It has been suggested that Davies only achieved what he did because Luton were so poor, but as Gerald Mortimer pointed out in the *Derby Telegraph*, 'They came to Derby with three wins behind them and a record only slightly inferior to the Rams' in the period since the two teams met in December.'

It was a remarkable feat by Davies as he took his season's goal tally from six to 11 in the space of 90 minutes, and just 48 hours later he moved on to 12 as the Rams once again scored twice.

This time Burnley were the victims in an Easter Monday massacre at Turf Moor with Hector adding two more in the 5-2 success, aided by Rioch and Nish.

Rioch scored twice in a Baseball Ground victory over Manchester City the day after that Burnley game and although Derby drew their next game 1-1 at Middlesbrough, successive 1-0 wins – at home to Wolverhampton Wanderers and West Ham United – put them on the cusp of regaining the title they had won in 1972.

Their penultimate match saw them draw 0-0 at Leicester City then news broke that their nearest challengers Everton, Liverpool and Ipswich Town had all lost.

One more point from the final game would be enough to clinch the title but once again Derby were crowned champions without kicking a ball as, on the Wednesday night before the final day, Ipswich dropped a point against Manchester City.

That was that and the celebrations at the club's annual awards night, at the Bailey's club in Derby, kicked off immediately.

No matter that the end of the season saw a drab 0-0 draw at home to relegated Carlisle United as it was all about milking the success.

Derby won the title on 53 points, the lowest successful total since Chelsea's 52 in 1954/55, but only tenth-placed Burnley scored more goals (68) than their 67, while only third-placed Ipswich Town – 23 against 21 – won more matches.

Davies finished the season with those 12 goals in the First Division, matching the return of Hinton and one behind Hector, but the leading scorer came from midfield as Rioch racked up 15.

And Davies's five-goal haul would be repeated in less than 18 months.

16 v Real Madrid 4-1

22 October 1975. Attendance: 34,839
Baseball Ground. European Cup Second Round First Leg

DERBY COUNTY:	REAL MADRID:
Boulton	Miguel Angel
Thomas	Sol
Nish	Rubinan
Rioch	Pirri
McFarland	Camacho
Todd	Velazquez
Newton	Amancio
Gemmill	Breitner
Lee	del Bosque
Hector (Davies 79)	Netzer
George (Bourne 79)	Martinez

Referee: Anatoli Ivonhal (Russia)

DERBY COUNTY v Real Madrid in the European Cup – make such a suggestion now and you will just be laughed at, as you would have been just a few years prior to 1975.

While Madrid were winning the first of their five successive European Cups in 1956, the Rams were fighting to get out of the Third Division North.

Even in the 1960s and with Derby in the Second Division, Madrid were still sweeping all before them on a regular basis and in that decade they added another European Cup and a staggering eight La Liga titles.

And then there was a strange bit of symmetry to the two teams' respective successes over the next few years.

In 1968/69, when Derby were promoted from the Second Division as champions, Madrid also won La Liga.

The Spanish giants did not win their national title again until 1971/72 – when the Rams were champions of England for the first time.

Madrid were not Spanish champions again for another three years, coincidentally the time it took Derby to win their second championship.

That took both clubs back into the European Cup – there were no places for teams coming second, third or beyond in those days – and with a straight knockout competition drawn each round, with no seedings or group stages to contend with, they avoided each other at the first stage.

Madrid were handed a tie against Romanian champions Dinamo Bucharest and came through 4-2 on aggregate, helped by a comfortable 4-1 win at the Bernabeu in the first leg.

Derby came up against Slovan Bratislava, of what was then Czechoslovakia, and lost the away leg 1-0 but turned things around with a 3-0 success at the Baseball Ground thanks to Jeff Bourne's strike in the first half and two late goals from Francis Lee.

There were some big names in the hat for the last 16, including Bayern Munich who had won the competition for the previous two seasons, but Derby landed the biggest of them all when they were paired with Real Madrid.

Occasions of that magnitude did not come along very often in that era so the Rams knew they were going to have to be on their best form against Madrid.

They had made a good start in their bid to retain the First Division championship and had only suffered three defeats with a run of six wins in eight games sending them into the Madrid meeting in good spirits.

They had a fully fit squad, too, whereas Madrid had a few injury concerns, notably over Spanish international centre-half Gregorio Benito who had already been ruled out of the first leg.

While Derby were beating Wolverhampton Wanderers 3-2 at home on the Saturday before the match, they sent chief scout Bert Johnson to take a look at Madrid in their 1-1 draw with Real Sociedad.

And Johnson told the *Derby Telegraph*, 'The draw was a fair reflection of the match. There is always a bit of needle between Real and teams from the Basque country although it was certainly not a dirty game.

'Any team that knocks them out of the European Cup is entitled to be very pleased. They have players who are familiar with the European scene and will undoubtedly raise their game in the European Cup.

'There will be two similar teams in action on Wednesday for both have a great deal of flair.'

Perhaps their biggest name at the time was Paul Breitner, who played at full-back for Germany but in midfield for Madrid, and he was passed fit to face the Rams.

And even though it was not a vintage Madrid side there was no doubting Derby manager Dave Mackay's excitement about the encounter.

He said, 'Their name is still magical. And once we did not draw the team from Iceland [IA Akranes], Real Madrid was ideal for me.

'We don't know how good they are although they have some exceptionally good players.

'But we will be going for goals tomorrow. It would be good for us to take a substantial lead to Madrid, even though we would not necessarily be in trouble if we did not win decisively at Derby.'

Despite all of Madrid's history and successes there was no way they could ever have come up against anything as unique as a fervent big-game Baseball Ground atmosphere, especially for a night match under the floodlights.

At that time in particular the famous old ground was often like an extra player for Derby and on this particular occasion the fans drove their players on right from the start.

With just nine minutes played the roof was coming off the stadium as the Rams took the lead.

There appeared little danger when Colin Todd lifted a ball out to David Nish on the left, and that still seemed the case when Nish found Archie Gemmill.

But Gemmill saw something the rest didn't and picked out a delightful low ball across the Madrid penalty area and in ran Charlie George to fire home a powerful left-footed shot into the corner of the net.

If that wasn't good enough, with 15 on the clock Derby's explosive start earned them a second goal.

Lee burrowed his way into the box and, showing all of his years of experience, knew just how to attract the tackle from Jose Antonio Camacho.

It was enough to send the experienced striker to the ground and a penalty was correctly awarded, so up stepped George to hammer his spot-kick past goalkeeper Miguel Angel Gonzalez.

Madrid were shell-shocked and had to dig deep quickly if they were to avoid being blown out of the water before the game was even a quarter of the way through.

This they did and in the 22nd minute captain Amancio Amaro's pass was chipped in to the Derby penalty area where Pirri took it on his chest and beat Colin Boulton to make it 2-1.

The Spaniards looked like they were taking over the match but three minutes before half-time they found themselves trailing by two goals once again.

This time Roy McFarland pushed forward from the back and laid the ball out to the left where Nish collected it, cut inside, and unleashed a low shot with his right foot that Angel somewhat dived over and allowed to squeeze in at the near post.

Angel made up for that error in the second half with a string of fine saves, twice denying Lee and also keeping out a powerful free kick from Bruce Rioch.

There was controversy midway through the second period when Madrid thought they had made it 3-2 through what would have been Pirri's second of the night.

The players went off celebrating but they soon spotted an offside flag which had, admittedly, been put up a little late – by linesman Tofik Bakhramov, the man who awarded Geoff Hurst's extra-time effort in the 1966 World Cup Final.

Madrid's ire was only compounded 12 minutes from time by Russian referee Anatoli Ivonhal's decision to award the Rams a second penalty, this time after Kevin Hector had been fouled by Gunter Netzer. It gave Lee the chance to complete his hat-trick and he took it in emphatic style to add the finishing touch to what was a truly remarkable night.

George took the headlines for his treble but the performance was based around the displays of Gemmill and Todd, who put in shifts that they possibly never surpassed in a Derby shirt.

'Derby County are good enough to win the European Cup' was the first sentence in the *Derby Telegraph*'s match report of what was arguably the club's most eye-catching result ever.

And a headline elsewhere in the following day's edition exclaimed, 'Our best in my time says Mackay'.

It was impossible to argue with such a sentiment after Derby made the whole of Europe sit up and take notice with not only their victory, but the manner of it too.

Mackay said, 'We were marvellous. I thought 4-1 was a fair result. Their second goal [the one ruled out for offside] was certainly a good one but then we should have had at least another penalty.

'The ref gave obstruction when Kevin Hector was hacked down but it was obviously a deliberate foul, and should have been a penalty.

'I don't care who had been playing for them last night – we'd have beaten them 4-1 again. They had a couple of injuries but if we have trouble like that we put in Steve Powell or someone and it doesn't make any difference to us.

'The crowd were excellent but the team did the crowd proud. I've always said that only the players can get the crowd going. The fans are in the right mood at the start but you've got to give them something.

'That first goal lifted them out of their seats. It was fabulous. Some national newspaper reporters asked me if we had practised the move. I said we had, but only with geniuses, and there aren't too many of them about.'

Mackay was keen to stress however that despite the resounding scoreline, the tie was far from over, and he added, 'Real are a very good side. We must have an excellent chance of going on to the next round – as long as we don't think it's all over now.'

His Madrid counterpart Miljan Miljanic also felt that the Spaniards did have a chance of turning things around.

The Yugoslav said, 'Our task is now formidable – but not impossible. Nothing is impossible at [the] Bernabeu.

'Derby County deserved to win tonight. They are a great side and they also had some, shall we say, sporting luck.

'But we did not play as well as we can. Two of the players who are crucial to us were missing through injury and we particularly missed Benito in defence.

'I do not want to comment on the decisions that went against us. The referee's word is final.

'Full credit to Derby and their magnificent supporters.'

Madrid did have Benito back in their defence for the second leg and whether that made the complete difference is impossible to say, but the boot was well and truly on the other foot in terms of the scoreline.

Roberto Juan Martinez put them in front on three minutes, added his second on 51, and when Santillana scored four minutes later to make it 3-0 on the night and 4-4 on aggregate, Derby's hopes of a quarter-final place were diminishing.

The Rams needed something special and found it just after the hour mark through another superb George goal and they were ultimately just seven minutes from going through but a controversial Pirri penalty took the tie into extra time.

Madrid, unbeaten in the Bernabeu since 1973, had one last say when Santillana scored his second on 99 minutes and Derby could not recover.

They had given it everything in front of a massive crowd of 120,000, the highest ever for any competitive Derby County fixture, but Madrid's might proved too strong.

Madrid went on to reach the semi-finals, where they were beaten by Bayern Munich who went on to win the title for a third successive season.

The Spanish side did not become European champions again until 1997/98 by which time the competition had been re-branded as the Champions League.

And Derby have not dined at European football's top table since that November night in Madrid.

17 v Leeds United 3-2

1 November 1975. Attendance: 33,107
Baseball Ground. Football League First Division

DERBY COUNTY:	LEEDS UNITED:
Boulton	Harvey
Webster	Reaney
Nish	F Gray
Rioch (Davies 26)	Bremner
Thomas	Cherry
Todd	Hunter
Newton	Lorimer
Gemmill	Clarke
Lee	McKenzie
Hector	Yorath
George	Madeley

Referee: Derek Nippard

THE modern game is beset by any number of managers and coaches who are almost as renowned for their personalities. It is a trend that started at the end of the 1960s with Brian Clough one of the first, alongside Malcolm Allison.

One of the big names of the old school was Don Revie. Seemingly given a charisma transplant at birth, he was the epitome of the dour northerner. Leeds fans and players loved him, but there was little popular support for him in the outside world.

It has to be pointed out, of course, that Brian Clough was not universally adored.

Rams fans knew what a brilliant job Clough had done for their club, but many – even among supporters – knew he could be brash, outspoken and arrogant.

You could argue that Clough was the footballing equivalent of Marmite. You either loved him or hated him, but you certainly couldn't ignore him.

The pair had much in common – as both were very successful managers who had turned mediocre teams into great ones, but their respective personalities meant that sparks flew whenever they were together. They detested each other, and the animosity spilled over on to the pitch through the players.

Anyone joining the ranks of Derby supporters over the last few years may think that the biggest rivalry for their club is against Nottingham Forest.

Derby and Leeds was far more intense in the early 1970s as anyone who was there at the time will tell you.

By the time the two clubs met at the Baseball Ground on 1 November 1975 Clough and Revie had moved on.

Ironically Clough, who had been so outspoken in his views on the methods and players of Leeds, had been appointed manager there but lasted a mere 44 days.

Revie, for his part, had taken up the role of England manager.

Jimmy Armfield was now in charge at Leeds, while Dave Mackay had replaced Clough and steered the Rams to a second title.

As they prepared for this meeting with Leeds they were in the middle of a two-legged European Cup tie against Real Madrid and would be taking a 4-1 lead to Spain after that amazing night at the Baseball Ground.

And while success in Europe was on the Rams' agenda, so was domestic domination and they were bidding to retain the championship they had won the previous season.

Their start had been impressive with only three defeats having been recorded up to the end of October.

One of those was the staggering 5-1 reverse at home to newly-promoted Queens Park Rangers in the season's first Baseball Ground encounter while they also went down 2-0 at Everton later in August, and 1-0 at Stoke City in September.

That Stoke defeat was the only blemish in a run of nine games that included six wins and two draws.

Burnley, Tottenham Hotspur, Manchester City and Manchester United were vanquished in successive matches prior to the trip to the Victoria Ground, which was followed by a 0-0 draw at Norwich City, a 3-2 win at home to Wolverhampton Wanderers and a 1-1 draw at Liverpool – plus that 4-1 victory over Real Madrid.

Francis Lee had scored three goals in his last four games including the draw at Anfield although only once in the previous five outings, the win over Wolves, had the Rams managed to net more than a single goal.

Leeds had also been beaten three times in their 13 matches prior to their visit to the Baseball Ground.

They had restored some order with a 2-0 win at home to Coventry City the previous Saturday but prior to that they had drawn 2-2 at Birmingham City, a week after going down 2-1 at home to Manchester United.

Every time it looked like they were going to go on a run they suffered a setback and twice went three games unbeaten before suffering a defeat.

But Leeds, as ever when they came to Derby, were up for the challenge from the first whistle as they looked to bring the defending champions down a peg or two.

They had already gone close through Allan Clarke and Peter Lorimer before they opened the scoring on 11 minutes, and it was no less than their start had deserved.

Lorimer lifted in a corner from the right wing and Trevor Cherry rose highest inside the Derby area to put his header beyond Colin Boulton.

Derby's equaliser arrived less than 15 minutes later with a move that started at the back with Colin Todd, who challenged Lorimer and Billy Bremner before pushing forward and slipping the ball right to Charlie George.

George went on and drove in a low cross that Leeds goalkeeper David Harvey could not hold and in stormed Archie Gemmill to bundle the ball home.

Bruce Rioch was then lost to injury and Roger Davies replaced him, with Hector dropping back into midfield, but it did not affect the Rams who were in front three minutes before half-time, albeit in controversial circumstances.

Francis Lee bundled his way past Norman Hunter and hit the turf. It looked like Lee was trying to win himself a penalty rather than the Leeds man giving anything away but referee Derek Nippard sided with the experienced number nine and pointed to the spot.

George made no mistake with the resulting kick to send Harvey the wrong way and raise the temperatures of the Leeds players, especially Hunter who reacted unfavourably to Lee's actions. And not long after half-time those frustrations boiled over with an incident that has gone down in football legend for all the wrong reasons.

It was described in the *Derby Telegraph* thus, 'Violence erupted seven minutes into the second half when, after Lee had put in a shot, Hunter clattered into him with a late challenge.

'Lee retaliated, Hunter hit back with a blow to Lee's lip which caused a cut requiring four stitches. Players from both sides separated them and referee Derek Nippard, quite rightly, sent both of them off the field.

'As the pair straggled away towards the dressing room, they began another fight and again had to be forcibly separated, although Billy Bremner seemed keen to have a dig on his own behalf.

'For two such experienced players, it was ridiculous behaviour but, in matches between Derby and Leeds, there is always a simmering undercurrent of passion, a legacy of the hostility which existed when Brian Clough and Don Revie were the managers.

'When that passion is expressed through the football, fine games have resulted and, apart from a few minutes of ugliness, this one provided wonderful entertainment.'

Entertaining this match certainly was as, after the fisticuffs, Leeds began to take control and the game was turning in their favour again after they had fallen behind following their excellent start.

They drew level with 17 minutes left through Duncan McKenzie, who hammered the ball home past Boulton after Bremner's pass had been driven into the area by Frank Gray.

A Leeds win was looking likely but Derby timed their response to perfection and got their reward having also seen Harvey save well from Hector and Todd.

It came with a minute to go as Davies chose the ideal moment to score his first goal of the season – and what a goal it was.

Todd drove forward with the ball and found Davies, who was surrounded by yellow Leeds shirts on the edge of the box but turned superbly then came across the line of the area before letting fly with a left-footed shot that flew well beyond Harvey's desperate dive.

It was a tremendous goal, worthy of winning any match, and it was even more poetic as it came in Davies's 100th Football League game.

But despite that, there was only one talking point in the aftermath of this match.

There may have been disputes about whether Lee should have been sent off in the first place but the unpleasant scenes as the pair made their way to the side of the pitch were roundly condemned as disgraceful.

There are two conflicting stories as to why fighting re-ignited between the two, with one source suggesting that Lee felt a hole in his mouth and instantly saw red while the other suggestion was that Hunter had pointed out that that the sending off meant Lee would miss the all important away leg against Real Madrid the following Wednesday.

But in 2012, in an interview with football website www.thehardtackle.com, Lee explained, 'Norman punched me and split my mouth open which I had to have stitched up after the game. He did that before the brawl. That's why it kicked off.

'It was something that I regret and its a shame people remember that moment after both me and Norman had very successful careers.

'Dave Mackay, the manager, knew I wouldn't have done it for no reason, but still that doesn't excuse my actions.

'Me and Norman made up a long while ago and have no problems with each other, it was just one of those things.'

Lee was indeed suspended for the second leg in Madrid, but despite that indiscretion he did not miss a First Division match and remained in the team for the four other encounters in November, which produced three wins and a draw.

Arsenal were beaten at Highbury thanks to Hector's goal, Rioch and George saw off West Ham United at the Baseball Ground, a point was earned with a 0-0 draw at Wolves then Lee was back on the scoresheet – alongside Archie Gemmill and Henry Newton – in a 3-2 win at home to Middlesbrough.

At that point the Rams looked like they would be serious contenders to retain their championship but consistency started to elude them through the winter and into the spring of 1976.

They were always there or thereabouts but an injury to one of their star players in March was to prove a massive blow, as you will read in future chapters.

Lee, however, would create headlines for all the right reasons on the final day of the 1975/76 season – and you can find out all about that a couple of chapters from now.

v Newcastle United 4-2

6 March 1976. Attendance: 38,362
Baseball Ground. FA Cup Quarter-Final

DERBY COUNTY:	NEWCASTLE UNITED:
Moseley	Edgar
Thomas	Blackhall
Nish	Kennedy
Rioch	Barrowclough
McFarland	Keeley
Todd	Howard
Newton (Davies 75)	Burns
Gemmill	Cassidy
Hector	Macdonald
George	Gowling
James	Hudson
	Unused sub: Cannell

Referee: Ken Burns

DEFENDING First Division champions Derby County were gunning for a first ever league and cup double in the 1976/76 season. Dave Mackay's men had their eyes on retaining the title they had won the previous season and were also making great progress in the FA Cup.

Their path in the world's oldest cup competition had not been easy as they faced the two Merseyside giants in their first two matches.

Everton were the visitors to the Baseball Ground in the third round, the first match of 1976, and they were duly beaten 2-1 with Charlie George scoring both of the Rams' goals. Three weeks later it was the turn of Liverpool to come to Derby and they, too, went home defeated, this time by a single goal scored by Roger Davies.

That put Derby into the fifth round for the second consecutive season and, having failed at the same stage 12 months previously when beaten 1-0 at home by Leeds United, this time they did get through with another single-goal victory, against Third Division side Southend United earned thanks to Bruce Rioch.

So Derby were into the quarter-finals of the FA Cup for only the second time since 1950 and their opponents would be fellow First Division outfit Newcastle United.

The Rams had beaten Newcastle 3-2 at the Baseball Ground earlier in the season but just a month before their FA Cup clash they were beaten 4-3 by the Geordies in the return fixture.

Despite that result, Newcastle were having a few problems and their only win before meeting Derby again was against Bolton Wanderers in the replay of their FA Cup fifth round encounter.

And they also travelled to the Baseball Ground with ten of their regular first-teamers on the injured list so would be fielding star names like Alan Gowling and Malcolm Macdonald even though they were not fully fit.

Mackay was, however, reading very little into the fortunes of the visitors as he knew just how much of a threat they could be.

He told the *Derby Telegraph*, 'I know Newcastle have their problems but whoever plays for them, they will still be a very dangerous side. The battle is on, whatever their injury situation.

'We have had two magnificent matches against them this season and the one at Newcastle, in particular, was a fine advertisement for football.

'Newcastle have done extremely well this season. They have scored more goals than anybody else and they reached the League Cup Final.

'They have had a lot of problems with injuries but they have not done any crying about them.

'Both sides are now so near Wembley that they must have the smell of it. We have home advantage and, if we get through tomorrow, we will have two matches on neutral grounds.

'We must fancy ourselves in these circumstances, and I have been so pleased with the performance of the team over the last eight weeks.

'This is a big opportunity for us and we must take it.'

Derby had injury concerns of their own with Steve Powell definitely out due to a shin problem while Leighton James was a doubt because of an ankle knock sustained in a tasty 1-1 draw at Leeds.

Rioch was fit to return however as the Rams went in search of a place in the semi-finals for the first time since 1948.

And it was Rioch who had a massive early impact on the game as he put Derby two goals clear with just a quarter of an hour on the clock.

His first came on four minutes following a move he started after Rod Thomas had won the ball from Macdonald.

Rioch laid it off to Hector and kept on running forward. Hector crossed in, George nodded it on and Rioch was there to apply the finishing touch.

If the first goal was all about craft, the second was about sheer power. George had been fouled on the edge of the box and up stepped Rioch to hammer a completely unstoppable shot beyond the dive of visiting goalkeeper Eddie Edgar and make it six goals in six games after a long run without finding the target.

Gowling got Newcastle back in the match from close range on 21 minutes but that gave his side just a flicker of a hope of a comeback, so dominant was Derby's performance.

The only real surprise was that it took them until the 64th minute to extend their lead, although they reserved the moment for what was another fine strike.

David Nish's corner was headed out by Macdonald but picked up by Henry Newton some 25 yards from goal.

Newton took a touch to bring the ball under control, steadied himself, and unleashed an effort that must have left Edgar wondering why he had got out of bed that morning as it was arguably even more emphatic than Rioch's second.

It was 4-1 only four minutes later. Goalkeeper Graham Moseley cleared the ball into the Newcastle half where it was headed on by George.

The defenders went to Hector, who cleverly back-heeled it into the path of George, who had a clear run into the box and finished calmly past Edgar to really wrap things up.

Gowling poached another back for Newcastle but they were never going to mount a recovery and could easily have found themselves further adrift with Davies twice wasting good opportunities for a fifth of the afternoon.

But that was not a problem as the Rams were through in relative comfort and, when you consider the goals, in some style too. Mackay was, understandably, purring about his team's performance as the Rams broke that long FA Cup semi-final duck.

He was particularly pleased with the quality of the goals his side scored, something that was becoming a hallmark of Mackay's men during the 1975/76 season.

Mackay enthused, 'I don't think I have seen four better goals from one side in any match.

'Bruce Rioch has started scoring again and it looks as if he has plenty of goals left in him this season.

'Leighton James had his best match for us. He stayed wide, as I have been wanting him to do, and took on the defenders. The run which ended with a centre to Archie Gemmill was magnificent – he really put his head down and went.

'Kevin Hector has done tremendously well since he came back in and I have been delighted with the team as a whole.

'And we have so many players waiting in the wings – people like Roger Davies, Francis Lee and Jeff Bourne.

'It is still very much on for us to do the league and cup double, especially if we can maintain the quality of recent performances.'

Derby would have to wait a little while longer to discover their opponents for the semi-final as the draw pitted them against the winner of the replay between Manchester United and Wolverhampton Wanderers.

United were back in the top flight and also seeking a league and cup double while Wolves were trying to avoid relegation.

The other semi-final was between Second Division side Southampton and Crystal Palace, who were playing their football in the third tier, meaning that for the third time in four years a club from outside the First Division would be reaching the FA Cup Final.

And Mackay admitted, 'If it's Wolves it's an all-Midlands game so the interest will be there, and if it's Manchester United we could fill the ground three times over.

'It takes a little bit of shine off the final when you haven't got two First Division clubs there. But the Leeds–Sunderland final [in 1973] was a great one. Everyone was involved in that, whether they were interested in football or not.

'If we get to Wembley, everyone will be rooting for Palace or Southampton, as they will be the underdogs.'

United won their replay 3-2 at Molineux to set up a semi-final against the Rams at Hillsborough, a repeat of the 1948 semi which the Reds won 3-1.

And they were victorious again, this time 2-0, though there was an element of controversy surrounding the April encounter at the same venue as an offside flag denied Nish what would have been a golden opportunity to level the tie at 1-1 in the second half. The incident is still debated by Rams fans to this day.

But perhaps of more cost to Mackay's men was the injury sustained by George 18 days after the quarter-final.

George's goal against Newcastle had been his 23rd of a prolific first season after joining the previous summer from Arsenal for £100,000, and he took his tally to 24 soon afterwards.

But after landing awkwardly in a 1-1 draw at home to Stoke City on 24 March he was carried from the field having dislocated his shoulder and would miss the rest of the season.

It was a hammer blow to the Rams and although they won their next match, three defeats from the following four ended their hopes of holding on to the championship, which was eventually won by Liverpool with Derby in fourth.

United went on to lose the FA Cup Final 1-0 to Southampton in another upset and, up to the time of writing, Derby have not been back to the semi-finals of the FA Cup since.

They did not reach another major semi-final until 2009 when they progressed through the League Cup where, in the last four, they were beaten 4-3 over two legs – by Manchester United.

19 v Ipswich Town 6-2

24 April 1976. Attendance: 26,971
Portman Road. Football League First Division

DERBY COUNTY:	IPSWICH TOWN:
Moseley	Cooper
Webster	Burley
Newton	Mills
Rioch	Sharkey
McFarland (Davies)	Hunter
Todd	Peddelty
Powell	Osborne (Johnson)
Gemmill	Talbot
Lee	Bertschin
Hector	Whymark
King	Lambert

Referee: Peter Walters

IF the signing by Brian Clough of Dave Mackay, seemingly coming towards the end of his great career, had been a master-stroke then Mackay produced a similar moment of managerial genius when he persuaded Francis Lee to spend the last of his playing days at the Baseball Ground.

Lee had enjoyed the best years of his playing days at Maine Road with Manchester City. Unlike many of his contemporaries he had invested wisely and was already comparatively rich thanks to investing in a paper plant which meant that he could live happily off the sale of toilet rolls and other products.

Although this was the source of good-natured banter and mickey-taking the truth was that Lee no longer had to play football to live.

Mackay realised this, and knowing that Lee liked to entertain and play open attacking football, suggested that he could sign for Derby and enjoy an Indian summer without any pressure.

The tactic worked and Lee won the title in his first season at the club, and in his second season the Rams almost managed a First Division and FA Cup double.

Unfortunately when Charlie George suffered a dislocated shoulder in March the campaign started to run out of steam and Derby faded away from the title race.

With no FA Cup Final to look forward to in the days when it was the final match of the season it became apparent that Lee would be making his final bow, not only as a Derby player, but as a professional footballer away to Ipswich Town on the final day of the 1975/76 First Division season.

Ipswich were, in many ways, a similar kind of club to Derby – a small-town set-up that had over-achieved when compared to the likes of Arsenal and Liverpool.

They played attractive football, and even if neither team had more to play for than pride there were worse places to bring the curtain down on a glittering career than Portman Road.

Ipswich had been promoted to the First Division in 1967/68, the season before Derby's elevation under Clough and Peter Taylor, and they had taken a few years to establish themselves but in 1972/73 they finished fourth, repeated the trick the following season, then finished third in 1975 and were one of the biggest challengers for the championship ultimately won by Mackay's men.

They had also been UEFA Cup quarter-finalists in 1974 and reached the last four of the FA Cup a year later but were off the pace somewhat in 1975/76 and were not among the teams in contention for the title.

They were, however, ending their season in good form and they had won four of the previous five before they welcomed Derby to Portman Road.

That run had included successive home victories over Manchester City and Manchester United, a triumph away to Arsenal and a 4-0 win in front of their own fans against West Ham United.

Derby, in the same five-game period, had seen their title hopes evaporate as their form deserted them following that injury to George.

David Nish, Bruce Rioch, Roger Davies and Leighton James had seen off Birmingham City 4-2 at the Baseball Ground on 27 March but a 4-3 defeat at Manchester City, a 2-2 draw at home to Leicester City, a 1-0 reverse at Aston Villa and a 3-1 loss at home to Everton meant they were dropping away from the top.

Lee had not really featured much in the team since the end of 1975 due to injury but he scored both of the goals in that draw with Leicester, getting himself on the scoresheet for the first time since a 3-2 win at home to Middlesbrough on 29 November.

And there was no doubt that, in his last match as a player, he was determined to mark the occasion in style – especially as it was his 500th Football League appearance.

It wasn't just Lee's day though as Derby also had a debutant, Jeff King, who was in the side for the first time since moving down from Scottish side Albion Rovers two years previously.

But it was two of the established legends who combined to open the scoring for the Rams early on.

Colin Todd was playing in midfield as an experiment and picked up a pass before moving forward into the Ipswich penalty area and squaring the ball across the six-yard box where Kevin Hector had the simplest of tasks to knock it over the line.

Then Lee and Todd were involved before the ball found its way to King, who was out on the right before cutting inside and being fouled by Brian Talbot inside the box.

Rioch, playing as one of the Rams' strikers, gave the spot-kick his typical hammering and doubled Derby's advantage.

Ipswich were soon back in the game when Roger Osborne found a bit of space on the right and rolled a neat ball in to Mick Lambert, who efficiently beat Graham Moseley from a narrow angle.

But no sooner had the game restarted than the Rams were two clear again after Rioch was sent away on a long pass from the back and once again he powerfully finished off the chance with his left foot.

The action continued as Ron Webster looked to have everything under control but, in a rare mistake, his back-pass was short of power and accuracy so Keith Bertschin nipped in, went wide as Moseley came out to cover, then squared the ball for Trevor Whymark to fire into the empty net.

Five goals had been scored in the first 20 minutes of the match – most definitely not a typical end-of-season affair.

It wasn't until well into the second half that the game's sixth goal arrived and it went Derby's way, giving them a 4-2 advantage.

Moseley cleared the ball forward and Lee laid it out left to Rioch, whose low cross was missed by the Ipswich defence and Hector took control before turning and beating home goalkeeper Cooper.

Time was ticking down for Lee to get his golden moment but it did come for him in the 89th minute.

He was involved in the build-up, playing the ball out to Archie Gemmill, then when the Scot crossed Lee's first header was blocked but the rebound fell nicely for him and he steadied himself before hammering it into the roof of the net and raising an arm in an understated celebration.

The icing on the cake came in stoppage time. Todd and Davies were involved, as was King, who fed Davies inside the area but to the right of goal.

Davies, on as a substitute for Roy McFarland, fired the ball in low and Lee dived in to bundle it home before taking the congratulations from his colleagues.

Lee had been an immensely popular figure from the moment he arrived at the Baseball Ground in 1974 so it was entirely fitting that he should have the last word – or words, in this case – on his final career appearance.

His goals bore the hallmarks of an experienced striker knowing how to sniff out an opportunity when it arises and be in the right place at the right time.

They took his tally to 12 First Division goals from 28 games, matching his haul from the previous season, and gave him an overall figure of 24 in 62.

Taking into account other competitions he ended his Rams career with 30 in 81 starts and two substitute appearances, a more than respectable ratio that was still up there with some of the best strikers around.

His tally of league goals, spread across those 500 matches, stood at 229, which was an excellent return and gave even more credence to those who said that Lee was one of the most underrated strikers of his generation.

He is widely – and rightly – regarded as one of the top 100 players to have ever pulled on a Derby County shirt, such was his impact over his two seasons at the Baseball Ground.

The win at Ipswich was enough to see Derby finish fourth in the table on 53 points, seven clear of the Tractor Boys in sixth but seven adrift of eventual champions Liverpool, and it qualified Mackay's men for the following season's UEFA Cup.

Lee went on to have an interesting career after finishing as a professional footballer, although he never moved into coaching or management.

His paper business continued to grow and at one point he employed a young man called Peter Kay, who went on to become the popular comedian and TV star he is today.

Lee later became chairman at Manchester City and remained at the helm for several years until being succeeded by David Bernstein, though he retained a shareholding after leaving the board of directors until selling those shares as part of the club's takeover in 2007 by former Thailand PM Thaksin Shiniwatra.

He was also a racehorse trainer and looked after notable horses such as Sir Harry Hardman, Allwight Then and Young Jason, though gave this up in 2001 as his business interests grew.

For King, the other notable name in Derby's side that day, life was not quite so exciting.

After making his debut he only totalled 14 starts and seven substitute appearances before joining Walsall in November 1977.

He later went on to play for Sheffield Wednesday, Sheffield United, Chesterfield, Stafford Rangers, Altrincham, Burton Albion and Kettering Town.

20 v Finn Harps 12-0

15 September 1976. Attendance: 13,353
Baseball Ground. UEFA Cup First Round First Leg

DERBY COUNTY:	FINN HARPS:
Moseley	Murray
Thomas	McDowell
Nish	Hutton
Rioch	T O'Doherty
McFarland	Sheridan
Todd (King HT)	Stephenson
Macken	D O'Doherty (Logan 55)
Gemmill	Harkin
Hector	Bradley (Mahon 63)
George	Healey
James	Carlyle

Referee: Antoine Queudeville (Luxembourg)

WITH the European Cup and that exit to Real Madrid over two legs but a mere memory, the Rams' next venture into football on the continent came in the UEFA Cup for the 1976/77 season.

Younger readers brought up in the era of the Champions League, where up to four teams from a country – three of which by definition could not possibly be champions – contested the premier international club competition, may find it a difficult concept to grasp that in the 1970s only the champions of each country challenged for the top prize along with the previous year's winner.

The best teams in the country based on league positions below the champions contested the UEFA Cup. This was a straight knockout contest with the aggregate score over home and away legs dictating who proceeded to the next round.

As with the European Cup all countries affiliated to UEFA were invited to take part.

There was an obvious drawback to this idea as some of the smaller countries had few if any teams of a high enough standard to stand their ground against the big boys.

The 1975/76 season had been one of disappointment for Derby County as having looked odds-on for an FA Cup and First Division double at one stage they won neither and finished fourth.

That was, however, a high enough spot to earn themselves qualification for the UEFA Cup and the Rams found themselves paired up with a Irish side called Finn Harps.

In local terms Finn Harps were among the big boys of the League of Ireland. They qualified for the UEFA Cup three times in the 1970s and never finished below halfway in the domestic table. The County Donegal-based club had only been formed in 1954 as a junior outfit and were admitted to the League of Ireland for the first time in 1969.

They had a slow start, losing their first game 10-2, though they did start to develop and had some success in the following years.

As well as their solid league form they won their first major trophy, the FAI Cup, in 1973/74, a triumph which earned them a crack at the following season's European Cup Winners' Cup where they were eliminated in the first round by Turkish side Bursaspor thanks to a 4-2 aggregate defeat over two legs.

That was their second season in Europe as they were also in the UEFA Cup in 1973/74 on account of finishing as runners-up in the League of Ireland in 1973.

On that occasion, too, they only lasted for the one round, as they lost 7-2 to Scottish side Aberdeen over two legs.

They were runners-up again in 1976 which earned them their place in the 1976/77 UEFA Cup where there were some plum ties to be had against former European champions AC Milan, Manchester United, Celtic or Ajax, while Barcelona and Juventus were also in the competition.

In the end they drew the Rams, perhaps not one of the leading names in the tournament but still with plenty of recent pedigree following their two First Division wins, the run to the 1973 European Cup semi-finals and the 1975/76 encounters with Real Madrid.

Dave Mackay's men were not in good domestic form as they warmed up to face Finn Harps but they were still expected to have no problems in dealing with the part-timers.

That appeared to be the case after just five minutes when Kevin Hector drilled his shot beyond Finn Harps goalkeeper Gerry Murray, who was going to have an unforgettable night – but for all the wrong reasons.

Bruce Rioch added a second on 12 minutes and then it all went crazy as between the 20th and 28th minutes, the Rams took their lead to 7-0.

Charlie George netted twice in that period, as did Leighton James, while Hector also helped himself to his second of the night.

His third and fourth goals arrived in the 36th and 39th minutes to take Derby to a record-equalling 9-0 scoreline – and it wasn't even half-time.

Finn Harps were not helping themselves with some pretty naive defending at times but there was still an enjoyable clinical and professional nature about the Rams' performance. They were not just rolling the ball around and waiting for things to happen, they were making them happen, and they continued in search of more goals in the second half.

Murray produced good saves from George and Rioch after the break but he was only delaying the inevitable and Derby racked up ten goals in a competitive fixture for the first time when Hector added his fifth on 66 minutes.

James and George also reached their own personal hat-tricks to take the tally to 12 for the night – and it could have been a whole lot worse had it not been for those Murray saves, plus the Rams hitting the woodwork on SIX occasions.

Having been totally annihilated in the first leg it seemed almost cruel to subject the League of Ireland club to yet more punishment – but the rules dictated that it had to happen.

Mackay said after the first encounter, 'My team played tremendously hard. To score 12 goals against any opposition isn't easy.'

And he showed real respect for his opponents by naming the strongest side he had available for the second leg.

Harps actually took the lead at their Finn Park home, even if it was an own goal from Roy McFarland's mis-placed header.

But that was only a minor blip on the night as Hector and George both added two more goals each, giving them personal hauls of seven and five respectively in a 16-1 aggregate victory.

The prize for what was virtually a walkover was a two-legged affair against AEK Athens of Greece.

The first leg was away and saw the Rams defeated 2-0. They came back to the Baseball Ground and scored first through George early in the second half to give themselves hope but the Greeks, having earlier stood firm in the face of plenty of pressure, scored three quick goals without reply.

Rioch got another one back for Derby but the comeback gathered no further momentum than that and they were out thanks to a 5-3 aggregate score.

AEK made it through to the quarter-finals, where they beat Queens Park Rangers on penalties, but lost 5-1 on aggregate to Juventus in the semis before the Italians beat Spanish side Athletic Bilbao on away goals in the final.

Finn Harps did, however, manage something that Derby did not do in the following years as they qualified for the UEFA Cup again, but in 1978/79 they went out at the first hurdle after being beaten 10-0 by Everton across two legs.

Derby, if you take out the short-lived exploits in the Anglo-Italian Cup in the early 1990s, have not qualified for one of the major European competitions since that exit at the hands of AEK.

They would have done so having finished fifth in the First Division in 1988/89 under Arthur Cox but the ban on English clubs because of the 1985 Heysel disaster was still in place.

And the 12-0 victory is still acknowledged as the club's 'official' record scoreline, beating the previous high which had stood since January 1891 when Wolverhampton Wanderers were beaten 9-0.

But it was actually bettered in January 2011 in what is accepted as a 'competitive' match as the Rams beat Shirebrook Town, of the Northern Counties East League, 14-1 in a Derbyshire Senior Cup match.

The competition has largely been the preserve of the county's non-league sides but for the 2010/11 season both Derby and Chesterfield opted to enter and use it as extra match practice for their second string sides.

The open nature of the draw meant something like this could always happen and Derby's starting line-up showed ten of the 11 players had Championship experience and they romped to victory – despite actually falling behind inside the first minute!

For the record, their list of goalscorers in the game played at Belper Town's Christchurch Meadow, read: Ben Pringle (2), David Martin, Jeff Hendrick (3), Tomasz Cywka (2), Miles Addison, Steven Davies, Callum Ball (2), Alex Witham, Gareth Davey (own goal).

Video of the first leg against Finn Harps can still be found on YouTube and even now, in 2013, it is surreal to see such a resounding scoreline.

21 v Tottenham Hotspur 8-2

16 October 1976. Attendance: 24,216
Baseball Ground. Football League First Division

DERBY COUNTY:	TOTTENHAM HOTSPUR:
Moseley	Jennings
Thomas	Naylor
Nish	Osgood
Macken	Hoddle
McFarland	Young
Todd	Pratt
Powell	Conn
Gemmill	Perryman
Rioch	Moores
George	Jones
James	Taylor
Unused sub: Bourne	*Unused sub:* Coates
Referee: Bert Newsome	

AFTER the disappointment of a fourth-placed finish the previous season, when Derby had hoped to retain their title and also add the FA Cup, supporters expected the Rams to bounce straight back.

It had been a recurring pattern after all – win the title, fall away again only to re-group and come back stronger and win it once more.

The 1976/77 season was different though for some reason. Instead of pushing back towards the top after nearly achieving the double, wins became increasingly hard to find.

From the start of the campaign the Rams could only manage five draws and three defeats out of eight league matches.

The single-pointers came with 0-0 stalemates at home to Middlesbrough and Manchester United, and away to Norwich City, while they also picked up a pair of 2-2 scorelines against Newcastle United at St James' Park and West Bromwich Albion at the Baseball Ground.

They managed to build up momentum in the League Cup – but against lower division opposition, having seen off Doncaster Rovers and Notts County on their way to the fourth round and a late-October meeting with Brighton & Hove Albion.

Goals had been hard to come by and in four of those eight First Division games the Rams had failed to find the back of the net.

There had, of course, been the record-breaking 12-0 victory over Finn Harps in the UEFA Cup, but in the one place where it mattered – the league – there was something not at all right.

Injuries played their part, and the situation got so bad that Bruce Rioch, one of the best attacking midfield players in the country on his day, had been forced into action as an emergency centre-forward. By the time Tottenham came along he was getting a real feel for the role.

Derby needed a good performance and decent result to kick-start their season as they remained winless and in their last match prior to the visit of Spurs they had taken a 5-1 beating away to Birmingham City with Leighton James scoring their goal.

In fact, so scarce were goals that only four Derby players had scored in those opening eight matches – James, Charlie George, Roy McFarland and David Nish, with McFarland and George the only men to have netted twice.

As for Spurs, they had at least managed something that Derby had not done and won a First Division match.

They had done so twice, and on successive Saturdays back in September as they followed up a 3-2 success at Manchester United with a 1-0 home victory over Leeds United.

On the back of that they were beaten 1-0 at Liverpool and drew 1-1 against Norwich at White Hart Lane before going down 4-2 at West Brom on 2 October and having to stew over that result for a fortnight before they travelled to the Baseball Ground, where they would be coming up against a Derby side managed by White Hart Lane legend Dave Mackay.

Mackay had been in charge of the Rams since October 1973 and had presided over three wins against his old club out of the five matches played, with the other two results going in the Londoners' favour.

It was George who opened the scoring in this encounter with his third goal of the season, although there was an element of fortune about it as his cross-shot went in past Pat Jennings.

Just a minute later George was the creator as he fired out a 40-yard pass described as 'miraculous' for Rioch, who touched the ball past two Spurs men before beating Jennings with a low shot.

In theory it was just what Derby needed to blast out their early-season problems but the visitors were back in it on 25 minutes as Steve Perryman scored from long range with a shot that beat Graham Moseley in the Rams' goal.

But it didn't take too much longer for Derby to go two goals clear again and Rioch was on target for the second time, finishing off well after McFarland's long free kick had reached him via George.

Spurs, to their credit, did not roll over and die and they got another goal back from the penalty spot four minutes from half-time as Osgood netted following Tony Macken's foul on Naylor.

Derby had enjoyed the better of the first half but Spurs were not out of sight, and it took until just before the hour for the home side's fourth goal to arrive.

Full-back Rod Thomas strode forward after collecting a rebounded pass and calmly stroked his shot beyond Jennings for his first Rams goal.

Four minutes later came the afternoon's most spectacular goal, one that wrapped up Rioch's hat-trick.

Steve Powell's throw sent James clear and the winger's driven centre was met with a powerful header from Rioch that arrowed in like a bullet.

George added the sixth from the penalty spot after Perryman's foul on Archie Gemmill, then it was seven on 70 minutes thanks to Colin Todd after more good work from James.

The eighth arrived four minutes later. James again provided the delivery, George saw his shot blocked and Rioch was on hand to ram home his fourth of the day.

It was becoming a bad season for Spurs, but in a season of lows this was to become the lowest of them all.

The 8-2 defeat remains a record as far as goals conceded by Tottenham away from home is concerned and their season never really recovered, although they won their next league game with a 1-0 victory against Birmingham.

The goalscorer on that day was Keith Osgood from the penalty spot. Osgood had contributed one of the two Spurs goals at Derby and later went on to play for the Rams.

They struggled to put two wins together consecutively and ended up relegated as the bottom club in the division having only managed to accumulate a total of 33 points from their 42 matches, two adrift of safety and going down with Stoke City and Sunderland.

Mackay said of the display, 'I knew it would come right. We have the players and we have the style. All week I've had a feeling that we would put it together today.

'We killed them off.'

It was impossible to disagree with that final sentiment, and there was sympathy from Mrs Mackay, the great Scot's wife Isobel, who offered some consoling words to Jennings having seen the Irishman play alongside her husband at Spurs.

She was quoted in the *Sunday Mirror* as having said 'I wish it hadn't happened to you', while Jennings, for his part, was shell-shocked by what had happened and could only describe the afternoon as 'a nightmare'.

After the result, Gerald Mortimer wrote in the *Derby Telegraph*, 'Derby's league season is underway at last.'

Mortimer, a well respected scribe and expert on all things Derby County, was not often wrong but this was one of those rare occasions where his prediction did not pan out as everyone had expected.

Derby's next First Division match saw them fail to score, again, as they went down 1-0 at Stoke, though a 2-0 success at home to Bristol City – George and Kevin Hector netting – followed by a 1-1 draw at Queens Park Rangers eased some of the frustrations.

The Rams also exited the UEFA Cup at the hands of AEK Athens and although they made it through to the quarter-finals of the League Cup, seeing off Brighton at the second attempt, the board soon decided that enough was enough and Mackay was relieved of his duties a few days after a 2-0 defeat at Everton.

Just like Brian Clough and Peter Taylor, Mackay had lasted a mere 18 months after winning the First Division championship.

Colin Murphy was installed on a caretaker basis while the directors tried to persuade Clough and Taylor to return to the Baseball Ground and leave Nottingham Forest, who were still in the Second Division at the time.

Clough openly flirted with the idea but it didn't happen and Murphy was given the job on a permanent basis.

It is fair to say he had a mixed time in charge as he won his first match, 1-0 at home to Sunderland, but did not see his players victorious on back-to-back First Division occasions before the season was out.

Bolton Wanderers, then of the Second Division, caused an upset with a 2-1 win at the Baseball Ground in the League Cup quarter-final at the start of December, and the Rams would only win twice across December and January in the First Division.

The second of those victories, 4-2 at home to Newcastle United, was significant in that it saw new record signing Derek Hales, the former Charlton Athletic striker, get off the mark with two of the goals.

Derby then lost five on the spin but drew their next four to take them up to the start of April, a period in which they beat Blackpool, Colchester United and Blackburn Rovers on their way to the quarter-finals of the FA Cup, where they lost 2-0 at Everton.

They were beaten twice during a hectic period of nine matches during April, though drew three and won one of their May encounters to at least give a bit of positivity to what had been a challenging season.

In the end they only lost two of their last 17 games but they finished 15th, four points above the relegation zone, on account of winning just nine matches all season – less than any other club – but drawing 19, which was the First Division's highest total in 1976/77.

Goals continued to be hard to come by and James was their highest First Division scorer on nine, followed by Gerry Daly – a spring arrival – with seven in his 17 games.

Hector could only finish with five, Hales added just two more to return a mere four, while Rioch's haul was the only time he would score in the First Division though his season was ended early by injury in December, and he did also net in the League Cup and UEFA Cup.

As for Clough and Taylor, their decision to stay at the City Ground paid off as they led Forest back to the First Division – and what happened at that end of the A52 over the next three years is best forgotten about.

Derby have not scored eight goals in a league match since this thrashing of Spurs.

They have managed six on numerous occasions, most recently in April 1996 when they beat Tranmere Rovers 6-2 at the Baseball Ground on the way to promotion under Jim Smith, and they did rack up seven in a 1993 League Cup tie at home to Southend United, but this remains the domestic high point for Rams goalscoring in many decades.

22 v Nottingham Forest 4-1

24 November 1979. Attendance: 27,729
Baseball Ground. Football League First Division

DERBY COUNTY:	NOTTINGHAM FOREST:
McKellar	Shilton
Langan	Anderson
Buckley	Gray
Daly (Emson 80)	McGovern
Webb	Lloyd
Osgood	Needham
Emery	O'Neill
B Powell	Mills
Duncan	Birtles
Davies	Francis
Clark	Robertson
	Unused sub: Bowyer

Referee: Michael Peck

DERBY COUNTY had struggled at the start of the 1979/80 season and had taken five games to register their first victory, 3-2 at home to high-flying Arsenal, though it did absolutely nothing to spark their campaign.

In eight of their first 11 games they failed to score while their defence was on its game in some matches and nowhere to be seen in others.

That was evidenced by the fact that in nine of the games prior to the visit of Nottingham Forest the Rams had conceded no more than a single goal, yet on two occasions they let in three and twice more they were breached four times.

Derby were clearly struggling with just five wins and two draws from 16 matches leaving Colin Addison's men 16th in the First Division.

Forest, meanwhile, were the defending league champions under Brian Clough and Peter Taylor having only won promotion in 1977 – but, more impressively, they were also European champions after winning the European Cup at the first attempt.

They came to the Baseball Ground challenging on three fronts as they were also making progress in the League Cup, and the month had started well for Clough's men with a victory over Ipswich Town in the First Division and Romanian side Arges Pitesti in Europe. A blip soon hit them as they suffered defeats at Southampton and Brighton & Hove Albion but they travelled to Derby feeling confident that a game against their local rivals would get their form heading back in the right direction again.

Derby made three changes, replacing Aiden McCaffrey with David Webb, bringing Gerry Daly back after his return to fitness following only 20 minutes of action since September, and filling the gap caused by Gordon Hill's departure to Queens Park Rangers with Jonathan Clark. The often-used argument is that form goes out of the window where a local derby is concerned although in this instance, with the directions of the two clubs so contrasting, it should have been an easy match to call.

Clough and Taylor may well have been forgiven for expecting their players to get the result, even if they would not have been naive enough to have anticipated an easy ride as they returned to the Baseball Ground.

What they got was an occasion on which the European champions were completely blown away inside the first 20 minutes. With 13 on the clock the visitors created their own problems and had the usually-reliable Peter Shilton to blame.

England international goalkeeper Shilton failed to hold a straightforward high cross from Steve Buckley which gave Daly the simplest of opportunities to score.

Two minutes later Shilton did not deal with another cross, this time from the right by David Langan, and rather than pushing it out for a corner he instead only saw it drop in front of goal where John Duncan applied the finishing touch. Duncan had been unlucky with injuries during his time at Derby and this goal against their big local rivals came during his longest run of consecutive matches – eight – of the entire season.

Steve Emery, an Addison signing from Hereford United, was the next to benefit from some poor away defending as Derby quickly extended their lead to three.

It was not his first goal for the club but it was his first experience of the local derby atmosphere and after making the step up from a lower-division club he might well have expected the defending to be of a higher standard than the work of Frank Gray, who failed to cut out what looked to be a simple through ball from Daly.

Emery was on it quickly and drew Shilton before placing his shot past him and sending the Baseball Ground delirious.

Derby's supporters, players and management were on a high, the Forest contingent less so, and later reports described Clough as being stony-faced and very angry as he left for the sanctity of the dressing room at half-time.

He would have plenty to say to his players during the interval and, having seen how he had galvanised struggling Derby sides in the past, the home faithful knew that their opponents would be coming back out with a different attitude.

It took Forest two minutes to get a foothold in the game. Gary Mills rampaged his way forward and reached the penalty area where he was fouled by Daly.

A penalty looked clear-cut and was duly awarded so John Robertson, who had missed from the spot the previous week, stepped forward again and this time made no mistake to bring the score back to 3-1.

But that was as good as it got for Forest as they never looked like mounting anything akin to a comeback.

Indeed, they were completely buried with 13 minutes remaining as Duncan bagged his second of the match.

Roger Davies was fouled by David Needham so Buckley lined up the free kick and delivered it into the box where it was met by Duncan with a header past Shilton that put the final seal on a rare highlight in what had been a poor season to that point.

And given the nature of the victory, a comprehensive thrashing of your local rivals who are also the defending English and European champions, there was barely any reaction to be found in the local media in the days following the match.

It was left to *Ram*, Derby County's own official newspaper, to deliver the goods and the next edition was not short of things to say.

An entire page in *Ram* was devoted to the success, including pictures of the goals and more action, a round-up of the match itself, though there were no direct quotes from either players or management.

But the newspaper's own editorial was not holding back and said, 'Well, yes, the most comprehensive and exciting Derby win in years was sparked off by defensive mistakes by the opposition.

'But considering the opposition were our fierce local rivals and neighbours Nottingham Forest the satisfaction was even more intense.

'This was a champagne day of champagne football that recalled the Derby County days of not too long ago.

'True, it needed Forest mistakes to get the adrenaline flowing, but after that it was all Derby except for a few minutes just after their early second half penalty goal cut the lead to 3-1.

'One great save from McKellar denied them, and Duncan put it safe at 4-1. Who will ever forget the exhilaration of three Derby first half goals in four minutes ... few, if any of us!'

Given that the earlier victory over Arsenal had been something of a false dawn, Rams fans were entitled to hope that this success would be something different and give their season new impetus.

If anything, however, it had the opposite effect. Derby did not win another game home or away for another three months, and by that point relegation was almost a certainty.

The run saw them play 12 times in the First Division and just once in the FA Cup, when they were thrashed 6-2 by fellow top flight side Bristol City in the third round.

Derby picked up just three points from three draws until they were next victorious when they beat Tottenham Hotspur 2-1 at the Baseball Ground on 23 February.

But they won just once in March, 2-1 at Bolton Wanderers, though with draws from their next two and a 2-0 win at Leeds United to start April hopes were briefly raised that they could survive.

Three defeats in the next four saw to that, including a 1-0 reverse in the return fixture at the City Ground, and they were relegated on the penultimate weekend of the season despite beating Manchester City 3-1 at the Baseball Ground.

A final-day 4-2 defeat at Norwich City saw the Rams finish second from bottom, five points from safety and sandwiched by Bolton and Bristol City who also dropped into the second tier.

Forest failed to retain their First Division championship but they went on to win a second successive European Cup with former Derby favourite John McGovern once again lifting the famous trophy as their captain.

The ultimate progress of the season did take the shine off the Rams' November victory over their great rivals but, as time has gone on, the result has been widely regarded as one of the Baseball Ground's greatest days.

The match was captured superbly by BBC Radio Derby commentator Graham Richards, whose own unique prose has gone down in legend among supporters.

His cries of 'Forest are in absolute ruins' after one of the goals will echo through the mind of anyone of a black and white persuasion and can still be found on the internet at http://www.bbc.co.uk/derby/rams/2003/derby_forest_audio.shtml

23 v Watford 3-2

15 May 1982. Attendance: 14,946
Baseball Ground. Football League Second Division

DERBY COUNTY:	WATFORD:
Banovic	Sherwood
Barton	Rice
Buckley	Rostron
Attley	Taylor
Skivington	Terry
McAlle	Bolton
Hector	Callaghan
Wilson	Blissett
Hill	Armstrong
Swindlehurst	Lohman (Johnson 72)
Emson	Barnes
Unused sub: Reid	
Referee: George Tyson	

DERBY COUNTY had been champions of the Football League in 1972 and 1975, were relegated from the First Division in 1980, and by 1982 they were fighting to avoid dropping down to the third tier of English football for the first time since the 1950s.

That, by anyone's standard, is quite a spectacular fall from grace but it was exactly the situation the Rams found themselves in.

Finishing sixth in the Second Division in 1980/81, albeit while never really being in the promotion race, was something of a false dawn and the following year they struggled.

Not once did the Rams win back-to-back matches across the entire 1981/82 campaign and their lack of ability to string results together on a regular basis was one of the main reasons why they found themselves in the wrong half of the table.

Goals had been in short supply too, with Kevin Wilson leading the way having scored nine in his 24 matches with David Swindlehurst, his regular strike partner, adding just six in 36 outings.

Even Charlie George, a legend from the 1970s, had returned to the Baseball Ground for the final weeks of the season but he rarely played in his favoured centre-forward role and notched just two goals in his 11 games.

Kevin Hector, the Rams' second-highest goalscorer of all time, had been playing more often in a deeper midfield position than as a forward and as the closing weeks of the season approached he had just four goals to his name.

Hector had also taken the decision to retire at the end of the 1981/82 season so he, perhaps more than anyone, would have felt the pain of relegation the hardest as it would have been no way to close the career of one of the club's greatest ever servants.

The man known as 'The King' hadn't scored since 26 September but had also not featured regularly since March, having been in and out of the team.

Through March and April the Rams recorded just three wins but, coupled with a sprinkling of draws, their form was just about enough for them to keep their heads above water.

May began with a 0-0 draw at home to Cardiff City before Derby then lost 3-2 at Bolton Wanderers, George scoring his final goal for the club, and collected a point from a 1-1 draw at Oldham Athletic.

That left them still with work to do on the final day though they knew that a draw would be enough to ensure survival regardless of what happened elsewhere.

And manager John Newman, who took over from Colin Addison in January, told the *Derby Telegraph*, 'Recent form does not matter. This is all about 90 minutes of football.

'We are all in this together. Every supporter will be behind 11 players, no matter who they are, and every player will be Derby County through and through tomorrow.

'Forget other games. We have bothered about them for too long. Our job is to come out of this game with pride, satisfaction – and the result we need.

'I have tried to prepare the players properly. Tomorrow, they must take over the situation themselves. But I will be there leading them.

'One thing is certain. Graham Taylor's team will be going as hard as in their previous 41 games. We know that and we must combat it.'

Derby's team selection issues saw Glenn Skivington take over from the suspended Frank Sheridan at centre-half while there were doubts about the fitness of George and Barry Powell.

Swindlehurst and John Barton were expected to be fit and also added to the squad were Tony Reid and Andy Hill, who had been out since November and February respectively.

Watford's season was ending in glory as their promotion to the First Division, completing the rise up from the Fourth Division under Graham Taylor, was already confirmed.

Derby had enough chances to have settled any nerves well before half-time with Kevin Wilson the culprit on more than one occasion.

First, he out-paced his man to chase down Paul Emson's long pass but Watford keeper Sherwood was out quickly to block his shot.

Then Bolton pushed over Andy Hill inside the penalty area and Wilson stepped up to take the spot-kick only to see Sherwood keep his effort out.

That could have seen the Rams crumble but they bounced back in tremendous style thanks to a powerful shot from full-back Steve Buckley, a man described as a 'scorer of spectacular goals' during his Rams career.

That put Derby into a comfortable position but with nine minutes of the second half gone they were anything but relaxed.

Hector's final outing looked like it was about to turn sour as he fouled future Ram Nigel Callaghan to give the visitors a penalty that Luther Blissett made no mistake with.

Then a foul by Skivington eight yards outside the Derby box gave the Hornets a shooting opportunity which Bolton snaffled up to put his side 2-1 ahead.

Suddenly it appeared as if disaster was about to strike the Rams and they knew that they had to turn things around quickly.

Fortunately they did so and were level again within four minutes. Emson was the provider, after a long run, and although Wilson did not hit his shot cleanly it still found the back of the net via a deflection off Rostron.

And when you need a real moment of inspiration you can always rely upon The King.

Just ten minutes after Derby went behind, Wilson created a crossing opportunity and there was Hector to head the ball in and make it 3-2 to the men in white shirts.

Yakka Banovic produced two fine saves to deny Blissett and keep the Rams ahead but that was all part of the story to ensure that Hector would be the ultimate hero.

Not that the game had an entirely straightforward ending as, with a couple of minutes to go, referee George Tyson theatrically blew his whistle for an offside decision.

Supporters streamed on to the pitch, wrongly thinking it was the end of the match, and that meant proceedings were delayed while the pitch was cleared.

Cleared it was, the remaining time was played out, and that was that – safety was secured and one of Derby's all-time greats had gone out in style.

To call it a 'fairytale finale' for Hector might be going into the realms of cliches but it would, in this instance, be an accurate phrase to use.

That was the headline on the *Derby Telegraph*'s interview with The King, who marked the occasion with the winning goal in the game that clinched survival.

Hector, now 37 and in his second spell with the Rams, had been presented prior to the match with two decanters to mark his achievements.

His goal was his 201st for the club, second only to the great Steve Bloomer and making him only the second Ram to top the 200 mark, and it came in his 589th and final game – setting a new all-time appearance record that was comfortably ahead of second-placed Ron Webster on 535.

And reflecting on his perfect ending, he said, 'It could not have been better if I had written the script myself.

'I scored on my Derby debut in 1966 and I have gone out with a goal which made sure we stayed in the Second Division.

'After I had given away a penalty, that winner was doubly welcome. It was a beautiful ending.

'I am glad I came back to Derby. I feel I did the right thing and I am certainly leaving far more happily than I did when Tommy Docherty sold me.'

And boss Newman added, 'I wanted Kevin to go out on the right note as much as I wanted the right result. What a player he has been and what a marvellous finish.'

It was also announced that, in honour of Hector's service, the sponsors' lounge underneath the Main Stand at the Baseball Ground would be re-named the Hector Suite.

But it was not an entirely positive way to end the season as the Rams were reported to the Football League by referee Tyson because of fans invading the pitch before the final whistle, while the *Telegraph* also reported that 130 seats had been smashed in the C Stand.

The pitch was at least cleared to allow the game to finish but an element of the supporters first went across to threaten those who had travelled from Watford.

Secretary Michael Dunford said, 'There are some mindless idiots pretending to be supporters.

'None of us want them and that goes for management and players as well as administrative staff.

'I am very concerned that season ticket holders should be subjected to this kind of trouble and it is a problem we must tackle.

'We have a good record of crowd behaviour this season. The only other trouble was at the Chelsea game and we blame that on Chelsea followers.

'But we must accept that some of Derby County's followers are as bad as any in the country and we must weed them out.'

Not surprisingly, no player since Hector has come anywhere near returning the sort of figures he did in a Derby shirt.

As for the trouble caused by pitch invasions, there would be an altogether more dramatic scenario unfolding just 12 months later.

24 v Nottingham Forest 2-0

8 January 1983. Attendance: 28,494
Baseball Ground. FA Cup Third Round

DERBY COUNTY:	NOTTINGHAM FOREST:
Cherry	Sutton
Barton	Swain
Attley	Bowyer
Gemmill (Dalziel 71)	Gunn
Foster	Young
McAlle	Walsh
Brolly	Proctor
Wilson	Wallace
Hill	Birtles
Swindlehurst	Hodge
Mills	Robertson (Davenport 70)

Referee: George Courtney

S O much is said and written about games between Derby County and Nottingham Forest, and so much is debated between both sets of supporters. But one thing that is always agreed on is that the management reigns of Brian Clough and Peter Taylor are the greatest in the histories of each club. What the pair did at Derby was remarkable enough in itself but to then go and do what they did at Forest was equally as staggering, perhaps more so given their triumphs on the European stage.

Their styles and abilities complemented each other perfectly but over the years cracks began to appear in their relationship and Taylor eventually retired from football in May 1982, with Forest having finished 12th in the First Division.

Six months later he was back in the game and on familiar turf as he was tempted with a return to Derby as the club's new manager to replace John Newman.

Taylor had cited reasons for retiring that Clough was sympathetic to but coming back and taking over at Derby was seen by Clough as little other than betrayal and their bond was never the same again.

Derby's Second Division situation at the time is well documented in the chapter and in a bid to remedy that, Taylor re-signed 35-year-old Archie Gemmill – a legend at Derby and Forest – for a second stint at the Baseball Ground.

It quickly looked to be a clever move and then the FA Cup threw up one of the stories of the season as Derby and Forest were drawn against each other in the third round.

The Rams, struggling in the Second Division, would host their biggest rivals, who were fourth in the top flight.

It was the first FA Cup meeting between the two sides since January 1936, when the Rams had been victorious 2-0 on home turf, but most importantly it was a case of Clough v Taylor rather than the more familiar Clough and Taylor.

And as well as the pair, plus midfield ace Gemmill, there was another connection between the two sides as Derby had Gary Mills on loan from the Seattle Sounders in

America, where he had gone after leaving Forest in 1982 having been part of their two European Cup-winning seasons.

Forest had in their squad Colin Todd, the great defender of Derby's glory days in the 1970s, but he was absent for this match so Bryn Gunn and Willie Young were given the task of keeping the Rams' attack quiet.

On paper that should have been a straightforward task owing to the unavailability of Bobby Davison and David Swindlehurst having to play in midfield, leaving the line to be led by Kevin Wilson and Andy Hill, the young Ilkeston-born striker who often played in other positions too.

Forest had a reputation for being solid at the back anyway but they were shaken up in the early stages by Wilson and Mills, while Hill might have put Derby two clear before the 20-minute mark had he shown more composure on a couple of occasions.

And the Rams were nearly made to pay for those misses when a deep Ian Walsh cross was met by Mark Proctor, who was only denied by a five save from Steve Cherry.

Mills, against his old club, was keen to prove a point and saw an in-swinging corner dip over Forest goalkeeper Steve Sutton but midfielder Steve Hodge was able to clear it off the line.

It was a tight affair, as is usually the case in matches between two great rivals like this, though the potency of the occasion was provided by it being in the FA Cup and those two famous names in opposite dugouts.

There were no goals before half-time but there was a feeling in the Baseball Ground stands that something would give – and give it nearly did on 57 minutes.

Right-back John Barton pushed down the wing and crossed for Wilson, whose shot hit the bottom of the post and bounced away to safety.

Wilson, who had been signed from non-league side Banbury United, was becoming increasingly influential and on 65 minutes he was hauled down just outside the box by Young in a central position. Had the tackle been a split-second later it would have been a clear penalty.

But the danger was still there and Swindlehurst ran over the dead ball to throw the Forest defenders off the scent before Gemmill stepped up and curled his shot beyond the dive of Sutton.

Forest had the supposed extra pedigree from being a successful top flight side but going behind really knocked the stuffing out of them and they struggled to mount a serious threat on Cherry's goal.

But when a goalkeeper is unemployed for most of the match is also when his concentration must be at its sharpest and while he probably had time to have written a match report from his own penalty area, he was called upon a final time.

Forest launched one last attack and Gunn fired in a long-range shot that Cherry had to be at his sharpest to turn away with a full-length dive.

The visitors offered nothing from that point but the final word of the afternoon went to the Rams.

Time was almost up when Ian Bowyer was caught in possession and Derby broke with most of the Forest players stranded at the other end of the field.

Mick Brolly had the time and space to power forward and he was supported by Hill, who applied the finishing touch to Brolly's cross.

It had been the most memorable of performances and victories by the Rams, though, surprisingly, there was very little reaction to be found in the press over the following days.

The next edition of the club's official newspaper produced the goods, however, with some interesting stories.

Ram did not hit the streets for another two weeks when Derby were next in home action and it also did not carry any direct quotes from players or management.

But it did run an editorial piece looking back at the Forest victory that also bemoaned the Rams' recent inconsistency.

The article read, 'Rams really are a conundrum, aren't they? They outplayed Forest in almost all departments, and knocked them out of the FA Cup here a fortnight ago.

'No fluke this, but it DOES happen in the Cup, to reply to Forest fans who couldn't believe what they saw.

'As Derby had also played as gracefully against QPR five days before, Rams fans thought we were on our way.

'Then came last Saturday's flop at Carlisle, to complicate the League issue. Will the real Rams please stand up today!'

The most interesting story, however, was an interview with Doreen Shadbolt, a clairvoyant from Uttoxeter, who had told BBC Radio Derby ahead of the Forest game that the Rams would beat their rivals. Doreen forecast plenty of success to come for Derby in 1983 – but only if certain circumstance arose.

'I know nothing at all about football,' she said in an interview with Notty Hornblower, the women's correspondent in *Ram*.

'But I do know about God, and the spirits. If there is a player on the team especially, or someone in the management or the administration who prays, then so much good will result.

'Don't worry about the present. If one or two Derby players really started to believe in themselves things would begin to happen.

'They could start by saying a little prayer to themselves, not in public, before they go on the pitch. Indeed the more players who do that, and the more fans too, the easier it will be.

'More things are wrought by prayer than this world dreams of. Yes, people will scoff, but I trust they won't be Derby County folk.

'That could do more harm than the good I am earnestly trying to invoke. Unbelievers could darken the light which is now beginning to shine over Derby County Football Club.'

Whether the 'real' Derby County stood up as demanded by *Ram* that afternoon is open to debate as Taylor's side drew 3-3 against Leeds United.

The next round of the FA Cup arrived on 29 January and Derby hosted Chelsea, then a run-of-the-mill Second Division club, with Wilson – who would later make the move from the Baseball Ground to Stamford Bridge – netting both goals in a 2-1 win.

The victory was, however, marred by serious crowd trouble and came just a week after Leeds fans had caused damage to the Osmaston End.

Beating Chelsea earned the Rams a last-16 home tie with Manchester United and they put up a good fight but went down to a solitary Norman Whiteside goal in the second half.

Derby were still struggling in the Second Division though and the story there is explained in the next chapter.

They earned another FA Cup giant-killing the following season when beating First Division side Norwich City on their way to that infamous quarter-final against

Plymouth Argyle, but would not beat top flight opposition while a division below again until December 2008 when winning at Stoke City in the quarter-final of the League Cup.

Less than two months after that success came the next FA Cup meeting with Forest – and you can read more about that one further on in this very publication.

Hill's Derby career never reached the same heights as that January afternoon against Forest and he never again scored for the club, before departing in 1983 for Carlisle United and later retiring through injury and becoming an accountant.

Though there was an interesting potential twist as Hill was later reported – though no confirmation was ever found – to actually have been a Forest fan and ultimately a season ticket holder at the City Ground!

The relationship between Clough and Taylor, however, never recovered, and was further disintegrated when Taylor signed John Robertson for Derby from Forest without first informing Clough.

It had not been repaired by the time of Taylor's death in 1990 though Clough did attend the funeral.

But Clough, regretting the breakdown in relations between himself and his former right-hand man, always maintained a place for Taylor in his heart from that point and made sure to praise him for his role in their successes together.

25 v Fulham 1-0

14 May 1983. Attendance: 21,124
Baseball Ground. Football League Second Division

DERBY COUNTY:	FULHAM:
Cherry	Peyton
Barton	Hopkins
Burns	Lock
Gemmill (McAlle 81)	O'Driscoll (Reeves 78)
Foster	Brown
Futcher	Gale
Brolly	Davies
Davison	R Wilson
K Wilson	Coney
Hooks	Houghton
Emson	Lewington

Referee: Ray Chadwick

I N a curious echo to the situation 12 months previously, Derby went in to their final game of the 1982/83 season needing a win to make sure they would retain their Second Division status.

They had struggled in the early months of the campaign and up to John Newman's departure as manager in November they had recorded just one win.

But the arrival of Peter Taylor had coincided with a change in their fortunes and Taylor slowly steadied the ship before masterminding a 15-game unbeaten run from the end of January to the start of May.

Only six of those matches were won so the nine draws meant that the Rams could never fully escape from the spectre of relegation, even if they were always just a step or two ahead of the real dogfight.

A 2-0 win at home to Burnley looked to have just about done the job with three matches left but successive away defeats at Blackburn Rovers and Crystal Palace meant that, with a home game against promotion-chasing Fulham on their last day, Derby were not mathematically safe.

Their 46 points in a remarkably tight Second Division table meant they were one of nine teams still in danger of relegation despite being 16th, but they had the consolation of knowing that a win would be enough while a draw would probably have been sufficient.

But Taylor was taking no chances and he was given a pre-match boost with the return of Archie Gemmill, Kenny Burns and Paul Hooks, who had all missed those defeats at Palace and Blackburn having picked up injuries in the victory over Burnley.

Steve Powell was still absent with a fractured cheekbone but Taylor was taking a positive tone in his pre-match briefing.

He told the *Derby Telegraph*, 'We want to go on a high note to justify all the good work which has been done here over the past six months.

'In that time, we have touched high points and we want to go out in the same way, leaving supporters looking forward to next season.

'All we tried to do in the team talk today [the day before the match] was keep the players relaxed. They're no good if they're tense and they have coped well with this aspect of the game considering how long we've been in trouble.

'The supporters will help us. Their backing can suck us out of trouble.'

As well as being vital to Derby's hopes of staying in the Second Division, the game – as touched on earlier – was crucial to Fulham's hopes of getting out of it.

The Cottagers were aiming for third place and promotion to the First Division at the expense of Leicester City, with the two teams starting the day level on points but with the Foxes holding a comfortable goal difference advantage.

For Fulham to go up they would need to take more points at the Baseball Ground than Leicester did in their home match with bottom side Burnley.

So with everything taken into account there was an air of tension around all four sides of the stadium as the players came out for a match so important for both clubs.

The early exchanges were tight as a result with few chances at either end though while Fulham pushed forward in search of the goal they hoped would take them into the First Division, they were met with a rock-solid home defence.

George Foster and Paul Futcher were outstanding in the middle of the back four, as was John Barton at right-back, which meant Steve Cherry wasn't troubled too often.

When he was called upon he showed just why his reputation was growing with good handling and fine saves as required, especially one early stop from Dean Coney's header.

Mick Brolly then hit the bar at the other end with his own headed effort but there wasn't much between the sides as the match reached half-time.

The woodwork was again on Fulham's side after the break with Brolly once more denied, this time by the post, and with so much at stake for both sides the tension was starting to increase.

It was eased for Derby as they took the lead on 75 minutes in impressive style through Bobby Davison, who had joined the club not long after Taylor's appointment as manager.

Barton's cross went through the Fulham box and was retrieved by Paul Emson, who was making his last appearance for Derby.

Emson put the ball back across, Brolly headed it on and Davison, falling while on the turn, rifled in his volley to give Peyton no chance in the Fulham goal.

But after that the atmosphere started to change as the game ticked by and Derby fans started pushing towards the front of the terraces.

Eventually they made their way beyond the terraces and started to gather around the edge of the pitch.

The closer the full-time whistle loomed, the more fans were getting ready to invade the pitch, and as the end neared they were almost solid against the touchlines on all four sides of the ground with one individual even walking on to the pitch to congratulate Cherry on a fine late save.

Fulham manager Malcolm Macdonald was clearly – and justifiably – annoyed by what was happening, especially when his player Robert Wilson was the recipient of a kick aimed at him while the ball was still in play.

It was beyond chaotic and when referee Ray Chadwick, a newsagent by trade, blew his whistle for an offside decision thousands of supporters flooded on to the pitch.

Order could not be restored so the players left for the sanctity of the dressing rooms and Chadwick took the decision to end the match there and then, despite there seemingly still being time to run.

All the post-match talk was about the circumstances that had surrounded the early end to proceedings but boss Taylor was not concerned with what had happened there.

Instead, he would only talk about the performance of his players, and their efforts in rescuing a difficult situation to ultimately finish 13th in the table.

He said, 'That was an incredible performance and I'm the only one that can say so because I know what side went out and in what condition.

'In terms of guts and determination, it was even better than the win over Burnley.

'We gambled and got away with it. Everything was right about the approach and the end result.

'That was our springboard. We have stayed in the Second Division and now we'll build. There's no telling where we can go from here.'

Chairman Mike Watterson said survival on the field was the second phase in the Rams' progression, having earlier ensured the club's financial status with £139,000 in season ticket sales having been taken already for 1983/84 – all but £3,000 of that coming before the current season had ended.

But the early ending to the match could not be avoided and Fulham, having seen their promotion hopes evaporate, were demanding a replay and a second crack at going up.

They would have come up against a weakened Derby side with most of the squad away on an end-of-season trip to Majorca while the Rams themselves were denying responsibility for the chaos that was caused.

They were supported by *Derby Telegraph* reporter Gerald Mortimer who, in an editorial comment piece, said that while the club was 'liable to carry the can', there were three main areas of blame – the police, match referee Chadwick, and 'irresponsible supporters'.

The last point was easy to quantify as supporters had encroached on to the edge of the playing area well before the end of the match, and one had kicked out at Fulham's Wilson, while Mortimer also wrote that Chadwick, officiating his final league match, seemed to lack common sense.

He backed that up by saying that the game should have been stopped when the fans encroached and not re-started until they were back on the terraces.

Chadwick had already played three minutes and 57 seconds of stoppage time before the abandonment and had said after the match that he had another minute and 18 seconds to go.

And Mortimer's comment that the police 'were not where they needed to be to control a situation which everybody could see developing' echoed the words of Rams chairman Watterson.

He said, 'The club is blameless. The police actually ordered our stewards to open the barrier gates to allow our fans on to the touchline well before the end.

'If the police had done their job properly, this would not have happened. I shall be making the strongest possible protest to the Chief Constable and I shall be asking for a refund on the £3,000 police charges for the game.

'Instead of helping our stewards, they kept most of their manpower, including mounted officers, in front of the empty terracing at the Osmaston End where there was no encroachment.'

A Football League commission deliberated whether the game should be replayed but ultimately decided that the result should stand, leading to Fulham launching an unsuccessful appeal.

The Football Association's role was to decide what, if any, punishment to hand down to Derby County.

It decreed that by 30 September 1983 all fencing should be brought up to FA-approved standard with each gate manned by a steward at all times and to be only opened from pitchside; the paddock seated area [the old A, B and C Stands] to be fenced to the same standard; the club to pay for the costs of the inquiry; and up to and including 3 September 1983 there would be no admission to standing areas within the ground.

The last point affected home fixtures against Sheffield Wednesday and Swansea City, which were attended by 10,240 and 9,711 respectively.

The abandonment also went down in history as the first English Football League match to finish early with the result still standing.

26 v Rotherham United 2-1

9 May 1986. Attendance: 21,036
Baseball Ground. Football League Third Division

DERBY COUNTY:	ROTHERHAM UNITED:
Wallington	O'Hanlon
Palmer	Barnsley
Buckley	Dungworth
Williams (Gee 36)	Gooding
Hindmarch	Smith
MacLaren	Pickering
Micklewhite	Birch
Christie	Emerson
Davison	Trusson
Gregory	Simmons
Chandler	Pugh
	Unused sub: Crosby

Referee: Tom Fitzharris

THE history of Derby County has always been a case of feast followed by famine, and never was this more so than from the gradual decline from the pinnacle of English football to relegation to Division Three, with the small matter of potential bankruptcy and the club being wound up and disappearing altogether.

The role the board played in persuading Arthur Cox to join as manager in 1984 should never be understated in Rams history, and the man who had re-ignited Newcastle United as a footballing force did an incredible job of turning things round.

It was never going to be instant success, Cox did not even inherit sufficient players to field a full 11 when he arrived at the club, but he wheeled, dealed, begged, and borrowed and slowly got the club on the right track with a seventh-placed finish in his first season, though these were the days before play-offs so promotion was never on the cards.

There were those who believed that Derby was too big a club to languish in the Third Division, but the statistics do not lie and although the Rams were safely ensconced in the top half of the table at the end of that first campaign they were never realistic challengers.

They actually finished up 17 points behind Hull City, who took the third and final promotion spot.

There were signs that Cox was getting to grips with the situation and there was much enthusiasm for the fact that players were being bought rather than borrowed for the start of the 1985/86 season.

Among those to come in was midfielder Steve McClaren, whose Baseball Ground impact would not be felt for another decade. Most important was the signing of John Gregory in November from Queens Park Rangers for £100,000.

Gregory was a class act able to run the game from midfield and had won England caps before dropping down from the First Division to the third tier of English football, swayed by what he felt Derby's potential for progress in the next few years was.

Things were running smoothly until a 4-1 defeat away to fellow promotion contenders Plymouth Argyle in March.

Derby suffered a collective lack of belief and staggered towards the finishing line with a mixture of draws, wins and losses as they found it difficult to string together a consistent run of results.

After the Plymouth defeat they drew three on the bounce, beat Gillingham, lost at home to Bristol Rovers, then won at Lincoln City before seeing off Bolton Wanderers at the Baseball Ground.

Three draws and a defeat followed before the rot was stopped with a 3-0 win away to Swansea City on 6 May with Trevor Christie scoring twice, one a penalty, and Jeff Chandler adding the other goal.

Bad weather had led to fixture congestion so the Baseball Ground found itself hosting a game against Rotherham United on the eve of the FA Cup Final.

The result at Swansea had guaranteed that, if the Rams then saw off Rotherham on home turf, they would secure themselves a top-three finish and a return to the Second Division at the second time of asking.

Unsurprisingly, the Baseball Ground's highest Third Division crowd of the season packed the terraces and seats for a nail-biting climax to the season.

But with that the tension was massive as the prize, for a club that ten years ago was aiming for the fabled double of First Division championship and FA Cup, of a return to the Second Division was potentially 90 minutes away.

It was almost as if the fans were too afraid to get behind the players in the first period as nerves were clearly spreading from stands to pitch.

Derby were not particularly fluent on the night and Rotherham, comfortable in mid-table, dug in and made it hard for the Rams despite their poor away record.

Gary Micklewhite found space through the middle but chose to try and cross when a shot would have been a better option, while behind him Charlie Palmer went from one extreme to the other and back again with some fine passes followed by several gifts of possession to the visitors.

One of the former occurrences was enough to send Micklewhite in again but Kelham O'Hanlon in Rotherham's goal blocked what was somewhere between a cross and a shot.

At the other end Mark Wallington had pretty much nothing to do though he should have been called into action when Mike Trusson and Daral Pugh both wasted good headed opportunities.

Early in the second half the Rams should have had a penalty – their fifth in four games – when O'Hanlon pulled down Jeff Chandler, but referee Tom Fitzharris chose not to point to the spot.

Rotherham then started to up their game and appeared to grow in confidence as more tension seemed to encase the Baseball Ground.

But it was lifted on 77 minutes and Derby were seemingly, finally, on their way back to the Second Division.

Christie dummied Ross MacLaren's clearance and Gee, on as a substitute in the first half for the injured Geraint Williams, raced clear of the Rotherham rearguard.

As ever, the Baseball Ground turf was cutting up in the rain but Gee glided over it before getting into the box and finishing past O'Hanlon for his first senior goal.

But if the home faithful thought the last 13 minutes would be a cruise to promotion, they were quickly told otherwise.

Andy Barnsley lifted an aimless and harmless-looking free kick into the Derby box but Wallington failed to claim it and the ball dropped loose for Trusson to hammer it into the roof of the net.

The Baseball Ground was famed for its noise, especially in night games, but at this exact point you could have heard a pin drop, so stunned were Derby's fans.

It was agony for those present and those listening at home, and with six minutes remaining the pain almost got too much.

Bobby Davison broke to the edge of the box where he was hacked down by John Dungworth, who had already been booked and was sent off for his troubles.

The free kick was taken but blocked by the wall and then cleared but, to the amazement of everyone, Fitzharris spotted an infringement and pointed to the spot with Dean Emerson having seemingly elbowed Chandler.

So this was the moment – one kick from 12 yards to almost certainly wrap up promotion, and it was Christie's responsibility.

The ground held its breath as Christie stepped up and placed the ball low to the right of O'Hanlon.

Thankfully the stopper had decided to dive to his left and the ball was in the bottom corner to put Derby 2-1 up.

Even then it was not an entirely straightforward run to the end of the game as a back-pass from Chandler almost put Derby in danger, then John Gregory appeared to trip Alan Birch inside the penalty area but once more, nothing was given.

So promotion was sealed with one game to go and it was time for celebration at the Baseball Ground.

Assistant manager Roy McFarland beamed with delight when he spoke to BBC Radio Derby after the match and said, 'The one thing that was important tonight was that the fans stayed behind us. We haven't played particularly well, a lot of tension and a lot of nerves, and the fans have been absolutely fantastic.

'We needed that goal [Phil Gee's strike] just to give us that little bit of confidence. It was a bad goal that we conceded, but we've kept our heads, we've tried to play a little bit of football, and at the finish we've got the result we wanted.

'I'll be quite honest with you, it's the first penalty, at every club I've been involved with, that I've never looked at.

'I just put my head down and said, "Please Trevor, please score". Thank God he scored.'

Chairman Ian Maxwell admitted it was an emotional night, and said, 'It's a double triumph since we also won the Central League so we're not just strong horizontally but vertically, every which way.

'I'm absolutely delighted. Listen to this crowd – 21,000, we haven't had that in ten years. It's an amazing night for the club.'

Winger Chandler said, 'It's a great evening for the fans, the club, for everybody. It was hard coming but we got there in the end.

'It was a cliff-hanger of a game and we fought all the way and got it in the end.'

Match-winner Christie said he always felt the Rams were going to get a penalty in the game and would be happy to take it as Chandler had missed two matches previously against Doncaster Rovers.

He explained, 'It's just a matter of keeping your cool and fortunately it went in the net and that's all I can say.

'I was just thinking "Don't miss it", there's going to be 12 of the lads on my back, but I went back to the way I used to take them at Notts County – just placing them – and the keeper went the wrong way.'

Prolific scorer Bobby Davison said, 'Look at these supporters who have come out in their thousands, it's brilliant. I'm chuffed for the lads that we've finally done it. It was a bit tight near the end but we've made it.'

Winger Gary Micklewhite could not keep the smile off his face as the celebrations rolled on and he said, 'At nine o'clock I wasn't sure this was all going to come true! I'm over the moon.'

Captain Rob Hindmarch said, 'We made hard work of it again. It took a long time coming and once it came I couldn't see us losing it but they got the goal back and I thought, "Here we go again".

'But fortune smiled on us, we got a nice penalty and Trevor stuck it away.'

Young striker Gee, after only his third first-team appearance for the club, said he would never forget the occasion.

He said of his goal, 'You've got lots of things going through your mind – whether to blast it, chip it, side-foot it or what, and I just decided to chip it and side-foot it.

'But it wasn't meant to be a chip – I went to side-foot it and mis-hit it but it went in!'

The final words were reserved for boss Cox, who said, 'The emotion at the end was very nice. It wasn't a particularly good football match, it was very competitive and they weren't going to let anything go without us earning it.

'The celebrations afterwards were very emotional, very nice. I'm pleased for the players because they've worked very hard, and the amount of support that we've had and that we get has stimulated opponents, it's made our players think they've got to do something special to win the game, and here are are at the end of it.'

It was a case of after the Lord Mayor's Show as an often-postponed match away to Darlington was finally played on Monday 12 May and the the troops could not be raised for one last skirmish.

Derby duly lost a disappointing encounter 2-1 at Feethams, though a positive came in the shape of Gee scoring once more and Derby ultimately finished third, three points behind Plymouth Argyle and ten adrift of runaway champions Reading.

Gee had netted 29 times for the reserves as they won the Central League title – the first time a club from the Third Division had done so – and his emergence was another good sign that the club was really starting to move forward.

But simply returning to the Second Division was not an end in itself as further chapters in this book will testify.

v Plymouth Argyle 4-2

9 May 1987. Attendance: 20,798
Baseball Ground. Football League Second Division

DERBY COUNTY:	PLYMOUTH ARGYLE:
Steele	Cherry
Blades	Nisbet
Forsyth	Uzzell
Williams	Law
Hindmarch	Burrows
MacLaren	Matthews
Micklewhite	Hodges (Summerfield 73)
Gee (Lillis 88)	Coughlin
Davison	Tynan
Gregory	Evans
Callaghan	Nelson

Referee: Trelford Mills

A STORMING run through the spring of 1987 had already confirmed Derby County's return to the First Division after seven years away. Promotion back to the top flight had been secured with a 2-1 win at home to Leeds United on 2 May that sent the Baseball Ground into raptures and completed the longest of journeys back from the club's near-oblivion documented in the previous chapter.

In truth it was no less than Arthur Cox's side had deserved as following defeat in their first game of the year, 1-0 at Crystal Palace, they did not lose again until 17 April when going down 3-1 at Blackburn Rovers – then they embarked on a trio of victories over Yorkshire opposition with 1-0 successes at home to Bradford City and away to Sheffield United followed by that defeat of Leeds to get over the finishing line.

And having confirmed their elevation to the First Division the final challenge for Derby was to go on and win the second tier title, something they had done three times previously in their history.

The first crack at wrapping it all up came just 48 hours after beating Leeds and perhaps the promotion hangover was still lingering as the Rams went down 2-0 away to Reading, so the championship race would go down to the final day as their nearest challengers Portsmouth lost 1-0 at Crystal Palace on the same night.

Derby would be hosting Plymouth Argyle at the Baseball Ground and knew that a point would be enough to clinch top spot regardless of what Pompey managed in their home game with Sheffield United.

And if the Rams were looking for any sort of encouragement to give them one last push they could find it in their home form with the Baseball Ground having been the proverbial fortress across the season.

Derby had only been beaten twice in front of their own fans throughout 1986/87 and, curiously, those reverses came in the first two fixtures, with 1-0 scorelines against Oldham Athletic and then Chester City – in the League Cup – being registered.

So all signs were pointing towards another day of glory for the Rams and another Second Division championship to go with the ones won in 1911/12, 1914/15 and 1968/69.

It was also a third promotion in four years for Cox after his success with Newcastle United prior to joining Derby and taking them out of the Third Division.

And Cox told the *Derby Telegraph*, 'I shall say to them [the players] what I have been saying all season. They have been consistent and genuine since last August and now they must take the final step.

'We want to win the title. The players are after it and so are the supporters, who are at the back of everything we are trying to achieve at the Baseball Ground.

'It would be nice for the players to have a medal and the photographs which show them as champions. In later years, they can look back and remember the days at Derby with, hopefully, something to show for it.

'We played extremely well at Plymouth in December. It was probably our best away performance of the season until we fell asleep in injury time and allowed them to equalise [the game finished 1-1].

'Argyle need the points if they are to have any hope of a place in the play-offs. We need a point to make certain of the championship and want to go out with a win.

'It has the ingredients of a match as good as the one against Leeds last week with another big crowd.'

The Leeds match had been attended by 20,087 fans, a figure that had only been beaten once at the Baseball Ground when 21,385 saw the 0-0 draw with Portsmouth at the start of March.

Another sell-out was on the cards this time with all tickets having been snapped up and, such was the magnitude of the occasion, the Baseball Ground turnstiles were opening early at 12.30pm while secretary Michael Dunford issued a plea for fans to arrive in good time.

There would be the chance for supporters to acclaim the champions – if Derby were successful – after the match, although with the destination of the title still unknown the Football League ruled that there would be no presentation of the trophy on the day.

The team line-ups also had some interesting side-notes to them as John Gregory, Ross MacLaren and Gary Micklewhite were completing a full house of appearing in all 49 matches for Derby while in Plymouth's goal was Steve Cherry, who had started his career with the Rams.

Cherry's Derby career was perhaps best remembered for the costly mistake against Plymouth in the 1984 FA Cup quarter-final replay at the Baseball Ground but, had he not been as inspired as he was in the first match at Home Park, there would never have even been a need for a replay.

And, as an aside, at the same time as Derby would be battling for the championship, Burton Albion were gunning for their own moment of glory with a visit to Wembley for the FA Trophy Final against Kidderminster Harriers.

All eyes were, however, on the Baseball Ground which was stunned into silence with just nine minutes on the clock when the visitors took the lead.

Garry Nelson was given far too much time and space to run through the defence and beat Eric Steele with his shot, and the Rams' title hopes could really have been hanging by a thread had it not been for a fine Rob Hindmarch interception later in the half.

Whatever was said at half-time did the trick as Derby came out for the second period with far more purpose only to be continually denied by Cherry.

It took something special to beat the former Baseball Ground stopper and Bobby Davison's equaliser was just that as he fired in his 97th goal for the club with a bullet of a left-footed shot.

The goal was enough to put Derby in pole position for the title once more but things could easily have changed if they had conceded again and matters at Fratton Park had gone against them.

But any nerves were well and truly shattered in the final ten minutes with the goals that encapsulated the season.

The first came from Nigel Callaghan, who broke from just inside his own half and reached the Normanton End penalty area before driving low past Cherry.

Callaghan then turned provider with a low run and cross that Micklewhite finished off from close range and although Plymouth got a goal back through Nelson, the afternoon's final word went to Gregory who turned on the edge of the six-yard box to hammer in his 12th of the season and ensure the final minutes would be played out in comfort.

As it turned out, the Rams would have been champions anyway had they not have come back to take something against Plymouth owing to Portsmouth's 2-1 defeat at home to Sheffield United.

Not that they would have wanted to confirm top spot because of another team's failure and the dramatic nature of the victory over the Pilgrims was a great way to bring the curtain down on the season.

It sparked scenes of real joy at the Baseball Ground and Cox called the afternoon 'pure theatre'.

Cox, who after the title success also signed a new long-term contract that was, according to the *Derby Telegraph*, 'believed to be worth over £200,000', added, 'We plumbed the depths in the first half. Our marking was poor, we lacked respect for the opposition and we got what we deserved.

'At half-time we suggested it was time to start playing properly and all the qualities which have stood us in good stead throughout the season came flooding back.

'Bobby Davison scored an excellent goal and it was followed by an even better one from Nigel Callaghan.

'Everything came to a rapturous finish and I am very pleased for the players. They did not deserve to win the Third Division championship last season. They have thoroughly deserved to win the Second Division this season.'

Promotion to the First Division capped a remarkable rise in the career of striker Phil Gee, who less than two years previously had been spotted playing non-league football locally for Gresley Rovers.

Having made four appearances in the 1985/86 campaign he was a mainstay this time around, scoring 15 goals in 41 Second Division appearances.

He said, 'Last August, my only target was to get into the team if I could. Mark Lillis had been signed and I knew he would be first choice.

'I started as a substitute and played once on the left wing. I had just signed a new contract and I had a nightmare. I was really embarrassed.

'Mark's injury gave me the chance to get in and I suppose what has happened since then will sink in when I see a medal on the sideboard.'

Exhausted skipper Jack Nicholas keeps hold of the FA Cup after the 1946 Final.

Supporters queue outside the Baseball Ground before the 1968 League Cup replay against Chelsea.

Captain Dave Mackay holds aloft the 1969 Second Division championship trophy.

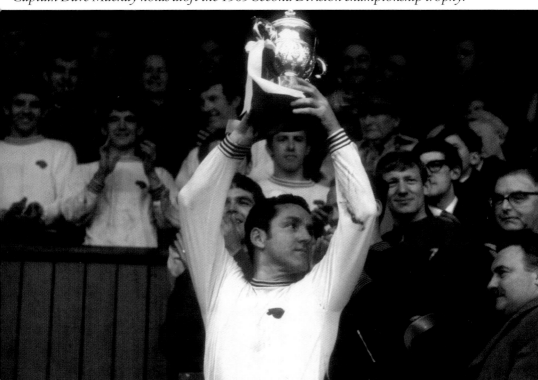

Derby's players celebrate a goal in the 5-0 victory over Spurs shortly after promotion.

John McGovern scores the goal that ultimately won Derby their first Football League title in 1972.

Roy McFarland heads home in the 3-0 European Cup victory over Benfica.

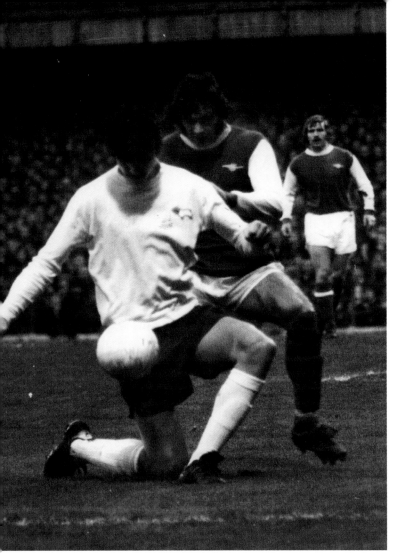

Roger Davies shields the ball in his memorable 1972 full debut against Arsenal.

Francis Lee gets his shot in during the away 1974 UEFA Cup match against Atletico Madrid.

Roger Davies heads in one of his famous five against Luton Town in 1975.

Charlie George gets ready to line up his hat-trick penalty against Real Madrid.

Tempers flare in the famous 1975 fight between Francis Lee and Leeds' Norman Hunter.

The Newcastle goal is breached in the 1976 FA Cup quarter-final at the Baseball Ground.

The Rams run riot against Irish part-timers Finn Harps in the UEFA Cup.

Kevin Wilson sets his sights from the spot in the 1982 season-ender against Watford.

Archie Gemmill curls his free kick into the Forest net in the 1983 FA Cup victory for Peter Taylor against Brian Clough.

Trevor Christie slots in the 1986 promotion-winning penalty against Rotherham.

Manager Arthur Cox celebrates
the 1987 Second Division
championship with the fans.

Marco Gabbiadini makes ground at
Wembley in the 1993 Anglo-Italian Cup
Final against Cremonese.

Robin van der Laan is mobbed after scoring the Rams' second goal on their way to
promotion against Crystal Palace.

Paul Simpson celebrates his dramatic equaliser in Derby's first Premier League game at home to Leeds.

Stephen Pearson is all smiles after putting Derby ahead in the play-off final against West Brom at Wembley.

It was also vindication for John Gregory who, the previous season, had dropped from the top tier to the third to sign for the Rams.

He said, 'It was a great finish to an excellent season. I did not have too many doubts when I came to Derby and what has happened speaks for itself.

'We've had setbacks but we have dusted ourselves down and tried again. As a group of players we don't fall out. We moan at each other on the pitch and we tell a few home truths but that's because we want the best for the team.'

Fans would have to wait a few more days for the trophy presentation as it was scheduled to take place at the Baseball Ground the following Thursday, before the reserves' final Central League match of the season.

Burton missed out on Wembley glory despite a heroic performance in holding their higher-ranked opponents Kidderminster to a 0-0 draw in their FA Trophy Final, only to lose the replay 2-1 at The Hawthorns three days later.

But for the Rams it was all about milking the moment – and then preparing for life back in a division they had been champions of just 12 years previously.

28 v Newcastle United 0-0

14 November 1987. Attendance: 21,698
St James' Park. Football League First Division

DERBY COUNTY:	NEWCASTLE UNITED:
Shilton	Kelly
MacLaren	Anderson
Forsyth	Tinnion
Williams	Wharton
Wright	P Jackson
Blades	Roeder
Callaghan	McDonald (O'Neill 74)
Garner (Gee 73)	Gascoigne
Davison	Goddard
Gregory	D Jackson
Cross	Cornwell
Unused sub: Penney	*Unused sub:* Bogie
Referee: Tom Fitzharris	

WHEN compiling a book of this nature there are various criteria to consider when deciding what makes a great game. Some are too obvious to require explanation such as cup final victories, promotion-clinching games or simply cracking spectacles that have had all watching on the edge of their seats from first to last.

Individual goalscoring feats such as the five scored by Roger Davies against Luton Town are also obvious.

There has to be something truly special about a scoreless draw to merit inclusion. That something special on this occasion was Peter Shilton.

He had kept goal a phenomenal 799 times in Football League games going into this match and was rightly considered to be England's finest goalkeeper of the era, a fact that could only be argued against by Ron Greenwood who as England manager had alternated between Shilton and Ray Clemence as he was undecided as to who was the better man. Shilton, along with England centre-half Mark Wright, had been signed during the summer from Southampton following Derby's promotion to the First Division and immediately proved invaluable to the team.

It was a hard season back in the top flight but the Rams managed to pick up enough points with the two new signings to keep their heads above water.

St James' Park held a special place in Arthur Cox's heart he had re-awakened a sleeping giant in the North-East during his time on Tyneside, and had done much the same in the East Midlands.

This was to be his first return to the club and media interest in the lead-up to this game focused mainly on the hero's return.

Cox had managed Newcastle to promotion in 1984 before leaving to take the Derby job, and in his time with the Toon Army he also signed Kevin Keegan while bringing through players like Chris Waddle and Peter Beardsley.

It was no surprise, therefore, that he received an emotional welcome from the passionate Gallowgate End crowd but he was focused solely on doing the business for Derby County.

The Rams had beaten Coventry City 2-0 in their last match, Andy Garner bagging both, but prior to that they had won only once in seven matches.

That victory over the Sky Blues was Derby's fourth since promotion back from the Second Division and they were doing just enough to keep out of the scrap to avoid relegation, even at a relatively early stage of the season.

They had beaten Luton Town 1-0 on the opening day thanks to John Gregory's goal, then Gregory netted a penalty to back up Bobby Davison's effort in a 2-1 win at Norwich City before three more points arrived on 17 October at Charlton Athletic with Steve Cross scoring the only goal.

In the 13 First Division games played to this point, Shilton had kept four clean sheets while also conceding 14 goals, but although Newcastle had drawn a blank in their previous two fixtures they had scored 16 times in ten of their 13 matches.

And who knows how many they would have scored on this occasion had it not been for Shilton's world-class – and that is a fair term in this instance – performance.

Paul Gascoigne, at 20 and still making a name for himself as a potential star of the future, gave a skilful and powerful performance from midfield and was behind most of the good things Newcastle did.

But regardless of his promptings, Shilton stood firm and simply would not be beaten.

In a five-minute period during the first half he produced three top-class saves to deny Darren Jackson, John Cornwell and Paul Goddard.

Even by half-time the home faithful must have been getting the feeling that their team would not be scoring and the events of the second half more than backed that up.

A close-range save from Goddard, who might well have had a hat-trick on another day, was up there with the best you will ever see.

Yet Shilton simply got better. A left-wing cross from Brian Tinnion was perfect and surely was going to be headed in by Goddard.

The number nine met it superbly with a header that went sharply downwards but, somehow, at the age of 38 and 21 years since he had made his professional debut for Leicester City, Shilton threw himself down and produced his most remarkable save yet.

It was the perfect example of why Shilton had already become a legend at Leicester, Stoke City, Nottingham Forest and Southampton and illustrated the benefits of his punishing training routines that had made him the world's best goalkeeper.

That was perhaps the point when Newcastle realised that they simply would not score past England's number one that day.

It wasn't all one-way traffic as Derby had their chances too, notably with Cross and Nigel Callaghan shooting wide and Garner seeing an effort cleared off the line.

But in a way a victory would have been harsh on Shilton as it would have given a goalscorer a share of the headlines on an occasion when he deserved them all to himself.

There is absolutely no doubt in the minds of anyone at the game that Newcastle should have won this match by a wide margin. It was Shilton alone who kept them at bay.

Cox ran on to the pitch after the match and even though he was usually a man of little outward emotion he planted a kiss on his keeper's cheek.

He later claimed Shilton's match day shirt as a trophy to keep with other souvenirs of great displays that he had witnessed.

Captain Wright did not need to wait to be asked his thoughts on what everyone had witnessed, instead seeking out *Derby Telegraph* correspondent Gerald Mortimer to ask, 'What about that?'

Mortimer later quoted Wright as saying, 'I have never seen a performance like that from anybody and if Peter doesn't score ten out of ten for that, nobody ever will.

'Without him, we'd have had a right tonking. He was unbelievable.'

The run of clean sheets went to three in Derby's next match as Cross and Gregory saw off Chelsea at the Baseball Ground, then Garner and Phil Gee ensured the points returned from The Dell after a 2-1 success.

A 1-1 draw at home to Watford with Wright on target opened up December and hopes were high that Derby would continue to work their way to safety and finish comfortably clear of the relegation scrap come the end of the season.

Then it all started to turn sour. The next eight games were all lost, a club record, and the Rams did not pick up another point until a 0-0 draw at Oxford United on 20 February.

Seven unbeaten games later they were looking up rather than down, only to lose four out of the next five – a 2-1 home win against Newcastle sandwiched by runs of two successive defeats either side.

But they did enough to get over the safety line as they won 2-0 at home to Southampton in game number 37 thanks to Gregory and Frank Stapleton, his only goal for Derby, then drew the final two to finish in 15th place, seven points clear of the relegation zone.

Shilton played in all 40 First Division games that season, conceding only 45 goals, and he remained at the club until February 1992 before he departed to take the player-manager's position at Plymouth Argyle after 211 appearances in a Derby shirt.

It is arguable that none was better than this one on Tyneside.

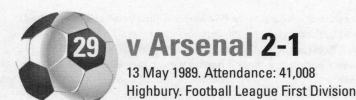

29 v Arsenal 2-1

13 May 1989. Attendance: 41,008
Highbury. Football League First Division

DERBY COUNTY:	ARSENAL:
Shilton	Lukic
Sage	Dixon
Forsyth	Winterburn
Williams	Thomas
Blades	O'Leary
Hindmarch	Adams
Cross	Rocastle
Saunders	Richardson
Goddard	Smith
Hebberd	Bould (Hayes 65)
Micklewhite	Merson (Groves 76)
Unused subs: Gee, Penney	
Referee: George Tyson	

NOT since the glory days of the 1970s under Brian Clough and Dave Mackay had Derby County been challenging at the right end of the First Division. But in the 1988/89 season, their second back in the top flight after promotion in 1987, that was exactly what the Rams were doing.

They were not contenders for a first championship since 1975 but they had been among the First Division's leading sides for much of the campaign and, under normal circumstances, would have been harbouring hopes of a place in the UEFA Cup.

But that avenue was not open to them or any of their rivals as English clubs remained banned from European competition following the Heysel disaster of 1985 which preceded the European Cup Final between Liverpool and Italian giants Juventus.

That took nothing away from how well Derby had performed across a season that had seen them unearth a man who was becoming one of the First Division's deadliest strikers – Dean Saunders.

The Welshman had scored twice on his debut against Wimbledon the previous October after becoming Derby's first million-pound player after signing from Oxford United.

His only absence from the side had been three days later when ineligible for a League Cup defeat at West Ham United so he had played in every match he was able to and been a prolific scorer.

Saunders's goals, and his partnership with Paul Goddard, had been key in Arthur Cox's side establishing themselves as a First Division force to be reckoned with.

Derby went into the visit to Highbury in the top six and looking to bounce back from the previous Wednesday's 3-0 defeat at Charlton Athletic, who were deep in relegation trouble.

But that was only their second defeat in seven games since the start of April, a run that included a 2-0 victory over Manchester United at Old Trafford on an afternoon that was overshadowed by the tragic events at the FA Cup semi-final between Liverpool and Nottingham Forest at Hillsborough.

And looking ahead to the game at Arsenal, manager Cox told the *Derby Telegraph*, 'Even if we had beaten Charlton on Wednesday we would have been looking for an improved performance.

'We have been pitched against several clubs with big incentives and Arsenal have an excellent chance of winning the title.

'There will be a big crowd and Highbury is a lovely place to play football. It is nice to be involved in a game of such importance and we shall do everything in our power to get something from it.'

The second paragraph of Cox's comments told the real story of just how important this match was shaping up to be for Arsenal. The Gunners would start the weekend five points clear at the top of the table with second-placed Liverpool, the only side now able to stop them from winning the championship, having a game in hand.

Arsenal had not been champions since 1970/71 when George Graham was a player at Highbury and, having taken the managerial hot-seat in 1986, he was seeking the club's ninth championship.

Their eighth had been an English record that was eventually overtaken by Merseyside rivals Liverpool and Everton, who were due to meet in the FA Cup Final seven days after this match.

Ordinarily the weekend of 13 May 1989 would have been the final day of the Football League season but the disaster at Hillsborough meant the fixture schedule was disrupted with the Gunners still having three more league matches to play and Liverpool having four.

The absolute final match of 1988/89 would come on Friday 26 May with the two title rivals meeting at Anfield but a lot would have to happen in the intervening games for that one to become a winner-takes-all title shoot-out.

So while Derby had little to play for the Gunners, having won five of their last six matches, definitely had plenty riding on this one.

And they were faced with a Rams side shorn of their central defensive talisman and captain Mark Wright, who was suspended for the second time in the season having been sent off in the 3-0 defeat on Luton Town's plastic pitch two weeks previously.

It was Wright's first absence since January although he did have more positive news in the build-up to the Arsenal game with a call to the England squad for the first time since the previous summer's European Championship.

His suspension meant that Paul Blades would switch across from right-back to partner Rob Hindmarch in the centre while Mel Sage, fit again after five months out of the side, would take over Blades's number two shirt.

It would be Derby's first changes to a starting line-up in eight matches though there was another alteration to contend with as flying winger Ted McMinn was out with a hamstring injury so Steve Cross took his place.

The re-shuffled defence might have been forgiven for taking a while to settle down but Sage, Hindmarch, Blades and Michael Forsyth stuck to their task resolutely right from the first whistle.

The early pressure was Arsenal's, especially when news broke that Wimbledon were ahead against Liverpool, but Derby were superb in repelling the Gunners' surprisingly direct approaches with Hindmarch and Blades heading and kicking clear with relish.

Alan Smith and David Rocastle wasted good opportunities before Derby showed them how to finish – and in spectacular style – with 29 minutes gone.

An angled pass from Geraint Williams arrowed towards Saunders who, from a very difficult position, let the ball drop over his shoulder before hammering an unstoppable shot past John Lukic.

If that goal was remarkable, so was a save from Peter Shilton as he kept out Kevin Richardson's header with Forsyth lying unconscious after a challenge from Steve Bould.

Shilton was in great form and twice denied Nigel Winterburn in the second half but could do nothing when Smith lined up his effort in front of an unguarded goal thanks to Paul Merson's good work – only to fire his shot against the crossbar.

Saunders wasted one chance to double the Rams' lead when he had been fed by the impressive-as-ever Goddard but the Welshman was right on the mark on 76 minutes.

He had tied Tony Adams up in knots with a run that saw the Arsenal defender bring him down inside the box and he stepped up himself to score with the resulting penalty.

That was enough to secure the points for Derby although home hopes were raised with a couple of minutes left when Smith netted from Richardson's corner, but it was no more than a consolation goal that, coupled with Liverpool's eventual win over Wimbledon, left the Gunners' title hopes under serious threat.

The result meant that Derby would finish no lower than fifth as they faced their final match of the season just 48 hours later when they travelled to Everton.

If they were to finish fourth, which they could still do, they would need to win at Goodison and Sheffield Wednesday would have to beat Norwich City at Hillsborough in order for the Rams to move above the Canaries. And that would also see them set a new club record of nine away wins in a single First Division season having equalled the previous best, registered in 1934/35, 1936/37, 1947/48 and 1971/72.

Manager Cox was proud of his team's performance at Highbury and he said, 'It was possible to see Arsenal's tension. They wanted to go by route one into our penalty area and we were determined to keep them out.

'Peter Shilton was formidable on the occasions when he needed to be and the first goal from Dean Saunders was fit to grace any game.

'Whichever of the great finishers you care to name would have been proud of that one. He was very busy around Tony Adams to win the penalty and now he must improve his football.

'We need to be more accurate with the ball when we are outnumbering opponents on the break.

'All credit to Micky Forsyth for carrying on after a nasty bang. There were a lot of bumps and bruises in an excellent team performance.

'The run of the ball and the rub of the green play a big part in professional sport but we have to do what we can to make them go our way.

'It is frustrating we have conceded ten goals in three away games, against Wimbledon [4-0], Luton [3-0] and Charlton [3-0], and only 19 in our entire away programme.

'After adverse results it would be easy to go overboard but if you want the team to be consistent, management attitudes must be the same.

'We need a bit of help from Sheffield Wednesday to finish fourth but we will do all we can to keep our side of the bargain.'

Unfortunately the trip to Goodison proved one match too far for Derby as they lost 1-0 thanks to a goal scored by Ian Wilson, who would have a loan spell at the Baseball

Ground in 1990/91, though Norwich's 2-2 draw at Hillsborough secured fourth place for them anyway.

Nottingham Forest were third and with most of the league fixtures completed, all eyes were then on the title race which still had some mileage to go.

Arsenal followed their defeat to Derby with a 2-2 draw at home to Wimbledon on 17 May which left them and Liverpool level on 73 points though the Reds also had a game in hand prior to that impending last-day encounter.

Having won an emotional FA Cup Final against Everton on 20 May, three days later Liverpool beat West Ham 5-1 to set up the final battle, when all they needed to do was avoid defeat by two or more clear goals to win the double.

With seconds of the season remaining it looked like they would do just enough as they trailed 1-0 at home to Arsenal, only for the Gunners to dramatically steal the title away from their hosts thanks to Michael Thomas's late, late goal.

As for Derby, they have not scaled such heights since.

30 v Nottingham Forest 2-1

24 November 1990. Attendance: 21,729
Baseball Ground. Football League First Division

DERBY COUNTY:	NOTTINGHAM FOREST:
Shilton	Crossley
Patterson	Laws
Pickering	Pearce
G Williams (Ramage 8)	Walker
Wright	Chettle
Forsyth	Hodge (Starbuck 69)
Micklewhite	Crosby
Saunders	Keane
Harford	Clough
Hebberd	Jemson
Callaghan	Parker
Unused sub: Kavanagh	*Unused sub:* Wassall
Referee: Colin Trussell	

FOR all the progress Derby had made under Arthur Cox in the second half of the 1980s, by the time the decade turned things were going in the opposite direction again.

Cox had taken Derby from the depths of the old Third Division to two successive promotions and a fifth-placed finish in the First Division in 1988/89 that would have earned a UEFA Cup spot had it not been for the ban on English clubs in Europe because of the Heysel disaster.

Just as an aside, in that season – the Rams' best since the glory days of the 1970s – Forest still finished third, showing how fortunes had changed in the intervening years and how at the time they continued to hold the upper hand on their great rivals.

But having finished fifth, the Rams had been unable to progress and found themselves battling to avoid a serious relegation scrap in 1989/90 though they managed to keep their heads above water, despite off-field troubles and uncertainty under Robert Maxwell's chairmanship.

By the time Derby and Forest clashed at the Baseball Ground in November 1990 Maxwell was keen on selling the club.

He had also been under investigation from the Football League having loaned money to Tottenham Hotspur through companies owned by himself and Spurs chairman Irving Scholar, though the ultimate result of the investigation was that he had done no wrong.

With that in mind, Maxwell was after an apology from the Football League's management committee and was asked at a sports writers' lunch whether, if he had indeed lent money to Spurs, Derby fans would be angry.

He was quoted in the *Derby Telegraph* as responding, 'If such a supporter exists, I would tell him to get stuffed. What right would he have to tell me what to do with my money?

121

'I could make Tottenham, Derby and Oxford suffer if the mis-management committee do nothing.'

A further editorial in the *Telegraph* added, 'It is scandalous that a threat against Derby County, from somebody who remains chairman of the club, should be used as part of an attempt to force an apology from the League.' Manager Cox was not, however, speaking publicly about the off-field matters and preferred instead to look at the football side.

He had his eyes on putting to an end Derby's poor recent record against Forest as the Rams had not recorded a victory against Brian Clough's side in the three seasons since they had been back in the same division.

Cox said, 'Since we came back to the First Division we have had six tries to beat Nottingham Forest and have not managed it once. That is not a record we are proud of and we would like to do something about it.

'There is always a crackle about a local derby and there have been some good matches at the Baseball Ground in the last two months. We are looking forward to it.'

Even though it had been a difficult start to the season with Derby having not won a game until 10 October, when they beat Carlisle United 1-0 in the League Cup at the Baseball Ground, they actually approached this match in decent form.

The Carlisle game was the first of a run of six unbeaten that included a 0-0 draw with Manchester United and a 6-0 victory over Sunderland, also in the League Cup, with only a 3-0 defeat at Leeds United blotting the copybook ahead of the visit of Forest.

Pre-match hype surrounded the likely battle between Derby skipper Mark Wright and Forest centre-half Des Walker with the pair having played together in England's defence during the run to the semi-finals of the 1990 World Cup in Italy.

Derby also added young defenders Steve Round and Jason Kavanagh to their squad for this match with injury concerns over Steve Cross, Mel Sage and Paul Williams.

And the Rams really had to dig deep and battle back to recover the points in memorable style having been in a familiar position with just 15 minutes gone.

Trailing in a match was hardly anything new to them that season, and being behind to Forest was almost customary as they had failed to beat them since winning promotion back to the First Division in 1987.

Forest's goal was one that Derby would have been disappointed with as they had more than enough chances to get the ball clear.

A low shot from Steve Chettle struck a post and was put out for a corner, which was again not dealt with and went back to Chettle who this time made no mistake with his second attempt from an almost identical position on the edge of the box.

Nigel Jemson passed up a good opportunity to make it 2-0 and even before going behind the Rams had been forced into a substitution that would ultimately turn the game in their favour.

Craig Ramage replaced the injured Geraint Williams after eight minutes and within two minutes of Derby going behind, the youngster collected a pass inside the Forest area and moved on to it before neatly lifting his shot over Mark Crossley and into the net.

Amazingly, that was Derby's first goal at home to Forest in the league since the famous 4-1 over the then-European champions back in 1979.

From there the game was always going to be a battle and it would be about who was able to wrestle the initiative away from their rivals first.

Wright's header from Nigel Callaghan's free kick hit the bar for Derby but at the other end the centre-half was superb in performing his defensive duties, and he had great support from Mark Patterson and Nick Pickering with the pair only in the team because of a lack of available full-backs.

Games like this can be decided on a single moment and it was no different in this instance. Thankfully it went in Derby's favour on the hour.

A ball was played long and nodded on by Mick Harford where Gary Micklewhite picked it up wide on the right.

Micklewhite's cross was perfect, as was the leap by Dean Saunders, and the Welshman powered his header past Crossley to the tune of ecstatic celebrations.

Then it was a case of making sure they didn't let their advantage slip and the Rams did so without any real scares, apart from when Nigel Clough lined up a shot that was saved by Peter Shilton.

Not only had Derby got one over on their rivals, they had also restored some pride after their hammering at Leeds the previous week – and lifted themselves out of the relegation zone, up to 17th, in the process.

The talk after the match was heavy in its praise of the impact made by Ramage and his perfectly-timed goal.

The headline on the back of the *Derby Telegraph* did not hold anything back, stating, 'DALGLISH STYLE FROM RAMAGE'.

The similarity was made between the way the young midfielder turned inside the Forest box and chipped his finish over Crossley and an almost identical goal by Kenny Dalglish to win the European Cup for Liverpool against Brugge at Wembley in 1978.

As another aside, in Brugge's line-up earlier in the tournament – and finishing as that season's second-highest goalscorer in the European Cup, with four – was former Derby man Roger Davies.

Ramage had been in the starting XI for the defeat at Leeds and had been named among the substitutes for the game against Forest as he continued to make his way as a professional having come through Derby's youth ranks. As it turned out he played for most of the match anyway and Cox was pleased with his response.

The boss said, 'Craig took his chance like Kenny Dalglish, a little chip when the goalkeeper committed himself.

'But he owed the other lads a goal because he has missed a number of chances this season.

'There are some very good and competitive players in both teams and we deserved to win because we were always that little bit more of a threat.

'Dean Saunders scored an excellent goal and Micky Harford always troubled Forest. Mark Wright was magnificent and the two full-backs were very effective.

'We had a good week preparing for Forest and the players were aware that we would have our backs to the wall if we lost. Instead, we have beaten a good side and we should take strength from that.'

And Saunders, who scored the crucial goal in front of the Normanton End, had plenty of praise for both Ramage and Micklewhite, who supplied the cross for the Rams' winner.

He added, 'Gary Micklewhite was involved in both goals and is in a purple patch. He has come back unbelievably well after a bad knee injury and looks better than ever.

'I think the doctors must have put an extra spring in his knee and his cross for my goal was perfect. I don't score many with my head but all I had to do was make sure I got a good strike on the ball.

'Craig showed his class by the way he took his goal. If people allow him to get on with his game, we may have a player who will be worth millions in the future.'

Unfortunately the result didn't really kick-start Derby's season as a victory over your rivals sometimes can do.

They backed it up briefly by drawing 1-1 at Sheffield Wednesday in the League Cup then picking up all three First Division points with a 2-1 win at Sunderland on 1 December.

The League Cup campaign was ended in the replay by Sheffield Wednesday, then of the Second Division in the season they went on to beat Manchester United in the Wembley final, before the Rams suffered a bizarre 6-4 defeat at home to Chelsea in their next First Division outing.

Nobody knew it at the time but that win at Sunderland would be Derby's last three-pointer until 4 May when they hammered Southampton 6-2 at the Baseball Ground in the third-to-last match of the season.

By then their relegation had already been confirmed, though they were doomed anyway well before the final nail was put in the coffin on 20 April with a 2-1 defeat at Manchester City that saw striker Niall Quinn go in City's goal after Tony Coton was sent off for a professional foul – then save Saunders's penalty.

That victory over Southampton was at least one final positive in a horrendous season and ended a 20-game run without a win that stood as a club record until the 2007/08 Premier League campaign.

Maxwell got his wish and sold the club in the summer of 1991, removing the shackles under which Derby had operated during the last two years of his tenure, with first Brian Fearn taking the chair before Lionel Pickering assumed the position.

Saunders's goal against Forest was one of 57 he scored in 131 appearances in a Derby shirt – 130 of those matches were consecutive as, after bagging a pair on his debut against Wimbledon in October 1988, he was ineligible for a League Cup tie three days later, meaning he actually played in every single game he was able to during his time at the Baseball Ground before moving to Liverpool with Wright in the summer of 1991.

Ramage never quite hit the heights expected of him, despite winning England Under-21 caps while at Derby, and he left the Rams in 1994 after 56 appearances to join Watford, where he enjoyed a good career before later signing for Bradford City and finishing as a player with Notts County in 2001.

He remains a popular figure at Derby, however, and in the summer of 2013 was announced as the new match summariser for BBC Radio Derby's commentary team.

But the final words must go to Graham Richards, the Radio Derby commentator who called Saunders's goal with his usual gusto for a sequence that became iconic among Rams fans.

'Micklewhite thumps it over, early ball, up goes Saunders ... goal! Goal! Goal! 2-1 Derby County! What a header! Forest are behind! Dig that one out of the net Mark Crossley, not a chance! In the back! 2-1!'

v Sheffield Wednesday 3-3

8 March 1993. Attendance: 22,511
Baseball Ground. FA Cup Quarter-Final

DERBY COUNTY:	SHEFFIELD WEDNESDAY:
Taylor	Woods
Patterson	Nilsson
Forsyth	Worthington
Nicholson	Palmer
Short	Harkes (Jemson 80)
Pembridge	Anderson
Williams	Wilson
Kuhl	Waddle
Kitson	Warhurst
Gabbiadini	Bright
Johnson	Sheridan (Hyde 57)
Unused subs: Goulooze, Comyn	
Referee: Gerald Ashby	

T is a recurring theme in the history of Derby County that FA Cup success has been pretty much consigned to individual matches and cup runs that have ended in disappointment a step or two from glory.

So it was with little enthusiasm that Rams fans discovered that their first opponents in the 1993 FA Cup would be Stockport County, a lower division side that Derby would be expected to beat before drawing a bigger name and going out of the competition.

A crowd of 17,960, a respectable number for a game at the Baseball Ground that season, saw the victory which earned them a fourth round tie away at Luton Town.

A hat-trick from returning Hatter Mark Pembridge plus strikes from Craig Short and Marco Gabbiadini made short work of their opponents, and when two goals from Short and one from Paul Williams saw off the fifth round challenge of Bolton Wanderers, another home tie for Derby, supporters started to wonder if perhaps something was going to happen that season.

The best anyone can ask for in the later stages of any cup competition is a home match, and prayers were answered when they were drawn at home to Premier League side Sheffield Wednesday.

Although initially pleased that the tie was to be contested at the Baseball Ground any students of the history between the two clubs would be aware of how poorly Derby had fared against the Owls.

The Rams' all-time playing record against their South Yorkshire rivals shows that they have won more games in all competitions but the pendulum swings heavily the other way in the FA Cup. The very first time they played each other was an FA Cup game which Wednesday won. That was in 1891.

Since then Derby had only beaten Wednesday once in the competition, 1-0 on their way to the semi-finals in 1923, and were knocked out by the Owls in 1986 and 1987.

Now, as it was in 1987, it was second tier v top flight but this time the Rams were hoping to cause an upset of their own having been on the receiving end of one last time around.

They had been having a mixed season in the First Division but after a 2-0 defeat at home to West Ham United on 10 January they started to turn things around and, coupled with their progress in the FA Cup, they had lost just twice in their previous ten matches by the time the Sky Sports cameras came to the Baseball Ground for this Monday night match.

They had also kept three successive clean sheets so would have felt confident of making sure that Paul Warhurst, the Owls' centre-half turned striker, could be kept quiet rather than continuing his prolific form.

Wednesday, for their part, warmed up for the game at Derby with a 1-0 defeat at Coventry City that came four days after a 1-1 draw at home to Liverpool.

But prior to that they had been on an amazing run of eight successive victories and overall they had won 13 out of 15, drawing the other two.

Their FA Cup run had seen them win 2-1 at Cambridge United in the third round, 1-0 at home to Sunderland in the fourth and 2-0 at home to Southend United in the fifth.

They were also into the semi-finals of the League Cup and had won their first leg 4-2 away to Blackburn Rovers on 10 February – but wouldn't be playing the return until the Sunday after their visit to the Baseball Ground, such was the nature of their fixture congestion.

It was no easier for Derby as along with their FA Cup run they had also earned themselves a place at Wembley in the final of the Anglo-Italian Cup, to be played on 27 March.

But all of the ingredients were there for an FA Cup classic under the Baseball Ground floodlights – and because the game was taking place on the Monday night, with the draw for the semi-finals having already been made, the winners knew that they would face Blackburn or Sheffield United in the semi-final at Wembley, where the semis were now being played.

Derby had not been to the semi-finals since 1976, when they lost to Manchester United at Hillsborough, though they had reached the quarters in 1977 and 1984.

Wednesday had the upper hand in the early stages with England winger Chris Waddle particularly dangerous, prompting all of their big moves.

There were only 12 minutes on the clock when he carved out the opportunity that saw Wednesday take the lead, though it came from the penalty spot and John Sheridan's right boot after Mark Bright was fouled by Mark Patterson after a pass from Waddle.

It was a powerfully struck penalty but nowhere near as powerful as the shot that led to the Rams getting themselves level before the half-hour mark.

A ball was played out to young left-back Shane Nicholson, in only his fourth game for the Rams, and as he pushed forward the Baseball Ground let out a collective cry of 'shoot'.

Not wanting to let his new fans down, Nicholson unleashed a piledriver from fully 30 yards that smashed against the crossbar, bounced down, and in off the trailing foot of the helpless Chris Woods.

If brute force had created the first two goals, the third came from two moments of class just seven minutes later to put Wednesday back in front.

Waddle's pass was measured to perfection in behind the Derby defence and Warhurst ran on to it, drew Martin Taylor and finished off with clinical efficiency.

Half-time came at the right time for the Rams who came back strongly after the interval, roared on by one of the Baseball Ground's loudest crowds in recent years, and they peppered the visiting goal.

Woods dropped a cross from Patterson and had to be bailed out by Carlton Palmer while the Wednesday rearguard blocked shot after shot.

The pressure eventually told in the 69th minute. Paul Kitson headed the ball on to Gabbiadini, who outmuscled Palmer and burrowed his way into the box before lifting his shot beyond Woods with an excellent finish.

Five minutes later the entire stadium seemed to be shaking in its foundations as Derby went 3-2 up.

There looked to be a shooting opportunity on the edge of the box for Pembridge but instead he rolled the ball sideways to Nicholson, who delivered an intelligent cross into the middle of the area.

It was crying out to be headed home and Kitson rose to positively bury it with an effort that flew past Woods's outstretched hand.

The Rams were just 16 minutes away from the semi-final but knew they would have to be on their guard for every single second before the final whistle.

Taylor saved a Danny Wilson shot then Wednesday introduced Nigel Jemson for John Harkes in a move that paid off for them.

With six minutes remaining, yet another delightful Waddle pass sent Jemson clear down the right and he pulled the ball back for Warhurst to hammer home his shot and silence the home crowd – his 11th goal in ten games since moving forward from the back.

Even then, both sides were going all out for the victory but a seventh goal on an amazing night just would not come and a replay would be required.

Though Derby may not have won this particular tie, any of the 22,511 fans who attended the game were treated to a spectacle that they would never forget.

It was certainly a night for football purists.

Gerald Mortimer summed everything up so accurately in his match report in the *Derby Telegraph* when he said, 'It was the kind of night when the watchers envied the players. It must be marvellous to be involved in a game like that and it is the province of the chosen few, whose ability earns them the right.'

Along with the elation of the match was a feeling that Derby's best chance of making the semi-final was to win at home as there is often a feeling that you don't get a second chance in matches like this – not least because the Rams had not won at Hillsborough in any match since 1936, including FA Cup semi-final defeats there in 1948 and 1976.

Both teams were then in action again just 48 hours later, the Owls winning 1-0 at Ipswich Town while Derby beat Bristol Rovers 3-1 at the Baseball Ground, then the Rams lost 1-0 at Millwall over the following weekend while Wednesday beat Blackburn 2-1 to seal their place in the League Cup Final.

The replay was also televised on Sky but any hopes the watching public had of witnessing a match as exciting as the first one were unfulfilled.

It took a single goal in the first half from Warhurst for the home side to go through and face their rivals from the Steel City for a place in the FA Cup Final.

Wednesday were at Wembley twice in April, beating Sheffield United 2-1 in their FA Cup semi-final but losing by the same score to Arsenal in the League Cup showdown.

Curiously, Arsenal would also be their opponents in the FA Cup Final after the Gunners saw off north London rivals Tottenham Hotspur in the last four.

Derby County's Greatest Games

The first attempt at separating the two sides ended in a 1-1 draw so the players and fans returned to Wembley the following Thursday night to see Arsenal win it 2-1 with a goal from Andy Linighan in the final minute of extra time.

Derby were first to Wembley, however, and you can read about their Anglo-Italian Cup exploits in the next chapter.

And they returned to the quarter-finals of the FA Cup in 1997 and 1999 only to be beaten again.

They have not been back there since 1999 so, at the time of writing, that wait for a place in the semi-finals goes on.

The two teams next met in the FA Cup in the third round in 2008 when Derby, then of the Premier League, came from two down at home to their Championship opponents to force a replay, where they again trailed but ultimately went through on penalties after a 1-1 draw.

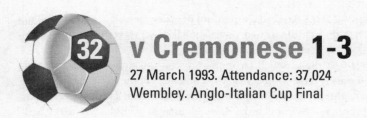

32 v Cremonese 1-3

27 March 1993. Attendance: 37,024
Wembley. Anglo-Italian Cup Final

DERBY COUNTY:	CREMONESE:
Taylor	Turci
Patterson	Gualco
Forsyth	Pedroni
Nicholson	Cristiani
Coleman	Colonnese
Pembridge	Verdelli
Micklewhite	Giandebiaggi
Goulooze (Hayward 83)	Nicolini
Kitson	Tentoni (Montorfano 85)
Gabbiadini	Maspero
Johnson (Simpson 81)	Florjancic (Dezotti 73)
Unused subs: Sutton (GK), Comyn, Stallard	*Unused subs:* Violini (GK), Feraroni, Lombardini
Referee: Joaquim Urio Velasquez (Spain)	

THE Anglo-Italian Cup was a strange beast. It was first played in 1970 on the back of the success of the Anglo-Italian League Cup, which was set up to allow third tier teams in England the chance to face continental opposition as, in 1967 and 1969, Third Division outfits Queens Park Rangers and Swindon Town won the League Cup but were not able to enter the UEFA Cup because of UEFA's rules.

Swindon won that first Anglo-Italian League Cup in 1969 by beating Coppa Italia winners Roma in a two-legged final and the Anglo-Italian Cup was then created for the following season to capitalise on the former event's success.

It was initially open to six teams each from Italy and England and ran for four years before being cancelled due to a lack of interest, only to re-start again in 1976 but only open to semi-professional clubs, by which time the Anglo-Italian League Cup – which had taken a break from 1972 to 1974 – was in its final season.

Derbyshire non-league side Matlock Town were the English runners-up in the 1978/79 tournament after qualifying having won the Northern Premier League Cup in 1978.

Once again the tournament faded from the horizon and was pulled in 1986 but it was re-instated ready for the 1992/93 season as a replacement for the old Full Members Cup (sponsored at different times in its existence by Simod and ZDS) – and this time things would be different.

It was open to clubs from the countries' respective second tiers, the newly-renamed First Division in England and Italy's Serie B, given a Wembley final and structured so that the final itself would truly be Anglo-Italian with a representative from each nation.

The 24 teams from the First Division were split into eight qualifying groups of three and Derby were handed games against Notts County and Barnsley with a place in the main competition the prize for topping your group.

Notts were beaten 4-2 at the Baseball Ground and Barnsley seen off 2-1 at Oakwell so Derby went through to the grandly-named 'international stage', where their opponents would all be Italian.

They beat Pisa 3-0 at the Baseball Ground and won 3-0 in both Cosenza and Reggiana, with their only reverse coming in a 3-1 scoreline at home to Cremonese.

But this is where things started to get complex as the final group tables were produced to reflect those results but in order of which English teams had done the best – thankfully Derby had done enough to finish top but they were shown to be ahead of Tranmere Rovers, West Ham United and Bristol City despite not having played them.

Cremonese were top of the group's Italian section so the two teams went through to the overall semi-finals where they would play opposition from their own country.

The Italians faced Bari and Derby were handed a tie against Brentford with the second leg to be played at the Baseball Ground.

They travelled to Griffin Park and came back just on the right side of a seven-goal thriller having won 4-3.

But as with any semi-final with Wembley the prize it is never straightforward and on a dramatic night at the Baseball Ground they were beaten 2-1 to set up a 5-5 aggregate score.

The away goals rule counted in the competition so Derby had done enough, just, to reach Wembley for the first time since the 1975 Charity Shield. Their opponents would be Cremonese, earlier victors at the Baseball Ground.

As the day of the final approached Michael Forsyth was hoping to become only the third Rams skipper to lead his side out at the famous venue.

Forsyth had handed over the armband to Martin Kuhl the previous January but with Kuhl ineligible the job was open once more.

He told the *Derby Telegraph*, 'I hope I will be given the job and that we can make it a great day for the supporters.

'More than 30,000 of them are going to Wembley to back us and that confirms the trophy is well worth winning. Not that we've ever had any doubts.

'The fans have turned out for all the games and we set out with the idea that we were going to Wembley.

'I've been there only twice before, once to see a schoolboy international and the second time to watch Liverpool in the Charity Shield.

'So this is a big day for me, although we know Cremonese will be tough. We started badly against them at Derby but they were the best of the Italian teams we faced.

'We have put some good performances into this competition and tomorrow is a working day for us. We want to bring the trophy back to the Baseball Ground.'

Derby, having been beaten by Cremonese earlier in the competition, knew they would have to get off to a good start if they were to win the cup and make it three wins from three at Wembley.

But they failed to do so and were quickly on the back foot so it was no surprise that the Italians took the lead on 11 minutes through their captain, Corrado Verdelli, who rose highest to head home a left-wing corner.

The game soon turned tetchy with Cremonese resorting to spoiling tactics early on and Derby made them pay with the equaliser on 23 minutes.

It was a neatly-worked goal with Marco Gabbiadini getting his head on Paul Kitson's cross and guiding the ball nicely in off a post to send the 30,000-plus Derby fans into celebration.

Five minutes later Cremonese were presented with a good chance to go back in front when Marco Giandebiaggi was fouled by Forsyth and a penalty was awarded.

Eligio Nicolini stepped forward but Martin Taylor was equal to the task and turned the spot-kick away superbly, then Derby might have taken a lead into half-time but Gary Micklewhite couldn't get enough purchase on his shot to beat Luigi Turci.

Unfortunately Derby also started the second half slowly and were made to pay four minutes in with another penalty, this time more dubious as Taylor was alleged to have fouled Andrea Tentoni.

And there was no repeat of Taylor's earlier save as Riccardo Maspero made no mistake from the spot.

The spoiling tactics soon returned and the battle between Gabbiadini and Luigi Gualco might on another day have seen the Rams awarded a penalty of their own and the Cremonese man receive a red card but the Spanish referee was not doing Derby any favours.

Cremonese's footballing class was always evident though and they might have added to their tally through Nicolini, who hit a post, before they finally did make it 3-1 with seven minutes left through the impressive Tentoni.

It was a tough defeat to swallow for Derby despite their opponents' superior performance across the 90 minutes.

Even if it wasn't one of the major competitions like the FA Cup or League Cup, nobody ever wants to lose a Wembley final and there were certainly tears among the Rams' players in the dressing room after the match.

But there was also a sense of Derby not quite having seized the occasion as manager Arthur Cox felt that his players could have performed better, although he had no doubt the Italians warranted their triumph.

He said, 'Their quality was too much for what we had and Cremonese certainly deserved to win.

'Over 90 minutes we can have no complaints about the result but it is a major disappointment for us. We did not do ourselves justice.

'There has been criticism of the Anglo-Italian Cup but we have enjoyed it. We scored plenty of goals on our way to Wembley and I believe the experience, especially of the final, will prove to be valuable.

'From the start of the competition we were determined to do well. We could have said we were not interested, that it would create too many extra fixtures.

'I do not believe that would have been the right approach and, even if we had been knocked out early, there is no guarantee that it would have improved other results. Nobody knows the answer to that.

'At half-time on Saturday I was not sure that Cremonese could play better but I knew we could. The second penalty set us back and Martin Taylor is convinced he made a legitimate challenge.

'Cremonese controlled and passed the ball so much better. We gave the ball away too often to establish continuity, while their midfield players and front two caused us a lot of problems.

'Marco scored a good goal and competed magnificently. He has had injuries and the thought of Wembley probably did as much to get him fit as Gordon Guthrie's efforts.

'It was very competitive between him and Gualco and the referee dealt with it as he saw fit.

'Mark Pembridge was hit in the face by Dezotti but he was out of order trying to pull him to his feet. That was the referee's job and Mark had no reason to interfere.'

Fans shouldn't have been too surprised at Gustavo Dezotti's reaction as the player had form for bad on-field behaviour. The Argentinean international defender had been sent off for his country in the 1990 World Cup Final against West Germany in Italy.

The revived Anglo-Italian Cup lasted for three more seasons with Notts County losing the final to Brescia in 1994 before winning it against Ascoli the following year.

Derby competed in each of those tournaments but failed to get past the qualifying stage on either occasion, though they did enjoy one notable result in the 1993/94 event as they came from two goals down to beat Nottingham Forest 3-2 at the Baseball Ground.

Genoa beat Port Vale in the last final in 1996 after a vastly reduced tournament in which the Rams were not involved, and the competition was scrapped after that because of fixture congestion and increasing violence at matches.

The 1993 final was also a memorable one for author Gareth but for all the wrong reasons as he actually missed the entire first half.

He had travelled to the game with his dad Richard, friend Mark and Mark's granddad Albert, and they had taken their seats in the Wembley stands when Gareth started to feel unwell shortly before kick-off.

Gareth takes up the story, 'All I can remember was the teams coming out of the tunnel, the PA man telling supporters to stand for the National Anthems, and as I stood I just felt really faint and pretty much collapsed.

'We were towards the end of the row so dad was able to get me out pretty quickly and he took me down to the medical room and told the staff what had happened.

'Then he said something along the lines of "I'll leave him with you – I need to get back for the kick-off"!

'The staff there gave me some water and a tablet but I was soon throwing up so they wouldn't let me go back to the stands.

'I knew we were behind as I had heard the announcement for the goal and later I heard a massive roar from the Derby fans followed by chants for Marco Gabbiadini so I took that to mean we had equalised.

'A few minutes later I heard loud boos, followed by cheers and songs of "there's only one Martin Taylor" so wondered if he had saved a penalty.

'Dad came back down for me at half-time and told me what I had missed. I was well enough to go back for the second half and when I got back to the seats people around us were asking if I was okay as they had seen me taken away before the match.

'Typically, Derby did not play too well in the second half and I had missed their best moments so while it was still a great experience to be there, my first visit to see my team at Wembley is slightly soured by what happened.

'There was no obvious reason for it to happen either. I was only 12 at the time though so I must have just been over-excited about it all!'

v **Millwall** 3-1

(Derby won 5-1 on aggregate)
18 May 1994. Attendance: 16,470
The New Den. Football League First Division Play-Off
Semi-Final Second Leg

DERBY COUNTY:	MILLWALL:
Taylor	Keller
Charles (Hayward 85)	Cunningham
Short	Van Den Hauwe
Williams (Kavanagh 85)	Stevens
Forsyth	Huxford
Harkes	Rae
Cowans	Hurlock
Pembridge	Berry
Simpson	Allen
Johnson	Moralee
Gabbiadini	Mitchell
Unused sub: Sutton (GK)	*Unused subs:* Carter (GK), Kerr, Goodman
Referee: Brian Hill	

AFTER the glory years of First Division football that Arthur Cox brought the Rams the club had to rebuild following relegation in 1991, and once Lionel Pickering took over as chairman they spent heavily to try and restore their top flight status.

They were not too far away from automatic promotion in their first season back down and finished third in the Second Division to earn a crack at the play-offs for the first time.

Cox's side went 2-0 up in the first leg at Blackburn Rovers only to lose it 4-2, and a 2-1 scoreline in the return at the Baseball Ground was not enough as Rovers went through to Wembley where they beat Leicester City in the final.

They finished outside the play-off positions the following year but were once again involved in the post-season showdown for 1993/94.

Derby ended the campaign struggling for a bit of consistency but they ultimately finished sixth though lost their final game 4-3 away to Southend United.

The defeat itself wasn't much of a problem, but fans spilling on to the Roots Hall pitch and into the stand as the game drew to a close suddenly gave the East Midlanders an unwanted reputation as troublemakers.

To add to the mix the Rams were drawn against Millwall in the play-off semis. Millwall have always had a reputation for courting trouble.

It is not my (author Phil) place to dig up old wounds, although I do remember in my days as purely a supporter going down to The Den when fans had not been advised to travel.

The players gave us tickets to get into the ground, but it was only when the Rams scored and we leapt to our feet and cheered that we realised we were the only half-dozen Derby supporters (other than those in the directors' box) in the ground.

We were a very restrained bunch of supporters after that!

I digress, but there was a certain air of tension before the home leg of the play-off semi-final at the Baseball Ground.

Despite the pressure of the event plus a certain hostility from the travelling support the Rams went into the second leg with a healthy 2-0 lead earned thanks to goals from Gordon Cowans and Tommy Johnson.

There remained a simmering under-current in the lead-up to the second leg, partially at least, due to accusations from the Millwall camp of racist taunts by a section of Derby supporters aimed at the Londoners in the first match.

Unlikely though the claims seem given the ethnic mix of players in the Rams squad it all fanned the flames for a volatile second encounter.

And there was criticism from Millwall manager Mick McCarthy who, while admitting that his side had been poor at the Baseball Ground, was not too pleased at Derby's players going on a lap of honour around the pitch and said, 'I hope they don't live to regret that action.'

Derby boss Roy McFarland, who had taken over when Cox resigned the previous October because of his back problem, offered in response, 'That lap of honour to reward our fans was planned in advance, whatever the result. We weren't trying to take the mickey.

'I'd have settled for 2-0 before kick-off and my team did their job splendidly. Gabbiadini and Johnson created havoc.

'We know it's not over yet – the New Den on Wednesday evening, with Millwall coming at us full blast, is going to be an intimidating place.'

Both of the 1993/94 season's First Division meetings between Derby and Millwall had finished goalless – a result that would have done the Rams just fine this time around.

As it happened a quiet 0-0 was about as far removed from this particular 90 minutes as you could get.

As a contest it was pretty much all over by the 23rd minute after Johnson and Marco Gabbiadini had exchanged assists to set each other up for the opening goals of the night.

That gave the Rams a 4-0 aggregate lead but it was the spark for hundreds of Millwall fans to congregate at the front of the East Stand and some got on to the pitch, leading to referee Brian Hill taking the players off for almost 20 minutes while the situation was calmed down.

Shortly after the players returned Derby's progress to Wembley was practically guaranteed through an own goal by Pat Van Den Hauwe – which had an element of retribution in the eyes of many Rams fans as it was Van Den Hauwe who put Ted McMinn out of football for 14 months with a challenge in 1989 while playing for Tottenham Hotspur. The uneasy atmosphere continued around the ground, even when Greg Berry got one back for the home side with a header in the second half, and on 74 minutes home fans invaded the pitch once more.

This time there was an even greater element of sheer stupidity to their actions as Millwall had just been awarded a penalty, but when the players returned 13 minutes later Hill restarted the match with a drop in the centre circle.

Derby made the wise move to substitute Paul Williams and Gary Charles, their black players, late in the match to avoid exposing them to any further problems, such was the racial nature of the abuse they were receiving.

Goalkeeper Martin Taylor had been floored by an invader as the second break started and he later described the night as 'the most intimidating atmosphere I have known'.

And the immediate aftermath of the game saw things turn very nasty indeed.

I was reporting on the night for Radio Link, the Derby Hospitals Radio Broadcasting service, and was sitting in the press box in the Main Stand and therefore away from the massed ranks of both Derby supporters and Millwall fans.

As we descended towards the press room we could see the violence starting to build when we peered through windows into the car park.

My first distinct memory post-match as we went down the stairs was of much respected football correspondent Brian Glanville pointing to a car in the official car park that had been turned over by an element of the home supporters. I had travelled to the game on one of the Roadriders, the official coach transport for Derby County supporters, and my brief was to return to the coach as quickly as possible on the final whistle.

To my horror I discovered that the outside of each stand had been closed off from all others by large gates and massed ranks of stewards, and I was behind one gate with the Derby fans 50 yards at the most away from me but separated by two gates and a strip of no man's land.

I formulated a plan in my mind that if I could not get back to the coaches I would beg a lift from my good friends Colin Gibson and Graham Richards in the BBC Radio Derby car – little realising that it was this very vehicle Glanville had minutes earlier described as being overturned.

My concern, along with that of thousands of others, increased with rumours that rioting had spread into the surrounding streets.

I will at this stage admit to never having witnessed anything quite so frightening at a game of football as a policeman on his horse galloping past me into action with both rider and animal fully covered in riot gear.

As the evening wore on and supporters remained penned behind the gates, my next memory was of a couple of stewards, quite possibly trying to make light of the situation, discussing whether they would get overtime pay for having to work longer than contracted.

Eventually the situation calmed a little and the gate was opened and I was escorted to the massed ranks of Derby fans and away to the coaches and a journey home.

And Richards, summing the night up for BBC Radio Derby, said, 'Last night was a night of infamy at The Den, Millwall, but Derby County go through thanks to a five to one goal aggregate to a game at Wembley on Whit Monday.

'As a contest it was soon killed off, Gabbiadini turning home Johnson's cross in the 17th minute, returning the compliment for Johnson to score in the 23rd.

'We then had a 19-minute delay thanks to a crowd invasion and when the teams returned, Pat Van Den Hauwe obligingly turned the ball back into his own net to give Derby a three-goal lead on the night.

'Berry scored in the second half with a header that was supremely irrelevant. What was not quite so irrelevant was a further ten-minute delay caused by malicious morons that came in from the main stand with evil intention plainly on their faces.

'As I say, it was a night of infamy for Millwall, but for Derby County and their supporters a night of discretion, of fine football, and of an absolutely blameless record.'

At the time it seemed almost irrelevant that Derby County had made it through to their first play-off final and had a trip to Wembley to look forward to.

It was an exciting thought that the club could do one over local rivals Leicester City and return to the top flight under McFarland.

It started brightly for them as Johnson opened the scoring in the first half but Steve Walsh equalised before half-time.

John Harkes missed a sitter late on and Leicester went straight up the other end to win it with Walsh's second of the game.

Sadly ultimate glory was not the Rams' this time as they fell to their second Wembley defeat in as many seasons.

But the events at Millwall that night will forever go down in infamy and are summed up perfectly by Gabbiadini, who said after the final whistle, 'We feel we have been through a war, not a football match.'

v Crystal Palace 2-1

28 April 1996. Attendance: 17,041
Baseball Ground. Football League First Division

DERBY COUNTY:	CRYSTAL PALACE:
Hoult	Martyn
Rowett	Edworthy
C Powell	Brown
Trollope	Roberts
Carbon	Anderson (Ndah 72)
Stimac	Hopkin
van der Laan	Pitcher
Sturridge	Houghton
Simpson (Ward 83)	Freedman (Veart 89)
Gabbiadini (Willems 63)	Dyer (Vincent 79)
Flynn	Rodger
Unused sub: Carsley	
Referee: David Allison	

JIM Smith's arrival as manager in the summer of 1995 hadn't exactly been warmly received by Derby fans. The man affectionately known as 'The Bald Eagle' had been out of management since losing his job at Portsmouth in January 1995, ironically his final league match in charge having come in a 3-0 defeat to Derby at the Baseball Ground.

He then took what he had termed as a 'desk job' as chief executive of the League Managers' Association and, at the age of 54 it was possible that his days as a boss were winding down.

Countless names were linked with the Derby job after Roy McFarland's departure at the end of the 1994/95 season including Martin O'Neill, then of Wycombe Wanderers, and Manchester United playing duo Steve Bruce and Mark Hughes in a joint role.

But in the end Derby chairman Lionel Pickering plumped for Smith and, despite some difficult early months, the Rams never looked back.

Some fans were calling for Smith's head after a 2-0 defeat at Barnsley in September 1995, a move never considered at all by the Derby board.

And the turning point came in October as the Rams unveiled the eye-opening capture of Croatian international defender Igor Stimac from Hajduk Split for a fee of £1.57m, at the time the second highest the club had ever paid for a player.

It was certainly a statement of intent to pay that sort of money for a man who played his international football for one of Europe's fastest-improving nations, particularly after a summer spent wheeling and dealing to ship out players like Mark Pembridge, Paul Williams and Craig Short and bring in the likes of Gary Rowett, Robin van der Laan and Ron Willems.

Stimac's debut was a troubling 5-1 defeat away to Tranmere Rovers in which he scored but operated as a central defender in a back four.

Derby County's Greatest Games

He was more at home as a sweeper and that was how he lined up the following week with Rowett and Dean Yates his central partners, then wing-backs on either side, skipper van der Laan and Darryl Powell in midfield, and clever Dutch forward Willems playing in behind Dean Sturridge and Marco Gabbiadini.

West Bromwich Albion were swept aside 3-0 at the Baseball Ground and the goals continued to flow, propelling Derby to the top of the table by Christmas during a run of ten wins from 11 including seven in succession into 1996.

By the time March arrived promotion was a serious possibility – and Derby were still unbeaten since that Tranmere game, extending their run to 20 with a 0-0 midweek draw at Watford to set a new club record for consecutive unbeaten games in a single season.

And in February there was a big announcement that confirmed the Rams would be leaving the Baseball Ground at the end of 1996/97 for a new stadium on the Pride Park area of the city.

Sunderland were the Rams' biggest threat for the title and they ended the run with a 3-0 win at Roker Park and Derby stuttered briefly, perhaps losing their nerve as they were overtaken at the top.

But they never dropped out of the automatic promotion places and might have sealed their spot in the Premier League on 20 April but for a late equaliser by Birmingham City at the Baseball Ground.

And in a way that was the best thing that could have happened as it set things up nicely for Sunday 28 April and the visit of Crystal Palace – who were in third place.

A win would have been enough to send Derby up, a draw would have kept them second going in to the final day, and a defeat would have seen them slip to third with that last game away to West Bromwich Albion their only hope of salvation and avoiding the play-offs but they would have then been relying on Palace slipping up too.

So a play-off final to a certain extent, but with a backup too, and how the sense of a big occasion was felt as the day of the game approached.

'YOUR CLUB NEEDS YOU' read the headline on the back of the *Derby Telegraph* the day before the match while the fans were urged to 'Roar 'til you're raw' and told to dress in as much black and white as possible in a campaign from the Baseball Ground.

It was almost lost that Derby were also celebrating 50 years since winning the FA Cup for the only time that same weekend, so high were the stakes.

'All our supporters are in the team for this one,' said Smith.

'This is a massive game for us. I took the players away this week to concentrate their minds but we're focusing on this one now.

'It is impossible to disguise the importance to Derby County. To us, it's bigger than the World Cup.'

Palace had won 12 of their 18 games since the February appointment of Dave Bassett as manager to storm from 15th to third in the table.

But it was entirely in Derby's hands and Smith had almost a fully-fit squad to choose from with Darryl Powell his only key absentee. Sean Flynn was expected to regain the right wing-back slot from Lee Carsley and the other choice was between Gabbiadini and Ashley Ward to partner Sturridge in attack.

As it turned out, Derby's squad was not in as good health as previously thought. On the morning of the game a headline came over on BBC Radio Derby saying that there was an injury blow to one of the Rams' defenders.

138

Thoughts immediately turned to Stimac with the talismanic Croatian having hobbled off for his country against England at Wembley in midweek but instead the unlucky man was Yates, who had injured a knee having played the previous 42 matches in succession.

It was a terrible blow for Yates, who was in tears after being declared unfit, and he received a rapturous reception before the match when he came out to collect the Player of the Year trophy.

Smith opted for the youth of Matt Carbon, given a first start since signing from Lincoln City, over the experience of Darren Wassall.

But just two minutes in the other end of the field was the centre of attention as Derby went in front.

Stimac stole in on a pass inside his own half and fed the ball to Paul Simpson, who in turn knocked it on for Sturridge to race away and place his shot into the corner beyond Nigel Martyn's dive.

But the joy did not last long. Within a couple of minutes Bruce Dyer escaped down the left for Palace and whipped a cross back that Kenny Brown ran on to and hammered home on the volley from the penalty spot.

The equaliser settled Palace more than Derby and the visitors went on to enjoy more of the play without really threatening to take the lead.

Indeed, though they had been on the back foot for most of the first half, Derby had the best two chances with Sturridge forcing Martyn into a save and Paul Trollope flashing a shot just wide.

The second half was just as closely-fought with neither side giving an inch as they searched for the goal that could take them to glory. It came in the 65th minute and went the way of the Rams.

Willems had only been on the pitch to replace Gabbiadini for two minutes and his first act was to control a throw-in and earn his side a corner on the right.

Simpson stepped up, swung his wand-like left foot through the ball and curled it to the far post, where van der Laan had been left unmarked by the Palace defence to meet it with a towering header into the back of the net.

But the celebration soon turned to tension as the Baseball Ground's clock still showed 25 minutes to play – meaning Derby were within touching distance of the Premier League.

Stimac cruised through the remaining time in his own style, Rowett was as polished as ever and 20-year-old Carbon impressed greatly having been thrown in for a full debut in the most testing of circumstances.

They repelled everything Palace could throw forward but the tension continued as the clock ticked over to 90 in the days before the amount of stoppage time was announced to the crowd.

It seemed to take an age but when the whistle blew after Palace goalkeeper Martyn pumped one last ball forward that was it.

Derby were in the Premier League and within seconds the Baseball Ground pitch was covered with celebrating Rams fans enjoying a truly memorable moment.

Promotion at the first attempt more than vindicated Pickering's choice of Smith for the manager's hot-seat less than a year previously.

And it also vindicated Pickering's backing of Smith in the transfer market for the big-money signings of Stimac and Ward, let alone the planned stadium move in 12 months.

Pickering said, 'Jim Smith has done it for us and proved that he is not yesterday's man, as some of the local press said.

'He is a very nice guy and very open. He's had total support from the board and responded magnificently.

'One or two things have not been right in the last few weeks but we got there. The team battled and I was proud of them.

'I've spent £12m, some of which has been recycled, and we've had three goes at promotion in five years. Arthur Cox missed by a whisker and Roy McFarland got us to Wembley.

'Jim's been able to clear the decks with a new team and they've gelled, which had not happened before.

'Now we have the problem of staying in the Premiership and building a stadium that could cost up to £20m.

'We don't have it, so it's interesting, but the team must be the first priority. We might pull in a few players from abroad – Jim knows Europe well.

'I'm convinced we'll play better in the Premiership because there'll be a bit of extra time for people like Igor Stimac and Ronnie Willems.'

And Smith, soaked in champagne and beer during the post-match celebrations, was equally delighted for Pickering.

'I don't quite know how it feels yet,' he said. 'But I'm delighted for Mr Pickering. He's put so much into this club and been super with me. He's a real Derby and Derbyshire fan.'

And there couldn't have been a more fitting scorer of the promotion-clinching goal than captain van der Laan, who had led by example all season and been a real inspiration – both on and off the field – after being handed the armband immediately after signing the previous summer from Port Vale.

The long-haired Dutchman said of his goal, 'I couldn't believe it. Everything seemed to happen in slow motion.

'As soon as Simmo hit it I thought "this is mine". I looked around and no one was with me. I knew I only had to head it down, hit the target and it was in.

'It's the biggest goal of my career. You know it will show up in the history books as the one which took us up but at the moment the full impact of what has happened hasn't really sunk in.

'It's been a great season and this again justifies coming here from Port Vale last summer.'

Their chance of the championship had gone the previous day with Sunderland's 0-0 draw at home to West Bromwich Albion, a result that secured top spot for Peter Reid's men, though Derby were not bothered having confirmed their place in the Premier League with a match to spare.

The final day saw a 3-2 defeat at West Bromwich Albion in which Smith fielded a much-changed team and gave several youngsters a run while the rested senior players sat behind the goal with the fans.

Instead it was about two things – whether Ward could score his first Derby goal after his million-pound move from Norwich City and whether Sturridge could become the first Ram to reach 20 league goals in a season since Bobby Davison in 1984/85.

Both things happened so all eyes were then Premier League-bound.

35 v Leeds United 3-3

17 August 1996. Attendance: 17,927
The Baseball Ground. Premier League

DERBY COUNTY:	LEEDS UNITED:
Hoult	Martyn
Laursen (Flynn 75)	Radebe (Wetherall 89)
Yates	Kelly
C Powell	Jobson
Rowett	Sharpe
Parker	Palmer
Dailly	Bowyer
Asanovic	Couzens (Tinkler 87)
D Powell (Simpson 75)	Ford
Gabbiadini (Willems 75)	Deane (Harte 56)
Sturridge	Rush
Unused subs: Taylor (GK), van der Laan	*Unused subs:* Beeney (GK), Wallace
Referee: Paul Danson	

F OR a game that has been around in its current form since 1884 five years can be a long time in football. When the Rams dropped out of the top flight in 1991 they were relegated from what was then called the First Division.

It would be wrong to suggest that all clubs were by now as equal as they had been in the 1970s when Derby were in their pomp.

In the 1970s the key to success was a good manager with an eye for talent, and a certain amount of financial backing, but a look at league tables of the day would show a mix of fashionable and unfashionable clubs vying for honours.

By the time the Rams returned there under Arthur Cox a divide between big and small clubs was starting to show, but when Jim Smith led them to promotion five years later everything had changed.

The First Division had re-fashioned itself as the Premier League, and the millions of pounds put in by Sky Television meant that there were already three divisions in one, with the top half-dozen contesting the title, the middle group looking for success in domestic cup competitions, and the rest trying to stave off relegation from the first whistle of the season.

Smith had done phenomenally well to take his team to promotion at the very first attempt, but even with his eye for spotting talent and making the most of what was available to him on the books already this was a new adventure for everybody, and one that even the most devoted fans met with a certain amount of trepidation.

Promotion had been achieved on the back of 20 goals from Dean Sturridge, along with magnificent displays from Croatian defender Igor Stimac, but what nobody knew was how either of them or any of the rest of the squad would be able to handle the step up.

Stimac had played for Croatia in that summer's European Championship in England, when they reached the quarter-finals – Stimac seeing red in the defeat to Germany at

Old Trafford. He was in the team alongside talented midfielder Aljosa Asanovic, whose displays in the tournament really caught the eye of the watching scouts and managers who were all keen to know where he was playing his football.

Thankfully for Derby, Smith had already been tipped off by Stimac and signed Asanovic for just £650,000 before Euro 96 began and the player's value rocketed.

Also in was Danish international defender Jacob Laursen, another Euro 96 man, along with highly-rated young Scottish midfielder Christian Dailly from Dundee United, and in the days before the start of the season Smith added Paul Parker on a short-term contract.

Parker, the former England international who had left Manchester United in the summer, was the only one of the new faces to have any experience of the top level of English football.

Returning to the top flight meant that the release of the fixtures was even more highly anticipated than normal and the Rams were handed a home match on the opening day.

But it was not just any home match as their opponents would be Leeds United, the old enemy from the 1970s and the era of Brian Clough and Don Revie along with the great fight between Francis Lee and Norman Hunter.

There was recent history between the sides too as Leeds had twice been to the Baseball Ground during the 1995/96 season, leaving victorious in both cup competitions.

The first match had been in the League Cup when they went through 1-0 thanks to Gary Speed's header but their second visit, for an FA Cup tie in January, was a cracker.

It was televised live to a nationwide audience who saw Derby recover from the dismissal of Gary Rowett and the loss to injury of Stimac in the first half to go 2-0 up early in the second period with quick goals from Marco Gabbiadini and Paul Simpson.

Leeds then scored twice in a minute on the hour to haul things level through Speed and Brian Deane, and just as it looked like a replay would be needed at Elland Road they won it in stoppage time with Gary McAllister and Tony Yeboah scoring.

Not that anybody really needed any extra motivation for the opening day of the Premier League season.

There were so many changes to the top flight compared to what Derby had left behind in 1991, not least little things like the addition of squad numbers to the backs of the players' shirts, but one thing that did not alter was that the opening day was bathed in sunshine.

The Baseball Ground was packed to the rafters as it embarked on its final season and the scene was well and truly set.

Parker was thrown straight in for his debut and played as a wing-back on the right with Laursen coming into the centre alongside Dean Yates and Gary Rowett, owing to the absence of Stimac through injury.

Dailly lined up in midfield alongside Darryl Powell and Asanovic, meaning skipper Robin van der Laan was only on the bench, and up top were Gabbiadini and Sturridge with Ron Willems a substitute and Ashley Ward out ill.

There was a fast pace to the game but very few clear-cut chances in the early stages of the first half though Nigel Martyn closed in quickly on Sturridge and at the other end Ian Rush, signed on a free transfer by Leeds after his legendary career at Liverpool, took too long after being found by Deane.

The opening goal had more than an element of fortune about it as Lee Bowyer crossed from the left and Laursen unluckily deflected the ball beyond Russell Hoult.

It deflated the Baseball Ground atmosphere for a while but the fans were soon back behind their team again and Derby were strong up to the interval and Yates drove one effort wide, Carlton Palmer cleared away after Sturridge hooked the ball goalwards before Dailly and Gabbiadini both went close to reaching Darryl Powell's low cross.

Leeds lost Deane to injury early in the second half and his replacement, Ian Harte, doubled the Whites' advantage within 20 minutes of his arrival after cracking a right-footed shot low past Hoult from just outside the box.

That might have signalled the end of Derby's hopes of getting something from the match but Smith threw caution to the wind and made a triple substitution – bringing on Willems, Simpson and Sean Flynn for Laursen, Darryl Powell and Gabbiadini.

Within two minutes the Rams had a goal back in stunning style through Sturridge, who unleashed a left-footer from outside the area that curled over and beyond Martyn.

That gave them hope and what followed over the coming seconds sparked amazing scenes of celebration.

Leeds took the restart and passed the ball back from forwards to midfield, then midfield to defence, where Richard Jobson continued the trend and rolled it back towards Martyn.

His pass was short of power so Simpson closed in and as he and Martyn challenged for the ball, it rolled loose and over the line to bring Derby level and send the Baseball Ground wild.

Calmness was the order of the day but after Yates hit the bar with a header that bounced down and then up, Derby were behind once more with just five minutes left.

Rush headed down a centre from Harte and in came Bowyer, with too much time and space to score on his Leeds debut after signing in the summer from Charlton Athletic.

Even then it wasn't all over. Simpson found Sturridge, who turned Lucas Radebe and slipped his shot past Martyn to once again spark off a mass outpouring of joy.

Those wearing the black and white shirts of the Rams, along with the red and white of Croatia in homage to their new heroes, could not believe what they had just witnessed.

Much of the philosophy of Smith's reign as Derby manager was shown on that afternoon as with all seemingly lost he refused to buckle and made the changes that ultimately saw his team earn a point.

Questions that supporters had on their minds at kick-off were largely answered.

Of course Stimac had what it took to be a Premier League player. Asanovic had won the crowd over before the final whistle, and two top quality strikes by Sturridge showed that he was able to cause top defenders as many problems as those a league lower.

Sturridge's goal would have been the best of any normal day but it came on the same afternoon that David Beckham scored his famous effort from the halfway line for Manchester United at Wimbledon.

But fans were urged not to get too carried away as in the words of *Derby Telegraph* reporter Gerald Mortimer, 'Of Derby's daunting first five fixtures, the home game against Leeds was always the one likeliest to produce a point or three.'

What maybe Mortimer could not have been expected to realise was that the confidence Derby gained when coming back from two goals down to earn a point lifted them into their next run of games, and they only lost one of their first seven outings.

They showed great character in coming from behind again in the next match, Dailly netting in stoppage time to earn a 1-1 draw at Tottenham Hotspur after Teddy Sheringham had put the hosts in front during the first half.

Derby County's Greatest Games

The first defeat came on the season's second Saturday as Smith's men went down 2-0 at Aston Villa with former Rams favourite Tommy Johnson adding the second goal from the penalty spot after Julian Joachim had opened the scoring.

Then came the first of the really big fixtures as Manchester United visited the Baseball Ground for a midweek game and were rocked on 25 minutes as Laursen hammered an unstoppable free kick beyond his international colleague Peter Schmeichel.

United were level before half-time with an equally stunning effort from Beckham but Derby gave as good as they got all night and fully deserved their point as even the great Eric Cantona was largely subdued.

Stimac seemed to enjoy the big occasion too and one particular photograph of him cleanly tackling a full-speed Ryan Giggs stands out as one of the iconic Rams images from the last couple of decades.

United and Blackburn Rovers were, at that time, the only two sides to have lifted the Premier League title and coincidentally Blackburn were the Rams' next opponents in a Monday night game live on Sky Sports.

Willems scored early, Blackburn equalised quickly through Chris Sutton, and both sides hit the woodwork before Flynn curled in a late winner from Gabbiadini's pass.

A penalty from Asanovic saw off Sunderland the following Saturday and then Derby took their solid start to Sheffield Wednesday, where they secured a 0-0 draw despite having the better of the play and the chances.

The ten points picked up from those games gave them a platform for what would become far more than merely a relegation fight.

v Manchester United 3-2

5 April 1997. Attendance: 55,243
Old Trafford. Premier League

DERBY COUNTY:	MANCHESTER UNITED:
Poom	Schmeichel
Laursen	G Neville (Irwin 70)
Dailly	Johnsen
McGrath	Pallister (Scholes 86)
C Powell	Butt (Solskjaer HT)
van der Laan	P Neville
Trollope	Giggs
D Powell	Beckham
Sturridge	Keane
Ward	Cantona
Wanchope (Simpson 65)	Cole
Unused subs: Hoult (GK), Carbon, Solis, Willems	*Unused subs:* van der Gouw (GK), Poborsky

Referee: David Elleray

DERBY COUNTY'S return to the Premier League for the 1996/97 season had been a relatively successful one without the serious threat of relegation that usually hangs over newly-promoted teams.

A mixture of the momentum gained from their promotion the previous campaign, solid form in front of their own fans at the Baseball Ground and some canny signings by manager Jim Smith meant that they had largely kept their heads above water by the time April 1997 arrived. They had done particularly well to stabilise after a difficult winter period that saw them go from 30 November to 15 February without winning a Premier League game but even still, through that time they never dropped in to the bottom three and were always a bit ahead of the relegation scrappers.

After breaking that bad run with a 1-0 victory at home to West Ham United they collected a 2-2 draw with Sheffield Wednesday four days later, lost 4-2 at Leicester City, beat Chelsea 3-2 at the Baseball Ground in a real thriller of a match then suffered a humiliating 6-1 beating away to Middlesbrough.

In that time they also beat Coventry City in the fifth round of the FA Cup, coming from 2-0 down to win 3-2 on a wet night in Derby, before bowing out of the competition 2-0 at the hands of Middlesbrough in what would be the Baseball Ground's last FA Cup tie – coming just three days after that heavy defeat on Teesside.

The disappointingly limp FA Cup exit was followed by a 1-0 defeat at Everton but the Rams did pick up another win going into the March international break when they beat Tottenham Hotspur 4-2 at the Baseball Ground in a game that swung one way, then the other, and back in the Rams' favour again. That left them in good heart during their two weeks off ahead of a first visit to Old Trafford since a 3-1 defeat in April 1991, days before relegation from the then-First Division was confirmed.

But what they did need to do was improve on their away record with their only Premier League win on the road coming at Blackburn Rovers – the only other team, besides United, to have won the top flight title since restructuring in 1992 – back in September.

The Rams' FA Cup campaign had started with a 2-0 win at Gillingham but it was their home form keeping them afloat in the league and they went into this match 14th, four points above the bottom three.

And Smith, mindful of the need to keep improving his squad, used the international break to sign three players – these were the days before transfer windows ending in January. Eyebrows were raised, however, at the nationality of the three men in question. One was an Estonian, goalkeeper Mart Poom, and two were Costa Rican, striker Paulo Wanchope and midfielder Mauricio Solis.

They were not complete unknowns. Wanchope had previously interested Queens Park Rangers but had been on trial at Derby and Solis was added to the deal as the pair both signed from SC Herediano in their homeland, while Poom had played for Smith at Portsmouth before returning to Estonia with Flora Tallinn, who Derby paid £500,000 for his services. All three were internationals for their countries.

The signing of a goalkeeper had been because of the inconsistent form of Russell Hoult, unchallenged as number one since the autumn of 1995, while Martin Taylor had played the Rams' previous three games but was still trying to get back to full fitness after that broken leg suffered at Southend United in October 1994. After Poom's arrival, Taylor was then loaned to Wycombe Wanderers.

Poom had already been told that he would be starting the Old Trafford clash, as intimidating a place to make your debut as it gets, but the Estonian was not concerned – especially as he was a United fan.

Speaking to the *Derby Telegraph*, he said, 'Manchester United were the English team I supported when I was growing up.

'We could pick up Finnish TV in Estonia and my favourites were Gary Bailey, Jesper Olsen and Bryan Robson.

'It's a hell of a place for a debut but I'm not worried. These are the occasions you dream about when you become a professional footballer and I'm going to make the most of it.'

At this time, clubs were restricted to only using three non-EU nationals in their match day squad and Derby had five on their books with the new trio plus Croatian pair Igor Stimac and Aljosa Asanovic.

Stimac's back injury had already ruled him out of the trip to take on the Premier League champions and Asanovic was a doubt with a calf problem, meaning there was a good chance all three of the signings would be involved.

Derby were also without the ill Lee Carsley and suspended Gary Rowett but Paul McGrath would be fit to face his old club while Ashley Ward was a definite starter and Matt Carbon was expected to return.

And Smith, who had never won at Old Trafford as a manager, said, 'We are going to have to be strong at United. The influx of new faces will have given us an extra spark and although it's going to be difficult it's far from impossible.'

During their most recent stint in the top flight, from 1987 to 1991, the Rams had won on two of their four visits to Old Trafford. Smith caused a bit of a stir with his team selection as Carbon did not come back in, meaning the Rams went with a flat back four of Jacob Laursen, Christian Dailly, McGrath and Chris Powell, in the days when they would normally have lined up with three centre-backs.

Paul Trollope, Robin van der Laan and Darryl Powell were in midfield with Ward and Dean Sturridge in the attacking line along with Wanchope, thrown right in at the deep end for his first match in English football.

By half-time the tactics could not have worked any better with the Rams 2-0 up but having missed opportunities to make it four.

Ward blew the first when through on Peter Schmeichel but made up for it on 29 minutes when he met Wanchope's nod-down with a shot into the floor that bounced up over the giant Dane and shocked Old Trafford.

And if that wasn't enough for the United faithful to take in, they were stunned into complete silence just six minutes later.

Darryl Powell snapped at Roy Keane and released the ball to Wanchope, who was still inside his own half.

Over the halfway line he went, apparently at no real pace but with no United man able to catch him, and by the time he reached a central position on the edge of the box, the seemingly impossible was about to become possible.

Wanchope took aim with the inside of his right foot and put his shot perfectly into Schmeichel's bottom-left corner before racing off in celebration with the United fans – and their Derby counterparts – scarcely able to believe what they had just seen.

The reaction had Ward made it 3-0 before the break, which he should have done as he saw two efforts saved by Schmeichel then hit the post, all in the same incident, would have been almost impossible to describe.

Instead, Old Trafford was up again two minutes into the second half with United pulling one back through Eric Cantona, who held off Trollope on the edge of the box before unleashing an unstoppable low shot.

From there it was anyone's game but Derby restored their two-goal advantage on 75 minutes in fortuitous circumstances.

Gary Pallister sliced a clearance backwards and seemed in control until Schmeichel charged out to the edge of his box, causing indecision between the pair.

Sturridge nipped in and headed the ball goalwards before chasing it down with Ronny Johnsen.

The United man slipped as the ball came back off the post, leaving Sturridge with the simplest of tasks from a couple of yards out.

United immediately roared back and within a couple of minutes Cantona turned provider, arrowing a ball forward that deflected into the path of half-time substitute Ole Gunnar Solskjaer who made no mistake.

Solskjaer and Ryan Giggs sent late efforts over the bar but Derby dug in and deserved their victory on effort and determination alone, let alone their all-round performance.

Wanchope's staggering debut goal had made him the talk of the Premier League and Smith was certainly pleased to have the youngster on board. He believed the goal showed just what Wanchope had in his locker, admitting after the match, 'He could be a special player. Paulo is 20 and a first appearance at Old Trafford did not faze him in any way.'

At the other end of the scale was McGrath who, at 37, was old enough to have been Wanchope's father.

'If Paul McGrath has the chance to rest before an important game, he can perform like that,' added Smith. 'He was magnificent.'

McGrath, part of a back four having normally played as a sweeper behind two centre-backs, truly was magnificent as he led by example in the face of growing United pressure and relished a return to his former manor.

The change in formation allowed Derby to put three men in midfield and also play three strikers, a move that paid off on many levels, as Smith explained.

'Due to the various injuries we had to play three centre-forwards with two of them playing wide,' he said.

'That was partly to stop United's full-backs being free to get forward but we should have gone in 4-0 up at half-time. Ashley Ward had three open goals in the same incident.

'Even so, I was cool at 2-0. A couple of minutes into the second half I was a lot less cool. When Cantona pulled a goal back, I knew we were in for a long, hard afternoon.

'To be honest, I might have settled for 2-2 at that stage but scoring a third gave us a great chance.

'We knew we'd have to defend well and work hard. The players did just that and we took three points we didn't have on our graph.'

As for Poom, the remarkable debut capped a hectic fortnight and he was thankful for the opportunity to make a couple of early saves to settle any debut nerves.

The 25-year-old said, 'I came to Derby and signed, then immediately had to leave to play against Scotland in the World Cup.

'After that, I went home before returning to Derby. I don't really know the players yet and a debut at Old Trafford was a big event for me.

'It is always good for a goalkeeper to make an early save. That makes you feel that everything will be alright.

'Everybody is very pleased for the win. It is always something special to beat Manchester United.'

The result lifted Derby to 12th and six points clear of the bottom three where Coventry City had been the big winners, lifting themselves out thanks to a 2-1 injury-time win at Liverpool that left Middlesbrough, Nottingham Forest and Southampton in the relegation zone.

Manchester United's next match was a Champions League semi-final first leg at Borussia Dortmund, highlighting the scale of the Rams' achievement.

The Saints escaped from the Baseball Ground with a 1-1 draw thanks to Darryl Powell's late own goal the following Wednesday but Derby then beat Aston Villa to pass the 40-point mark that is perceived as almost certain to guarantee safety.

They confirmed survival with a third away win of the season, 2-1 at Coventry in their final match, then a last-day defeat to Arsenal in the Baseball Ground's final competitive match left them 12th in the table, comfortably clear of relegation trouble.

United lost in their semi-final to eventual European champions Dortmund but won the Premier League again while Coventry staged a remarkable recovery act to survive on the final day, leaving Sunderland and Middlesbrough joining Forest in dropping to the First Division.

Wanchope didn't score again that season but his haul in 1997/98 included another cracker against United, this time at the new Pride Park Stadium, when he ran from deep and evaded several challenges before flicking his shot past Schmeichel.

And in 2009, as part of the club's 125th anniversary celebrations, his goal at Old Trafford was voted by the fans as the greatest in Derby County's history.

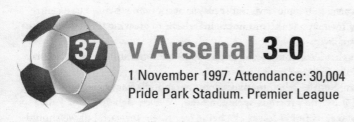

v Arsenal 3-0

1 November 1997. Attendance: 30,004
Pride Park Stadium. Premier League

DERBY COUNTY:	ARSENAL:
Poom	Seaman
Carbon	Winterburn (Wreh 69)
Rowett	Adams
C Powell	Dixon
Laursen	Bould
D Powell	Vieira
Solis (Kozluk HT)	Platt
Carsley	Parlour
Sturridge (Trollope 86)	Petit
Wanchope	Anelka (Boa Morte 69)
Baiano (Burton 86)	Wright
Unused subs: Hoult (GK), Hunt	*Unused subs:* Manninger (GK), Grimandi, Hughes

Referee: Paul Alcock

PAULO Wanchope was making quite a name for himself in the autumn of 1997 as he continued his spectacular introduction to English football. The Costa Rican striker had announced himself to the Premier League in April with that unforgettable goal at Old Trafford after signing from SC Herediano in his homeland.

And by the time the 1997/98 season was in full swing so was Wanchope with goals in each of his first three starts.

A fourth followed in the League Cup against Southend United to start October – a month that saw him named as the Carling Premier League Player of the Month, the first Ram to win the prize.

After that Southend game he was a massive handful in a televised 2-1 Monday night victory at Leicester City, scored both in a League Cup success at Tottenham Hotspur by the same scoreline, added another remarkable solo effort in a 2-2 home draw with Manchester United and created the Rams' first goal for Francesco Baiano that afternoon, just as he did in the 1-1 draw against Wimbledon four days later in the match re-arranged after Pride Park's opening league night had been cut short by a floodlight failure.

Baiano was in a run of eight goals scored in six consecutive games spread across September and October but it was Wanchope who was making all the headlines for his form.

He was recognised by the 17-strong panel that voted for the award, which included Premier League managers, national journalists and England head coach Glenn Hoddle. Arsenal's Dennis Bergkamp was the previous winner for September. And in a rare interview, 21-year-old Wanchope spoke of his pride at winning the prize.

'I feel very honoured to win the award and it's nice to be recognised individually,' he said. 'But it is a reward for the whole team and the way we have been playing.'

But tellingly, he warned, 'People have not seen the best of me yet.

'I make too many mistakes at the moment and I have to start cutting them out to become a better player.

'The award shows that I am doing some good things but I can still do more. I have a lot of hard work to do to improve my game.'

And manager Jim Smith, who uncovered his rough diamond when bringing Wanchope over to Derby the previous spring, added, 'We are delighted for Paulo to gain this recognition so early in his career.

'He has that bit of magic and star quality and while it would be hard for him to maintain that standard all season, we genuinely believe there is a lot more in his locker.

'He's added goals and the unexpected to the team and his number of assists is excellent. He's been involved in nearly every goal we've scored since he came in for the Sheffield Wednesday game [a 5-2 win at Hillsborough in September, in which Wanchope scored].

'The most pleasing thing from my point of view is his work-rate. He plays for the team.'

Smith, who was also honoured before the Arsenal game by the League Managers' Association with a new set of golf clubs to mark his 25 years of service as a boss, then set about warning that his team needed to take lessons from their two Italians – former Fiorentina striker Baiano, and midfielder Stefano Eranio who had arrived from AC Milan – on how to see out games.

Derby had lost leads to draw each of their last two home games, 2-0 to 2-2 against Manchester United and 1-0 to 1-1 against Wimbledon.

But they were still in fine form and their 4-0 defeat at Liverpool the Saturday after drawing with Wimbledon was only their second loss in their last 12 games.

Smith said, 'Our two Italians cannot understand the way we keep piling forward when we are in the lead at home. They are used to teams tightening things up and that's what we have to do.

'We have to be confident when we're ahead so we can beat these teams. Against Manchester United, although less so against Wimbledon, a little bit of self-doubt crept in and we lacked the belief to finish the job.'

Smith would be without Scottish international defender Christian Dailly against Arsenal due to a bout of tonsillitis, and with Igor Stimac also missing there was likely to be a re-shuffle at the back.

The Gunners were missing Bergkamp, who was starting a three-match ban, so Arsene Wenger opted to give teenage striker Nicolas Anelka his first Premier League start alongside Ian Wright, who was expected to be fit despite a heavy cold.

Elsewhere, there was more positive news from the Derby camp with midfielder Paul Trollope's call-up to the Wales squad for a forthcoming friendly in Brazil.

Derby's defensive problems meant they were unable to return to the usual formation of three centre-backs flanked by two wing-backs so they continued with the 4-3-3 line-up that they had used in the last four matches.

That also saw a rare start in midfield for Mauricio Solis, who had joined the club as part of the Wanchope deal but found his opportunities limited due to the restrictions on non-EU players in match day squads.

The Rams were struggling to find their most fluid football with the different shape and Arsenal certainly had the best of the first half.

Their golden moment arrived on the half-hour when Patrick Vieira went down after Lee Carsley's late challenge, and referee Paul Alcock pointed to the penalty spot.

There were few complaints from those in the white shirts but the feeling changed to relief seconds later when up stepped Wright, having recently become Arsenal's all-time record goalscorer, to smash the penalty against the bar before Anelka headed the rebound over an empty goal with Mart Poom having dived away to his right.

For all the Gunners' pressure they were lacking a real creative spark and when Derby switched things around at the break, introducing young Rob Kozluk in place of Solis and returning to three at the back, the game changed.

Just a minute into the second half Wanchope embarked on one of his long, loping runs through the middle and having reached the edge of the box he didn't quite catch his shot cleanly but it still had enough power to reach the bottom corner beyond David Seaman's dive.

With Baiano prompting everything and Dean Sturridge looking dangerous it came as no surprise when Derby doubled their lead in the 66th minute.

Sturridge had powered his way in from the left and drove in a low cross that Nigel Winterburn failed to deal with in his own six-yard box, leaving Wanchope with an easy finish.

Poom's first real save came from a powerful David Platt volley but the icing was added to the cake eight minutes from time.

Matt Carbon played a long ball up to the halfway line where Baiano collected it and nicked it on to Sturridge, who left the Arsenal defence for dead before cutting in and classily lift the ball over the advancing Seaman to make it 3-0.

Wanchope may have once again chosen the perfect occasion to turn on the style but after a result that left Derby sixth in the table, four points adrift of the second-placed Gunners and with a game in hand, Smith instead handed down praise to Baiano.

The little Italian had arrived shortly before the start of the season for £1.5m, a recommendation from his compatriot Eranio after Derby's move for Azzuri legend Roberto Baggio had failed at the last minute.

And he had quickly shown his worth after settling in nicely to a role in behind the front two akin to that occupied by Dutchman Ron Willems in the 1995/96 promotion season.

Of Baiano, Smith said, 'Francesco didn't really want to come off near the end because he hadn't scored.

'But he is instrumental in the way we play. He is very bright and clever, the one who keeps the ball for us.

'At times he is frustrated if the other players do not pass to him. He takes great positions and wants the ball.'

The win was Derby's ninth in their last 13 matches, a run stretching back to the end of August, and was rated by Smith as the best of the season so far.

He added, 'In the circumstances, I was very pleased. Christian Dailly falling ill before the match was beginning to stretch us and we were under the cosh in the first half.

'I changed the system for the second half. Injuries forced us to play with four at the back but they are far more comfortable with three central defenders and wing-backs.

'A goal so soon after half-time gave us a lift and Paulo does frighten people. You saw even senior players in the Arsenal team nervous when he got the ball.

'Jacob Laursen was outstanding. He's been Mr Consistency.'

Laursen had indeed been Mr Consistency, a fine signing by Smith from Danish side Silkeborg in the summer of 1996.

He was also wearing the captain's armband in the absence of Stimac and modestly said after the match, 'I know when I've played well or badly. If I get good feedback from the coaches, that will do for me.'

The Dane did, however, look at Arsenal's much-vaunted defensive unit as something for the Rams to emulate in the future.

'Arsenal's back five have been together for years and I think we could do the same,' he added.

'Only Igor Stimac is 30 and the rest of us can develop together. If we do that, build on solid foundations, Derby can stay in the top ten for a long time.

'It is the way to do it, rather than push everything towards one season, and the manager is steadily bringing in better players.

'Against Arsenal, we changed the system after half-time and were better with three at the back. It helped that Matt Carbon came in and played so well.

'If there are injuries, you rely on people like Matt being able to do the job and it was good for Rob Kozluk to play again. Liverpool was not the best place for him to start last week but now he has something behind him.'

Derby reverted to three centre-halves from the start the following week at Leeds United and were once again 3-0 up, this time after only 33 minutes, but they collapsed in spectacular style and ended up losing the game 4-3 in the final minute.

It could be argued that they never really recovered from that defeat as consistency eluded them for the rest of the season and they only won one of their last ten matches to finish ninth, having harboured hopes of a tilt at UEFA Cup qualification.

They remained unbeaten at their new Pride Park home until February, when Dwight Yorke secured a 1-0 victory for Aston Villa in stoppage time.

Laursen was rewarded for his fine season by going to the 1998 World Cup with Denmark, one of five Rams to take part in the France tournament.

Dailly lined up for Scotland in the opening game against Brazil, then Croatian star Stimac and Jamaican duo Deon Burton and Darryl Powell ended up in the same group and were all on the pitch at the same time as the Croats picked up a 3-1 win.

Stimac and his former Derby team-mate Aljosa Asanovic then starred as Croatia reached the semi-final and took the lead against France, only to lose 2-1, though they did win the third-place play-off against Holland.

But back to Derby and Wanchope finished as the Rams' leading scorer in 1997/98 with 17 goals in all competitions, and Baiano added 13 to his assists and all-round starring displays which saw him voted as the fans' Player of the Year.

What made the victory over Arsenal even more remarkable was that it was their first loss of what was their first full season under Wenger.

The Gunners more than recovered as they surged through the last three months of the season to win the Premier League and FA Cup double in emphatic style.

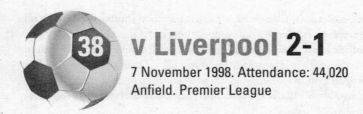

38 v Liverpool 2-1

7 November 1998. Attendance: 44,020
Anfield. Premier League

DERBY COUNTY:	LIVERPOOL:
Hoult	James
Carbonari	Staunton
Dorigo	Carragher
Elliott	Heggem (Thompson 67)
Laursen	Bjornebye
Powell	Redknapp
Harper	Ince
Bohinen	McManaman
Delap (Kozluk 73)	Berger (McAteer 32)
Wanchope (Bridge-Wilkinson 90)	Fowler
Burton	Owen
Unused subs: Poom (GK), Launders, Christie	*Unused subs:* Friedel (GK), Harkness, Kvarme

Referee: Uriah Rennie

MUCH has been made in this book and many others of the years when Derby County were genuinely a big club in the world of football. There were a number of periods in their history when they had enjoyed sustained spells in the top flight and were the equals of anyone.

Unsurprisingly the golden period was the spell from when Brian Clough and Peter Taylor took the club into the top division until the final stages of the Dave Mackay reign when they nearly pulled off a league and cup double.

Derby were imperious at home in those halcyon days, but even at the very pinnacle of their time they struggled to beat Liverpool at Anfield.

A 2-0 victory on 28 February 1970 was the first of the modern era, and you had to go back as far as 1937 for a previous win there.

Of even more concern was the fact that not only did the Rams lose regularly at Anfield, but it was frequently by an embarrassing amount. Conceding plenty of goals on the red half of Merseyside was far from uncommon.

Scoring at Anfield was also a rare occurrence. Ashley Ward bagged a late consolation in an October 1996 2-1 defeat there in a televised Premier League fixture but prior to that you had to go back to February 1977 for the last time the Rams found the target – Kevin Hector netting in a 3-1 defeat under Colin Murphy.

The 1997/98 fixture at Anfield was another of the bad days as Derby were comprehensively beaten 4-0 by a rampant Reds side.

So there was absolutely nothing about this fixture that suggested anything other than a regulation victory for the hosts.

Liverpool were the one remaining English side in the UEFA Cup and were in good domestic form too although they had lost on their last Premier League outing, 1-0 away to Leicester City on 31 October, though prior to that they had thumped Nottingham Forest 5-1 and were unbeaten at home in all competitions so far through 1998/99.

Derby, on the other hand, were struggling for a bit of form. They had beaten Leicester 2-0 on 19 September and won at Manchester City – then of League 1 – four days later in the League Cup, but their next three Premier League games all ended in defeat, 1-0 away to Aston Villa and at home to Tottenham Hotspur then 2-1 at Newcastle United.

They stopped the rot with a 1-1 draw at home to Manchester United, only a late Jordi Cruyff goal denying them the points, and a League Cup exit at the hands of Arsenal's second string followed before an exciting 2-2 draw at home to Leeds United.

So not only were the Rams without a win in six matches in all competitions as they headed to Anfield, they also went there knowing that the club had been defeated on ten successive visits going back as far as the 1970s.

And worst of all manager Jim Smith was without six senior players because of injury, including frontline strikers Francesco Baiano and Dean Sturridge, defenders Igor Stimac and Spencer Prior, and a further player in Stefan Schnoor who was suspended.

It all meant that Smith's resources were decidedly stretched as they prepared for a trip to one of English football's most iconic – and, on its day, intimidating – grounds.

Smith was likely to have to call upon some of his younger players to make up his squad such as 19-year-old striker Malcolm Christie, who had only been signed from non-league side Nuneaton Borough less than two weeks previously.

Christie made the bench, alongside youth products Robbie Kozluk and Marc Bridge-Wilkinson, and young Irish midfielder Brian Launders.

Kozluk and goalkeeper Mart Poom were the only two of the five who had actually played first-team football for the Rams.

And there was a first start for Kevin Harper, the Scottish winger signed from Hibernian for £300,000 earlier in the season who had to this point made a handful of substitute appearances.

Harper was included as part of a front three alongside Paulo Wanchope and Deon Burton as Derby set out with the ability to attack their hosts but also with the option to switch to more defensive tactics if they needed to.

As it turned out, that was something of a Smith master-stroke akin to giving Wanchope his debut at Old Trafford less than 18 months previously.

Only six minutes had gone when Burton fed Tony Dorigo on the left and the former England man's cross was calling out for a towering header at the far post.

In the end the man who rose to meet it was Harper, surely the smallest player on the pitch, but he guided the ball perfectly past David James to stun the home fans in the Kop behind the goal.

Liverpool pushed on in search of a quick response and Derby had Horacio Carbonari to thank for two interventions after Russell Hoult had got caught out of position but the pair could do nothing when Jamie Redknapp headed against a post.

Steve Elliott, just beyond his 20th birthday, produced a fine tackle to deny Robbie Fowler but before the half-hour mark Derby eased the pressure on them with a second goal.

Once again it came from a wider area, this time the right, where Rory Delap whipped over a perfect cross for Wanchope to get above Vegard Heggem and head home powerfully in true number nine style.

Derby held their advantage into the second half which saw Liverpool attacking the Kop and they used the impetus from that to mount some early assaults which saw Hoult save well from Fowler, who also headed wide when well placed.

Everything Liverpool threw forward was repelled with relish by the Rams' back three of record signing Carbonari, the ever-dependable Jacob Laursen and Derby-born youth product Steve Elliott, who enjoyed an outstanding afternoon.

Only with six minutes remaining did the home side finally break through as Redknapp netted from close range after Steve McManaman crossed low but even then Derby had an immediate chance to wrap things up but Wanchope shot just wide.

From that point it was one-way traffic as the Reds looked to salvage something to appease their restless fans but the best they could muster was another Fowler effort that went beyond the post and Derby hung on.

This was a victory against all the odds, a team given no chance who out-played, out-fought and even out-thought their illustrious opponents.

And after the game, a delighted Smith said, 'Towards the end we were under a little bit of pressure but the lads, as they did all afternoon, battled magnificently.

'We had three up front, one a natural outside-right, one right up and another front player on the left. It was to push their back four back and not let them have so much play and on the defensive side it worked very well because Wanchope scored and Harper scored from crosses into the box, with good headers.

'We had six of our senior players out and we had to re-jig the side on Friday morning to be honest. We decided to go this way and young people like 20-year-old [Steve] Elliott at the back did magnificent, Kevin Harper making his [full] debut, and [Horacio] Carbonari did well.

'They all did well but it was a very encouraging performance. I think the win was the most pleasing thing but to see young Elliott – we get labelled with all these foreign players – but it's lovely to see a local lad, an English boy, in the team.

'Our ambition has been from day one to try and improve on last season's points total and that's all you should be looking to do.'

If Derby lacked any belief going into the match they certainly came out of it with bucket loads.

Their next game was to be a Monday evening clash with old rivals Nottingham Forest at the City Ground. There was a nine day gap between the fixtures and the confidence brought back from Anfield was fed during that period.

The side gained a 2-2 draw from the televised local derby clash, and although losing the following weekend at home to West Ham United they put together a six-game unbeaten streak with two wins and four draws that they then extended to just two defeats in 11 going into the spring.

That put them in with a serious shout of qualifying for the UEFA Cup, something they had threatened to do the previous season before tailing off and finishing ninth on 55 points.

They also made progress in the FA Cup through the spring of 1999, reaching the quarter-finals for the third time in seven seasons with victories over Plymouth Argyle, Swansea City and Huddersfield Town after a replay.

Their Wembley hopes were again ended by Arsenal, though this time by the Gunners' first team and a last-minute goal at Highbury, which sent Arsene Wenger's holders through to that classic semi-final against treble-hunting Manchester United.

Derby immediately bounced back with a 2-1 home win against Aston Villa then did the double over Liverpool with a thrilling 3-2 success in front of what was then Pride Park Stadium's record attendance.

That put them right in the hunt for European football but they faltered from then on, winning only two of their final nine matches – though they did have the consolation of recording both of those victories against local rivals.

The first came on 10 April when a late Carbonari goal earned a 1-0 success over Nottingham Forest, the big Argentine's second goal against the Reds in his debut Rams season, and the second came on 5 May with a 2-1 scoreline at Leicester earned by Mikkel Beck's winner, his first goal for the club.

A 0-0 draw at home to Coventry City and a 2-1 defeat at Chelsea ended the season with Derby having finished eighth, improving their position from 1997/98, but with three less points.

As for the young players on the bench that day at Anfield, Christie went on to become an England Under-21 international in a successful Rams career, Kozluk also played for the Under-21s but joined Sheffield United in March 1999, and Launders made two substitute appearances but was released at the end of the season.

Bridge-Wilkinson, who came on for his Rams debut in the last minute, did not actually touch the ball and never made another first-team appearance for the club – surely giving him one of the most unique Derby County careers there has ever been!

v Bradford City 4-4

21 April 2000. Attendance: 18,276
Valley Parade. Premier League

DERBY COUNTY:	BRADFORD CITY:
Poom	Clarke
Elliott	Wetherall
Dorigo	Westwood (Saunders 71)
Laursen	Jacobs (Rankin 77)
Carbonari	Halle
Powell	O'Brien
Johnson	Dreyer
Delap	McCall
Burley	Beagrie
Christie	Blake
Strupar (Kinkladze 65)	Windass
Unused subs: Oakes (GK), Jackson, Schnoor, Riggott	*Unused subs:* Davison (GK), Todd, Sharpe
Referee: Alan Wilkie	

AFTER the year on year rise enjoyed by Derby County the 1999/2000 season showed the team hitting a brick wall. It took them five matches to register their first Premier League win, 2-0 away to Sheffield Wednesday, and by the turn of the year they had only managed three more victories – one of which, against Everton, had come just three days after that success at Hillsborough.

The magic touch in the transfer market seemed to have deserted manager Jim Smith. Granted, the signing of Seth Johnson had plenty of plus-points to it as the former Crewe Alexandra man made 36 league appearances that season and when eventually sold netted the club a record fee.

Not so successful was the signing of rising star Lee Morris for £2m, as the youngster only managed two starts and one substitute appearance before being ruled out of the campaign through injury. Morris was a good player, as was Argentinean forward Esteban Fuertes who cost a hefty £2.3m from Colon de Santa Fe and scored the winner on his home debut to see off Everton.

He had been a target since the summer but the red tape so often involved with international transfers held up his first appearance until the game at Sheffield Wednesday.

The player claimed European ancestry which allowed him to ply his trade in this country by virtue of his passport.

Fuertes did not have any of the other qualifying requirements necessary to come from a non-European Union country and play in England.

Unfortunately for both player and club an early-season break to a training camp in Portugal during one of the periods scheduled for international teams to meet up proved an absolute disaster.

Fuertes was stopped by officials at Heathrow who denied him entry back into the country on the grounds that he was carrying a forged passport. He was put on a plane and sent back home to South America.

The uncertainty around the club caused by this, along with the fact that scoring goals was proving hard to do, led to a season of struggle.

As a sign of how difficult things were in the striking department Rory Delap, who was moved from right-back to central midfield, was their most regular goalscorer.

A heavy round of spending took place over the Christmas period as it became increasingly obvious that there was a real possibility of the season ending in relegation.

In came Belgian international striker Branko Strupar and Scotland midfielder Craig Burley, each for £3m from Genk and Celtic respectively, and the enigmatic Giorgi Kinkladze on loan from Dutch giants Ajax.

Also down at the wrong end of the table were Bradford City, a club that had done remarkably well to reach the Premier League under their highly-rated young manager Paul Jewell.

There was nothing about the recent playing records of either team to suggest what was about to occur on this particular afternoon.

Derby had beaten Wimbledon 4-0 at Pride Park Stadium on 4 March but then did not pick up another win until 2 April, when they beat Leicester City 3-0 in front of the TV cameras, but they followed that up with a drab 0-0 draw at relegation-threatened Watford – when Stefan Schnoor missed a penalty – and a 2-1 defeat at home to West Ham United to set up the Bradford game.

Bradford, for their part, were coming in with even worse form having lost their last six matches and suffered an overall run of seven defeats in nine, with just two draws being collected in that time.

They were, however, looking to do the double over Derby having won 1-0 at Pride Park back in September thanks to a Horacio Carbonari own goal in the 66th minute of an afternoon that also saw Fuertes, plus the visitors' Andy Myers, get sent off.

Such was the importance of this particular meeting that the Rams decided to beam back pictures and commentary from Yorkshire to a giant video screen set up on the Pride Park pitch so Rams fans who hadn't travelled to Valley Parade would be able to see the action. Smith had called for his struggling players to show how strong their hearts were and they rewarded him with the best possible start.

Only 21 minutes were on the clock when Darryl Powell combined with Strupar and picked up a return pass only to see his shot palmed away by Matt Clarke, but Malcolm Christie – quickly making a name for himself in his first run in the team after signing from non-league Nuneaton Borough in the autumn of 1998 – was on hand to roll the ball back across for Delap to finish off from close range.

Strupar soon missed a chance to make it 2-0 but he was not downhearted and quickly made amends with a curling free kick into the bottom corner that left Clarke helpless.

That should have been the signal for Derby to tighten their performance up and ensure they saw the job through, even if it was still early in the game, but things soon went the other way. A further 20 crazy minutes passed and the Rams found themselves trailing 3-2 and down to ten men.

Dean Windass gave the Bantams a lifeline with a crisp, low shot beyond Mart Poom and the equaliser arrived on 18 minutes through Windass again, whose powerful shot from 30 yards found its way low into the bottom corner.

Nine minutes later, Robbie Blake netted from Stuart McCall's free kick but Blake had been pulled back in the action of shooting by Delap and although the Bradford man had scored, referee Alan Wilkie consulted with one of his linesmen before sending Delap off and awarding a penalty.

Peter Beagrie beat Poom from the spot and before half an hour had passed this match had packed more into it than most do across the entire 90.

But the action did not stop there. Derby were awarded their first penalty of the afternoon on 36 minutes, when Ashley Westwood hauled down Christie inside the box, and up stepped Burley to hammer it home and put Derby on level terms.

Amazingly they then found themselves 4-3 down before half-time when Windass completed his hat-trick.

Derby stepped things up again after the interval and it took them just seven minutes to level once more and yet again the goal came from the penalty spot. John Dreyer handled and Burley made no mistake with his second spot-kick of the afternoon.

Bradford came roaring back, sensing the need to win a game against one of their relegation rivals, but the more they poured forward the more Derby finally found their defensive stability with Carbonari particularly outstanding.

Christie and Seth Johnson both passed up good opportunities to put the Rams 5-4 ahead but they were presented with a great chance on 82 minutes – their third penalty of the match after Gunnar Halle took down Powell.

The Rams could have changed their penalty taker but Burley, after his two successful kicks, showed that he was up to facing the pressure and stepped forward once again with the intention of completing a rare hat-trick from the spot.

Unfortunately, this time he was foiled as Clarke produced a wonderful save to tip his effort away from goal.

And still the drama was not complete as right at the death, Poom had to produce a world-class save to deny Derby legend Dean Saunders what would surely have been the winning goal against his old club – though with the way this game went, nobody could have been certain until the final whistle.

It led midfield man Burley to admit afterwards, 'We don't know whether to be happy or disappointed because from 2-0 up we should have been professional enough to win the game but we weren't.

'It was a crazy game and both teams showed why they are in relegation trouble because they gave away too many goals.

'I thought attacking-wise we were very good, we created a good few chances, but it was disappointing the amount of goals we gave away.

'I put my hands up and said I would take the responsibility [for the penalties] and I was pleased to get the one in the first half but I didn't expect to get another one in the game.

'Again in the second half I got another one and we were behind so I tried to go for the same side, which worked, and then when you get the third one you're thinking "where do you go here?"

'So I decided to stick that one down the middle with power, and the keeper has dived again the same way and got a hand to it in the middle of the goal.

'We created a lot of chances and someone has got to take the penalties, especially when we're in a situation of being behind in a relegation battle, and I'm one of the more experienced players so I'll put my hands up.

'I'm disappointed to have missed but that's the way it goes. It's a battle of wits and the keeper out-witted me on the last one.'

History shows that 4-4 draws are pretty rare in modern football and author Phil was lucky enough to commentate on this game for the club's own official website.

Those who travelled up to Bradford were treated to a true spectacle. Less fortunate were those unable, or unwilling, to travel who instead went to watch the live beam back of the game to Pride Park.

Beam backs had been very popular and successful, but on this one unfortunate occasion technical gremlins meant that fans back in Derby had blank screens and no dedicated commentary of the game, causing some disturbance later on as angry supporters surrounded the ticket office in search of a refund on their admission fee – of £1.

Both sides then went on to finish the season with relatively solid runs to ensure their survival in the Premier League, though it took Bradford until the last day to do so.

After the draw with Derby they won their next two, including a crucial 3-0 success at home to Wimbledon, and on the final day they beat Liverpool 1-0 at Valley Parade to mean their first season in the Premier League would end safely with the Dons joining Sheffield Wednesday and Watford in going down to the First Division.

Derby beat Southampton 2-0 in their next game thanks to goals from Christie and Powell before drawing 1-1 at Tottenham Hotspur, conceding a last-minute equaliser when a win would have confirmed survival, though they were safe on the penultimate day with a 0-0 stalemate at home to Newcastle United.

The season ended on a low note with a 4-0 beating at Chelsea that left them 16th, one place and two points above Bradford.

If Burley had been successful with his third penalty then he would have been the first Derby player to have ever scored a hat-trick from the spot in the same game – something not even the great Steve Bloomer ever managed.

And it would have also been the Rams' first hat-trick of any kind since Paul Simpson's treble on Easter Monday 1996 in a 6-2 beating of Tranmere Rovers at the Baseball Ground on the way to promotion from the First Division.

Although Arturo Lupoli, Nathan Ellington and Tito Villa have scored trebles in cup matches, that haul of Simpson's remains – at the time of writing – the Rams' last hat-trick in a league match, more than 17 years on.

And the aforementioned Fuertes went on to have an interesting career after leaving Derby for French club Lens in 2000 – amazingly at a £500,000 profit on his original transfer fee.

He had two more spells with Colon de Santa Fe, becoming their all-time leading goalscorer having earlier won the 2003 Torneo Clausura – the second championship, in Argentina's convoluted league system – with River Plate.

And at the age of 36, in May 2009, he won his one and only cap for the Argentinean national side against Panama before eventually bringing his career to a close with Colon in 2012.

v Reading 3-0

10 August 2002. Attendance: 33,016
Pride Park Stadium. Football League First Division

DERBY COUNTY:	READING:
Poom	Whitehead
Barton	Murty
Higginbotham	Williams
Riggott	Shorey
Boertien (Jackson 74)	Mackie
Bolder	Igoe (Cureton 59)
Murray	Watson (Parkinson 86)
Lee	Harper
Morris (Twigg 80)	Salako
Ravanelli	Hughes
Christie (Evatt 85)	Butler (Henderson 81)
Unused subs: Grant (GK), Strupar	*Unused subs:* Ashdown (GK), Rougier
Referee: Graham Laws	

THE previous spring, with Derby County in the Premier League and Reading in the Second Division, there had been plenty of space between the two clubs in English football's league system. But there was always the likelihood that they would be playing each other in 2002/03 at some point as Derby were limping towards an inevitable relegation after struggling for the previous two seasons while Reading were well set for automatic promotion having missed out in the 2001 play-off final.

And in the end that is exactly what happened – the Rams, with John Gregory their third 'permanent' manager of a troubled 2001/02 season, embarked on a seven-match losing streak from March that saw their drop from the top flight confirmed.

Mind you, Reading almost didn't make it with their automatic promotion in the balance right through to the final minute of the final game of the season.

Their last ten games had realised just one win, at Chesterfield on 16 March – the same day as Derby's last win of the campaign, 3-1 at Bolton Wanderers – though the Royals did draw the other nine in that period.

It sent them into the final day second in the table, a point clear of third-placed Brentford, who coincidentally were their opponents in West London with automatic promotion up for grabs behind champions Brighton & Hove Albion.

With 13 minutes left the Royals were trailing 1-0 and facing the play-offs once again but Jamie Cureton had come on as a substitute and scored the goal that clinched second spot and a return to the second tier for the first time since relegation in 1998.

The fixture list, as it so often does in these occasions, threw up a match between a relegated side and one newly promoted to the division on the opening day – but even between the drop and 10 August so much happened to the Rams.

They were quickly feeling the financial squeeze that comes with dropping out of the Premier League and were not helped by players on some big wages, not least Fabrizio

Ravanelli's reputed £40,000-a-week deal that still had another year to run. Derby had tried and failed to move on their big earners over the summer so they were starting a second tier campaign with the experienced Italian still in their ranks along with other expensive buys like Craig Burley, Giorgi Kinkladze, Branko Strupar and Francois Grenet.

Goalkeeper Mart Poom, defender Chris Riggott and striker Malcolm Christie had all attracted attention from the Premier League but they, too, remained at Pride Park and all played a full part in a pre-season campaign that had culminated in a 2-1 defeat at home to Serie A giants Lazio the previous Monday night with Adam Murray scoring the goal.

Derby's squad also showed no new faces from those who had finished the previous season – though it wasn't for a lack of trying.

Former Wimbledon man Neal Ardley had been on trial at Pride Park over the summer, as had ex-Middlesbrough midfielder Robbie Mustoe, scorer of Boro's winner at Derby the previous April, but no deals were done as the Co-op Bank imposed a transfer embargo on the first-team squad until costs were cut.

The Rams had pinned most of their transfer hopes on the signing of the then-unheralded Nigerian striker Yakubu Aiyegbeni from Israeli side Maccabi Haifa.

Yakubu was very highly rated by the Derby staff and a deal in the region of £2m was agreed with his club but a work permit could not be obtained and the transfer fell through, though whether it would ever have been completed due to the financial problems is debatable.

But off the field there were major issues too, especially given the money crisis that was surrounding the club.

Former Coventry City chairman Bryan Richardson had arrived as an executive director two days before the Reading game, with the specific remit of agreeing deals to get the Rams' highest earners off the books.

A takeover offer from former directors Peter Gadsby and John Kirkland, who had left the club after relegation from the Premier League, had been withdrawn with chairman Lionel Pickering having allowed the 8 August deadline imposed by Gadsby to expire.

All of that meant the word 'turbulent' was the ideal one to apply to Derby's situation as they approached a season outside the top tier for the first time since 1995/96.

But by the opening day, manager Gregory had his eyes firmly fixed on football matters and the visit of Reading.

'Reading will come here as the underdogs and all the pressure is on us, but we don't mind that kind of pressure,' he said.

'We will be the team everyone wants to beat in Division One. Teams will raise their game when they visit Pride Park and will look forward to playing in front of 30,000. But we have to cope with that and I am sure we can.

'We know all about Reading. They are a strong team and are used to winning games after promotion from Division Two last season.

'They have the winning habit but we are looking forward to getting started.'

Gregory's point about attendances was a pertinent one as the game was heading towards a sell-out and the Rams' highest opening-day attendance in 29 years.

The manager had predicted that Reading would come and make life difficult for his players and he was proven right as Derby had to wait until beyond the hour mark before they got the first goal of what was, in truth, a comfortable victory.

Left-back Paul Boertien had battled his way forward and found Rob Lee, at 36 the oldest player on the park.

The former England man let fly from 25 yards with a bullet of a low shot that arrowed into Royals goalkeeper Paul Whitehead's bottom-right corner.

Derby deserved their advantage and doubled it two minutes later with Ravanelli repeating his feat of 2001/02 by scoring on the opening day.

This time it was a finish from open play, as opposed to a curling free kick against Blackburn Rovers 12 months previously, and after his shot from Christie's pass the Italian raced down the touchline to celebrate with Gregory.

It was Christie who then wrapped up the scoring on 72 minutes with a composed effort to beat Whitehead after he collected Boertien's pass.

A fine save from Poom prevented Reading getting a consolation goal between Derby's second and third strikes but the visitors could have been a long way out of sight well before they even found themselves one behind.

Getting the season off to a 3-0 winning start was the perfect way for the Rams to set the standard for 2002/03.

But the main talking point after the match was the goal – and all-round performance – from Ravanelli, who was continuing to impress with his attitude to life in the First Division.

'The White Feather' had looked fit and sharp throughout the pre-season campaign as he tried to follow up nine Premier League goals with enough strikes to fire the Rams back to the top flight.

He shared the man of the match award against the Royals with fellow goalscorer Rob Lee, who said, 'Rav has been fantastic in pre-season and now against Reading. His attitude is first rate and the way he trains is a great example to everyone.

'There are some people who say Rav will moan and mope about but that is not true at all. He is great in the dressing room. He could be our biggest player this season.

'He has scored goals wherever he has been and I expect him to score a hatful of goals in this division.'

Lee's sentiments were backed up by boss Gregory, who said, 'Rav led the line really well against Reading.

'We've worked hard in pre-season to keep him in the centre of the pitch. He's so committed in everything he does that he sometimes finds himself out on the wings chasing back full-backs – which is somebody else's job.

'His enthusiasm to please and work hard is so great that he doesn't quite use his head in the manner in which he should.

'While he is in the centre of the pitch, he will cause problems to opponents.'

And Gregory was pleased with his side's performance to open the good season, adding, 'We said at half-time that we must keep persevering, keep patient and keep plugging away.

'At the same time we needed to keep the back door shut and not do anything silly. We didn't want to concede a goal.

'We just felt that if we kept the pressure on we might get the break – and it came with Rob Lee's goal.

'We could then have gone on and scored more than three but overall it was a good afternoon for us.'

Despite getting the season off to an ideal start, it turned into something of a false dawn as Derby came back down to earth with a bump three days later with a 1-0 defeat at Gillingham.

Consistency was hard to come by with the Rams winning five and losing six of their first 11 games, and they didn't win back-to-back matches until the end of October and the start of November.

They never went more than three matches unbeaten across a season that saw them rarely in serious relegation danger but always a little too close to the bottom three for comfort.

Gregory's reign ended in March 2003 after being sacked for alleged misconduct, a charge that was never proven and he later won a settlement against the club for unfair dismissal.

On the field, Ravanelli contributed five goals as one of 36 players to pull on a Derby shirt during 2002/03, ten of which were debutants.

Yakubu went on to score a Champions League hat-trick for Haifa and then net against Manchester United before moving to Portsmouth, by virtue of having a Portuguese wife, scoring twice for Pompey in a 6-2 thrashing of Derby at Fratton Park on their way to promotion to the Premier League where he became a prolific goalscorer with them, Middlesbrough, Everton and Blackburn Rovers.

But off the field Derby were really up against it and the turmoil in the boardroom continued.

Debt levels were reported to be as high as £35m, with an annual wage bill of £17m, and the Co-op Bank withheld the club's money for August's player salaries, leading to defender Danny Higginbotham threatening to go on strike.

Gregory put his hand in his own pocket to cover a £2,000 hotel bill for an away game at Rotherham United while Bryan Richardson departed in October having offered up a £30m 'bond' to re-finance the club without a takeover.

That came to nothing and there were no changes at the top until October 2003, and the ill-fated arrival of the group who came to be known by fans as the 'Three Amigos' – by which time the landscape of Derby County was changing again.

v Nottingham Forest 4-2

20 March 2004. Attendance: 32,390
Pride Park Stadium. Football League First Division

DERBY COUNTY:	NOTTINGHAM FOREST:
Grant	Roche
Kenna	Louis-Jean
Jackson (Boertien HT)	Dawson
M Johnson	Impey
Mawene	Morgan
I Taylor	Williams
Huddlestone	Jess
Costa (Holmes 71)	Barmby (D Johnson 33)
Osman	G Taylor
Peschisolido	Sonner
Tudgay	Reid
Unused subs: Oakes (GK), Tome, Whelan	*Unused subs:* Formann (GK), Thompson, Doig, Westcarr

Referee: David Pugh

WHICHEVER way you look at it, Derby County had big problems prior to the visit of Nottingham Forest to Pride Park Stadium in March 2004. They had been struggling at the wrong end of the table all season and were in the bottom three following a 2-1 defeat at Watford the previous Tuesday night, two points from safety with only ten games remaining in what was then the First Division prior to the re-branding that summer.

One thing George Burley's men did have in their favour, however, was their home form as they were six without defeat in front of their own fans and had not been beaten at Pride Park in any match during 2004. And they also had a new favourite in the shape of experienced Canadian striker Paul Peschisolido, who had arrived from Sheffield United in a swap deal that saw youngster Izale McLeod join the Blades on loan.

Derby had moved for Peschisolido following a 0-0 draw at home to Crewe Alexandra, in which they battered the visitors' goal but could not find a breakthrough.

Peschisolido repaid Burley's faith with the only strike on his debut, a 1-0 win at home to Rotherham United, and was also on target in that defeat at Watford.

However, most of the hype in the Derby camp was about teenager Tom Huddlestone, an absolute giant – a boy-mountain, if you will – having been a fixture in the team since the start of the season when he was still only 16.

Huddlestone, 17 by the time of this match, had been born in Nottingham and represented Forest as a youngster before joining the Rams as an Under-13.

There were no split loyalties for Huddlestone though, despite his red connections, and for him it was all about the Rams in what was his second taste of the derby occasion having played in the 1-1 draw at the City Ground the previous September.

He said, 'Some of my mates are Forest fans and they give me stick sometimes, but I hope to keep them quiet on Saturday.'

'The atmosphere at the City Ground back in September [the game finished 1-1 with Junior on target for Derby] was good and hopefully we'll be able to better that at Pride Park.'

Derby's team also included Michael Johnson, another Nottingham lad who had been born in the city and grew up supporting Forest too but started his playing career with Notts County, who he left to join Birmingham City before signing for the Rams in August 2003.

Johnson, the former Jamaican international, admitted, 'I was born and raised in Nottingham and spent a lot of time as a kid following Forest and the local derby games.

'I know some Rams say they could cope with relegation so long as we beat Forest. I can't quite believe that's true, but I do know how much this game means.'

And while Derby were struggling in the table, Forest were not in much better shape as they had four more points than their hosts and sat 17th.

Their recent form had seen them lose one of their last eight games and they headed along the A52 after four points from two home games, culminating in a 1-1 draw against Burnley 24 hours after Derby had lost at Watford.

Forest had been beaten by Sheffield United in the play-off semi-finals the previous season – Peschisolido scoring a memorable goal for the Blades to win the second leg before celebrating wildly with his shirt waving above his head – but with Joe Kinnear in charge they were struggling to match their form in 2003/04 and had spent most of the campaign in the bottom half.

Kinnear was confident, however, that his side would not be dragged into a relegation battle and felt instead that all of the pressure was on the Rams on this particular occasion.

And, having been in charge of Forest for a little over a month, he was looking for his first taste of an East Midlands derby.

He said, 'We've got everything to play for and I'm sure it will be a fantastic occasion. I'm looking forward to it because I haven't been to a game between the two clubs before.

'I must admit I don't know too much about games between Forest and Derby. I've been told that it's the only game that matters to both sets of supporters because of the rivalry that exists between the two clubs.

'They tell me the atmosphere is good and I'm sure all the players are looking forward to it.

'Games between Forest and Derby have been very tight over the last couple of years but bring it on. Let's go for it. We will go there well prepared and although I wouldn't say that confidence is sky high, it's certainly very good.'

But any hopes Kinnear had of getting a memorable victory for his new club were dashed by an enthralling first 40 minutes by Derby that saw them three clear and a terrace legend become crowned – 'the coffee cup goal'.

Burley's men were already a goal to the good when, on 28 minutes, a harmless-looking pass was rolled back to Forest goalkeeper Barry Roche who took aim with a first-time clearance.

What he hadn't reckoned with were the strong winds swirling around Pride Park which had amazingly blown a coffee cup on to the pitch, right in the path of the ball as it arrived at Roche's feet.

Roche aimed his clearance but the ball deflected off the cup and as the keeper swung his foot he only succeeded in spooning it up into the path of Peschisolido, who had the simplest of tasks to tap home into an empty net.

If that wasn't funny enough, replays later showed that as the ball struck the cup, the lid came off and coffee spilled out on to the pitch.

Derby had already opened the scoring in the fourth minute when skipper Ian Taylor ran on to a pass and hammered his shot low past Roche, then nine minutes after the moment that went down in folklore the score went to 3-0 with all three goals having been scored in front of the Forest fans.

Peschisolido was on target again, making it four goals in his first three appearances with a crisp finish from Marcus Tudgay's through pass.

It looked like it was game over and Derby would cruise to a victory but they were given something to think about when Forest's Gareth Taylor bundled one in for the visitors.

And nerves were getting seriously frayed on 68 minutes when Forest made it 3-2 with Gareth Williams on target.

Derby could have been forgiven for trying to hang on to what they had but to Burley's credit he put the emphasis on attack rather than defence, a move that paid dividends as they wrapped things up with nine minutes to go.

Youth product Tudgay was the scorer with a rasping drive from the edge of the box that put the seal on one of the more remarkable wins over Forest.

The game itself had been exciting enough, and it was a big victory for Derby towards their hopes of staying in the First Division, but there was one incident that stood out above everything else and became a real talking point in the post-match briefings.

Rarely has there been anything as bizarre as the 'coffee cup goal' anywhere in football, let alone through the storied history of Derby County, but for those with black and white blood it became one of the most iconic and talked-about incidents in generations.

It was one of the more unlikely assists you will ever see in a match and it was evident in Peschisolido's under stated celebration just how bemused he had been by the whole incident.

Speaking to the media after the match, he said, 'I felt really sorry for the keeper. It must have bobbled up as he hit it and he shinned it to me. I turned, expecting him to have the ball, and there it was in front of me so I stuck it in the net.

'I was pleased to have a part in the goals and to have scored two. We know what a win over Forest means to the supporters and we wanted to go out and do our best for them.

'We are in a situation where we need to win every game so today was useful.'

But while Peschisolido had shared the headlines with the coffee cup for his two goals, experienced midfielder Taylor had started it all off with his early effort.

Taylor had already become a fans' favourite after moving from Aston Villa the previous summer and said following an emotional 90 minutes, 'I'm feeling a mixture of frustration and elation really. We played really well – but why can't we do that every week?

'The conditions were awful. It was really windy but I think we adapted better than they did. We tried to stick the ball in behind them for most of the game and it worked for us.

'I just gambled on the ball through and with the wind helping by holding it up I was through on goal. I just took my time and whacked it!'

It was an important win in the wider context of Derby's season but they took their time building on it and collected just two points from their next four games, a period that included a 1-0 defeat at home to relegation rivals Walsall – though that proved to be their only home defeat of the second half of the season.

But it left them in big trouble as it kept them in the bottom three while teams above them had games in hand.

The last of those four games without a win came in a televised 0-0 draw at West Ham United which preceded successive home wins, 3-2 in an exciting game against fellow strugglers Bradford City and 5-1 in resounding style against Preston North End.

That put Derby up to 19th with safety in sight only for a 1-0 defeat at Burnley, also in trouble themselves, to leave them still with plenty to do in their final two games.

Their penultimate match saw them host Millwall on a Saturday tea-time and after Walsall had been beaten that afternoon the Rams knew that a win would confirm their survival.

A 2-0 scoreline was enough in a televised clash against that season's FA Cup finalists and it sparked scenes of celebration centred more around relief than any sense of achievement as the Rams were safe and stayed up by a single point.

Off the field the club got as much PR as they could out of the victory over Forest, including bringing out the game on video and DVD along with all the build-up and post-match reaction, titling the production *Gone With The Wind*.

And the cup itself was retrieved by a member of staff and later signed by Peschisolido before being put on display in the stadium!

42 v Nottingham Forest 3-0

11 December 2004. Attendance: 30,793
Pride Park Stadium. Football League Championship

DERBY COUNTY:	NOTTINGHAM FOREST:
Camp	Gerrard
Kenna	Impey
I Taylor	Rogers
Bisgaard	Nowland (King 63)
M Johnson (Mills 90)	Morgan
Peschisolido (Reich 86)	Dawson
Smith	Reid
Jackson	Evans
Huddlestone	D Johnson (Robertson 74)
Rasiak	G Taylor
Idiakez (Bolder 90)	Lester (Thompson 49)
Unused subs: Grant (GK), Tudgay	*Unused subs:* Doyle (GK), Hjelde
Referee: Graham Laws	

THE arrival of George Burley as Derby manager in the spring of 2003 had been initially a short-term measure to save the season as the Rams' fall from grace, which began with relegation from the Premier League the previous season, looked like continuing.

Burley took over on an interim basis when John Gregory was suspended after 55 games in charge over allegations of misconduct, and eventually sacked, though the nature of the allegations never came out in public.

The charges were eventually dropped and Gregory compensated but that story was for another day as it was all about staying in what was then the First Division for Derby.

Burley managed that and was handed the job on a permanent basis at the start of the 2003/04 season, one in which the Rams were fighting a constant battle against the drop to the third tier and only succeeded in confirming their survival with a victory at home to Millwall in their penultimate match.

Burley's tactical awareness and some shrewd signings helped their cause, along with the wind swept victory over Nottingham Forest covered in the previous chapter.

That season the club was also taken over by a consortium that included John Sleightholme as the new chairman, Jeremy Keith as chief executive, and Steve Harding as a director.

Under the new board Derby were able to make some smart moves in the summer of 2004 and they snapped up Tommy Smith, Morten Bisgaard and Inigo Idiakez all without a penny paid in transfer fees.

Burley's eye for a bargain and ability to seamlessly mix players signed from domestic football and the European leagues meant that he was beginning to mould one of Derby's potentially most attractive sides in many years.

Derby County's Greatest Games

It took them a little while to warm up however and they lost five of their opening seven fixtures, including a humiliating 3-1 defeat at League 2 side Lincoln City in the League Cup.

They eventually found their stride and by the time Forest visited Pride Park in December the Rams had won eight fixtures in what was now known as the Championship following a summer re-brand, and they had lost only four times through September, October and November.

December started with a home match against Coventry City and Derby showed their powers of recovery by coming from two goals down to strike twice at the death and earn a draw, the fourth time already during the season that they had overturned a two-goal deficit – although one of those occasions, at home to Crewe Alexandra, had ultimately ended in defeat.

One of the goals against Coventry had been scored by another of Burley's shrewd captures from abroad, Polish international striker Grzegorz Rasiak, who the Rams had embarked on a long pursuit through the early weeks of the season for before ultimately landing the tall front-man.

The Coventry draw left Derby tenth in the table while Forest were in the relegation zone with only 20 points to their name and had failed to win a game since the middle of October.

But there was very little across the whole division as apart from Rotherham United, who were adrift at the bottom, only 13 points separated second-bottom Gillingham and Leicester City, who were up in eighth.

The Rams' position was, points-wise, right in the middle of the Championship as they were ten clear of the relegation places and 11 behind the automatic promotion spots.

Burley made a couple of changes to the side for his second game against Forest of the calendar year and re-introduced Ian Taylor in place of Marco Reich, while Paul Peschisolido – who had scored the equaliser as a substitute against Coventry – was handed a start alongside Rasiak.

Michael Johnson was fit to go from the off and he partnered Tom Huddlestone at the heart of the defence, meaning the Rams went into a clash against their rivals with two Nottingham-born centre-halves starting.

Conditions were perfect for football and Derby almost took the lead inside the first minute when Rasiak and Peschisolido threatened but Andy Impey cleared for the visitors.

There is often an early goal in these fixtures, as shown by the previous season's meeting, and it was no different this time around as Burley's men showed their best flowing football to steam past Forest and go in front.

The move started in front of the two benches inside the Derby half and involved Taylor, Jeff Kenna and Bisgaard as it swiftly reached the Forest penalty area.

Bisgaard laid the ball back to Idiakez, who in turn squared it on for Smith, running in from the left, to neatly finish with a perfectly-placed shot beyond Paul Gerrard.

Despite falling behind so early Forest were not willing to give an inch and Wes Morgan headed over from a corner as they threatened an equaliser.

Then Morgan was in more familiar defensive action to deny Bisgaard with a good challenge shortly after Rasiak had taken too long when a chance looked to be opening up on the edge of the box.

A golden chance to double their lead fell Derby's way on 20 minutes when they were awarded a penalty.

The initial opportunity came from a free kick that Taylor met but his header was handled by Impey, leaving referee Graham Laws little choice but to point to the spot.

Forest protested and Gerrard was then booked for time-wasting, which may well have contributed to what happened next as the usually-calm Taylor, having waited to take his kick, blazed the ball well over the bar and into the Forest fans behind the goal.

Derby's early momentum deserted them after Taylor's miss and Forest pushed on in search of an equaliser with Impey and David Johnson both looking to carve out chances.

But gradually the Rams did restore some of their superiority and began to create some half-chances for themselves while the visitors' frustrations were starting to boil, as evidenced by an exchange on the sidelines between coach Mick Harford and midfielder Andy Reid.

It was Reid who had Forest's best opportunity of the first half but he narrowly missed the target with a free kick from 20 yards, and at the other end Gerrard was scrambling to keep out Rasiak's powerful shot on the turn.

Yellow cards began to come either side of half-time as the flow of the game disappeared for a while, then there was a delay early in the second period as Forest's Jack Lester went down with a serious-looking knee injury and received treatment before being replaced.

Then tempers started to flare with players from both sides squaring up to each other on a couple of occasions before eventually the football returned and Michael Dawson cleared a dangerous cross away from in front of his own goal.

Idiakez became the seventh player to be cautioned but the Rams were soon showing their better side again and they doubled their lead with 15 minutes left.

Another fine move sent Smith away down the left and he beat John Thompson with ease before delivering an inviting cross to the far post where Rasiak met it with his head and applied the finishing touch.

It wasn't quite game over as Forest showed some fight with Thompson seeing a shot tipped over and Gareth Taylor heading wide but you always felt that if another goal was going to come, it would be scored by the home side.

And that was exactly how things panned out as Derby made it 3-0 with a couple of minutes remaining.

Ian Taylor picked up the ball in midfield and played it out to the right where Bisgaard had time to line up his first-time delivery which arrowed low across the Forest penalty area for Rasiak to touch home and net his second of the game.

Substitute Adam Bolder almost added a fourth but Forest were well and truly beaten as Derby recorded their biggest victory over their rivals from along the A52 since November 1979.

It was a performance the Derby supporters knew their team was capable of, a feeling backed up by Burley when he spoke after the match.

'I think we have shown the fans this season that we have come a long way and today we were on top from start to finish,' he said.

'I'm pleased for the fans because it's been a difficult few years. Because we hadn't won any of our previous three games I think there was a bit of tension, but we came through.

'You couldn't single anyone out. Going forward we were outstanding and everyone played a part today.

'You don't mind how you score but today we hit three very good goals – the build-up play was outstanding.

'The penalty miss could have knocked us back but we came back well in the second half.'

The two teams did not meet again until the return fixture at the City Ground in February, by which time their respective seasons were really taking shape.

Derby had put themselves in contention for promotion to the Premier League by getting right into the race for the play-off places while Forest faced an altogether different fight to avoid relegation to League 1.

It finished 2-2 in Nottingham with Rasiak again scoring twice, cementing his status as a hero among Rams fans if just for his goals against the old enemy.

That under-sells the Pole's contribution somewhat as, although he only scored twice more in 2004/05 after that February brace, his tally of 17 goals saw him top the club's charts and play a crucial role in guiding Derby to fourth place.

That earned them a crack at the play-offs but they suffered heartbreak with a 2-0 aggregate defeat to Preston North End, managed by Billy Davies, who would later have influential spells at both Derby and Forest.

Rasiak missed a penalty in the second leg against Preston and scored two more goals at the start of 2005/06 before joining Tottenham Hotspur in a £2m deal at the end of the August transfer window.

His four goals in a Derby shirt against Forest put him level with Rob Hulse and Archie Goodall as the club's second-highest return – behind the great Steve Bloomer, who is well ahead on 27.

Forest did eventually get relegated at the end of 2004/05 and spent the next three seasons in League 1, meaning hostilities did not resume until 2008/09 which produced some more memorable encounters and interesting stories.

v Southampton 2-3

(AET, 4-4 on aggregate, Derby won 4-3 on penalties)
15 May 2007. Attendance: 30,602
Pride Park Stadium. Football League Championship Play-Off Semi-Final Second Leg

DERBY COUNTY:	SOUTHAMPTON:
Bywater	Davis
Mears	Makin (Belmadi 71)
Moore	Pele
Leacock	Baird
McEveley	Cranie
Fagan (Currie 105)	Viafara
Oakley	Skacel
S Johnson (Jones 86)	Guthrie (Idiakez 83)
Pearson	Surman
Macken (Barnes 62)	Best
Howard	Saganowski (Rasiak 74)
Unused subs: Camp (GK), Edworthy	*Unused subs:* Bialkowski (GK), Wright-Phillips
Referee: Andy D'Urso	

THERE is always an argument that play-off games are among the most exciting and dramatic you will see anywhere in the English football system, especially in the Championship where promotion to the Premier League is the ultimate prize for the winners.

This was Derby County's fourth crack at the end-of-season mini-tournament having been beaten in the 1992 semi-finals by Blackburn Rovers, the 1994 final at Wembley by Leicester City, and the 2005 semi-finals by Preston North End.

That 2005 occasion had a remarkable amount of connections to the 2007 showdown against Southampton.

Two years previously, Derby were managed by George Burley while Preston were guided by Billy Davies.

By the 2007 event Davies was in the Derby hot-seat while Burley was in charge of Southampton.

In Burley's squad were Spanish midfielder Inigo Idiakez, Derby's Player of the Year in that 2005 campaign, and Polish striker Grzegorz Rasiak, who was their leading scorer.

Both were big fan favourites as was midfielder Matt Oakley during his 12 years with the Saints – he left the South Coast club in the summer of 2006 to join Derby and had been an inspirational captain across 2006/07.

Southampton also had in their ranks defender Chris Makin, who had played 13 games for Derby in 2004/05, along with goalkeeper Kevin Miller who joined the Rams shortly after Makin and sat on the bench regularly as cover for first-choice stopper Lee Camp.

The two teams had met on the opening day of 2006/07 and shared the points in a televised 2-2 draw that saw Seth Johnson put Derby in front, Bradley Wright-Phillips and 17-year-old Gareth Bale turn things around, only for Paul Peschisolido to climb off the bench and equalise in stoppage time.

Derby County's Greatest Games

By the time they faced off at the St Mary's Stadium in February 2007 Derby were in command of the Championship and a 1-0 win, earned by Steve Howard's late strike after Davies's team soaked up plenty of early home pressure, left them six points clear at the top of the table.

Curiously, they didn't then keep another clean sheet until 20 April by which time their hopes of automatic promotion were hanging by a thread and a 2-0 defeat at Crystal Palace the following week in their penultimate match confirmed them in third, with Birmingham City and Sunderland taking the top two spots.

The Saints beat Southend United 4-1 on the final day with Derby seeing off already-relegated Leeds United 2-0 to set up the play-off match, with the first leg of the semi-final to be played on the South Coast.

That match took a similar form to the Championship encounter in February as Southampton came out of the traps quickly and this time they opened the scoring through Andrew Surman's curling effort.

But once again Derby battled back and Howard headed them level on 36 minutes before notching his second of the afternoon and 19th of a season in which he was voted as the fans' Player of the Year with a penalty in the 58th minute.

That was enough for the Rams to take a 2-1 lead back to Pride Park Stadium for the second leg.

But as anyone who has seen play-off games will know, bringing an advantage home from an away tie first up – especially a slender 2-1 scoreline – guarantees precisely nothing.

Both managers were also well aware of the ups and downs of play-off football with Burley having taken Ipswich Town to defeat in the semi-finals three times before earning promotion to the Premier League in 2000 via a Wembley final against Barnsley, before his experience with Derby in 2005.

Davies was in his third successive tournament as after getting past Derby in 2005 his Preston side lost to West Ham United in the final, and a year later they were beaten by Leeds in the semis.

And this time around he was solely focused on finishing the job and getting Derby to Wembley.

Prior to the second leg he told the *Derby Telegraph*, 'We had a very good performance and result on Saturday but we start again – we know the game is far from over and there's lots to play for.

'It's a play-off game and both teams will go out trying to win. I expect it to be end-to-end, I expect there to be lots of chances and a number of goals.

'I said before the first leg that we had to try and win both matches. We managed to do that in the first game and now we are focused on the second match.

'Anything is possible in the play-offs, we know that. The ones who turn up on the night will be the fortunate ones who go to Wembley.

'We are very much looking forward to it because of the position we have put ourselves in.'

There was an added twist for the winners as they would go forward to play in the first Championship play-off final at the newly-rebuilt Wembley Stadium with the previous six finals having been played at Cardiff's Millennium Stadium.

In a curious echo of 2005, Derby went into the semi-finals with a major injury headache to contend with.

Back then, Idiakez and Rasiak had missed the first leg at Preston before being rushed back for the second when clearly not fully fit.

This time around the concern was teenager Giles Barnes, whose season was apparently over after being carried off on a stretcher in that defeat at Palace with a knee injury.

Barnes missed the first leg at Southampton but was a surprise – and welcome – name on the bench for the second as Derby kept the same starting XI while the Saints made several changes, notably goalkeeper Kelvin Davis replacing Bartosz Bialkowski.

Davis's first act was to pick the ball out of the back of the net with just three minutes gone after Darren Moore had met Oakley's corner with a towering header that put Derby 3-1 up on aggregate.

But any hopes of the Rams cruising to Wembley from here on in were dashed within 90 seconds.

Moore's back-pass to Stephen Bywater proved a challenge and the goalkeeper could only head the ball out to around 40 yards from goal, where Jhon Viafara volleyed it straight back over the stopper to bring Saints level on the night.

Derby remained on the front foot as Davies saved Howard's header before Seth Johnson and Craig Fagan went close with low drives while at the other end Surman also fired one wide.

The Rams went in at half-time still with the advantage overall but they knew that things could change for them in a single moment.

And that moment arrived in the 54th minute. They were caught cold by a ball from Leon Best that sent Viafara away on the right and the big Colombian midfielder steadied himself inside the area before hammering his shot beyond Bywater for 3-3 on aggregate.

From there it could have gone either way but Davies didn't wait too long before trying to regain the impetus as he introduced Barnes for Macken with 62 minutes gone.

And that move paid dividends very quickly as Barnes forced the visitors into conceding a corner that Johnson swung in and the teenager challenged for with Best, who got the final touch to head it past his own goalkeeper.

From that point the tension was unbearable as every minute ticking by on the scoreboard seemed to take an hour to complete.

Saints introduced Rasiak on 74 minutes and Idiakez later with both men looking to perform a salvage job against their old club while Rams fans were fearing the twist of their former favourites ending their promotion hopes.

And Wembley was just minutes away when the first of those nightmares became a reality.

The stadium clock showed 89 minutes but Derby failed to clear the ball and it fell inside the box to Rasiak, who drove it home for a 4-4 aggregate score and extra time.

Fagan was Derby's biggest threat in the extra period, just failing to reach one cross from Stephen Pearson and also hitting the bar from Howard's flick, while Rasiak also went close to a winner but the two sides could not be separated so a remarkable night went all the way to penalties, which were taken in front of the massed visiting fans in the South Stand.

Nottingham-born Best stepped up first and put his kick wide of Bywater's left-hand post and then it went back and forth with Howard, Barnes, David Jones and Jay McEveley all scoring for Derby leaving Saints needing to net their fourth penalty otherwise the Rams were through.

The man tasked with the challenge was Idiakez, who had scored several times from the spot in his Derby career – but who had missed a few as well.

By this time the rain was pouring down as the Spaniard walked forward and he went for power rather than placement with his shot. That proved a bad move as he blazed his effort way over the crossbar, sending Derby to Wembley and sparking wild celebrations that involved a mass pitch invasion from the stands, the supporters not caring about getting a soaking in the most torrential of downpours.

The scenes witnessed at Pride Park that night have remained firmly in the memory of those who were either there and involved or witnessed them from the stands or on TV.

Davies had not been able to watch the penalty shoot-out, so high was the tension, but after Idiakez's wayward effort he leapt to his feet to join the celebrations.

And he admitted that what followed was an emotional occasion when he spoke in the post-match aftermath.

He said, 'It was an unbelievable sight and made the hairs stand up on the back of your neck. The emotion and what it means to the fans is quite incredible.

'It was chaos in the tunnel and on the pitch. There were fans laughing, crying and hugging each other. I have never seen so much emotion in my life.'

Guiding his side to Wembley gave Davies the chance to win promotion two years ahead of schedule having spoken of a 'three-year plan' after his appointment the previous summer.

The Rams' opponents were unknown at the time with Wolverhampton Wanderers and West Bromwich Albion – the Baggies holding a 3-2 lead from the first leg at Molineux – playing their second match at The Hawthorns 24 hours later.

Though Davies wasn't concerning himself with that just yet as he basked in triumph after an amazing night.

'We are at Wembley, and one game away from the Premiership,' he said. 'It's difficult to describe how I feel and how far we have come in such a short period of time.

'Great credit goes to everybody – the players, the board, the staff and the fans, whose support was absolutely fantastic. Everybody has put in so much work.'

And the match itself had panned out how Davies had expected it to do with five goals, lots of chances, and a breathless pace from first whistle to last.

He added, 'It was a great game, end to end, but I thought over the two legs we thoroughly deserved it.

'The players did not stop and we have shown great character all season and did so again with the penalties.

'Great credit to both sets of players and it is an absolute nightmare for Southampton to lose on penalties in the play-offs. It is a sickener for them but I'm just delighted we got through.'

And in every great game there also has to be a loser with Burley once again suffering play-off agony.

But the Scot, who had been in charge of the Saints since December 2005, was magnanimous in defeat.

He said, 'It's been a terrific season. The team are moving forward and there are a lot of encouraging signs.

'I'm very proud, there's no regrets. We worked our socks off, the players played as best they could and really deserved to get to the final but in football you don't always get what you deserve.'

Derby's night of celebration continued before attentions turned to the Wembley final over the next couple of days, by which time their opponents had been confirmed with West Brom winning their second leg 1-0 to complete a 4-2 aggregate success.

And author Phil, who had been commentating on the game for Ram FM, became something of a mobile phone sensation as his description of the match-winning penalty was released by the radio station as a text message alert tone, leading to him having the bizarre experience of being in a shop and hearing his own voice blaring out when someone near him received a text!

44 v West Bromwich Albion 1-0

28 May 2007. Attendance: 74,993
Wembley Stadium. Championship Play-Off Final

THERE was never any real doubt when compiling the list that the 2006/07 play-off final was going to be included. It was not the greatest spectacle of those in the book, and neither was it among the greatest performances.

Many, including most neutrals, would argue that Derby weren't the better team on the day and that by all normal rules of fairness West Bromwich Albion should have won promotion on that rainy May afternoon.

It is a reasonable viewpoint and could equally have been made of the semi-final matches against Southampton.

It was symptomatic of the season as a whole. Billy Davies's Derby County side on many occasions came away from games with victories that left supporters asking themselves 'how did we manage that?', and even those of us in the media were perplexed.

I (author Phil) was covering the club on a daily basis for Ram FM at the time and regularly I would sit down with Steve Nicholson of the *Derby Telegraph* and Colin Gibson from Radio Derby, and we would ask each other how we got away with it again. The number of times we did that must have run into double figures.

It was ever the way with the side that Davies and his team of loyal assistants put together. They were solid as a team, worked for each other, and dug deep for victory.

The first half of the season had seen the Rams put down solid foundations, and although they wobbled a little after the turn of the year, partially caused by bringing in more new players and seemingly upsetting the mix that was in place, they amassed enough points to earn a place in the post-season shake-up.

For me it was an incredible time. My commentary of the penalty shoot-out in the second leg of the semi-final, as Inigo Idiakez blasted his spot-kick over the bar, was turned by Ram FM into a downloadable ringtone.

I have to admit that I totally lost it as the ball sailed skywards, and for weeks afterwards as I wandered around supermarkets and public places I frequently heard the sound of me going mental as complete strangers answered calls on their mobiles from loved ones.

As a bizarre footnote, Dino and Pete from the radio station breakfast crew rang me up a few days after the ringtone was created to tell me that if ringtones had actually counted I was number 37 in the national download charts that week!

The play-off final itself was billed as 'the most valuable prize in football in the world', a claim that was easy to justify as with television rights and parachute payments it was conservatively estimated that the winners would make in the region of £60m even if they went straight back down again as the worst-placed Premier League side the following season. But none of that was concerning Davies or his players as they came down off the massive high that was the semi-final victory over Southampton before preparing for the big day.

They had finished third over the regular 46-game season, eight points clear of West Brom in fourth, and the points had been shared between the two sides in the two meetings.

Derby won the first, 2-1 at Pride Park Stadium in November having come from behind to earn the victory with a Matt Oakley screamer and Giles Barnes's header, then a month later they lost 1-0 at The Hawthorns as a result of John Hartson's late strike.

That was in the back end of 2006 and come May 2007 it was all about the history of the first Championship play-off final at the newly-rebuilt Wembley Stadium, and the glory of earning a place in the Premier League, from which Derby had been relegated in 2002 while the Baggies were aiming to go back up at the first attempt.

And in the build-up, Davies said, 'It's as simple as that – 90 minutes away from Premier League football, a 50-50 chance, a wonderful occasion for the fans and players, and everyone at the club.

'It has been an outstanding season so far and we want to finish that off by putting in an excellent performance on the day, getting the breaks that matter and trying to take this club to the Premier League.

'We have prepared very well this week, we have worked extremely hard on the details we need to look at and we're very much ready.

'The players are buoyant as you can imagine, they are ready for this game, the spirit is excellent and at this moment in time we have a clean bill of health.

'We have prepared the team very well. Once you cross the white line that's it. There's nothing the manager can do, or anyone else, it's down to the individual players to perform to their best and do what they're good at.

'These guys have been a pleasure to work with and we'll keep that going until Monday but once they cross that white line all they can do is what they have done all season and hopefully they can do it one more time.'

And popular midfielder Seth Johnson, in his second spell with the Rams, added, 'The fans have been great. It's a football city, a one-team city, and everyone is pulling in the same direction and rooting for us to go there and get the win.

'It's an exciting time for the club and the main thing that we want is to go there and get the win.

'It's going to be a great day out for the supporters but it's not a place to go and lose. We want to go there and make sure that we win this game, and come home knowing that the club is going to be in the Premier League next season.'

Derby County's Greatest Games

Amid the excitement as the final approached there was controversy over the sale of tickets with each club allocated around 33,500 seats at Wembley.

But the new Club Wembley seats, totalling around 15,000 of the stadium's 90,000 capacity, were likely to remain largely empty on the day because an agreement could not be reached between Wembley Stadium and the Football League over their sale to supporters of the clubs involved.

None of that mattered come Monday 28 May, however, and neither did the miserable weather as supporters of both clubs felt optimistic that this would be their year, creating a cracking atmosphere inside Wembley as kick-off time neared.

Ten of Derby's starting line-up basically picked itself but the final decision would be who to partner striker and Player of the Year Steve Howard.

In the end Paul Peschisolido got the nod ahead of Giles Barnes and Jon Macken, who were both on the bench, and it was the Canadian who had the Rams' first chance on ten minutes when he found himself bearing down on goal with time on his side but he couldn't produce the finish and shot straight at Dean Kiely.

But Derby might have already been behind as Diomansy Kamara served notice of his trickery with a mazy run and shot that Stephen Bywater turned away.

After Peschisolido's chance, the Baggies started to get the upper hand and with Jason Koumas particularly dangerous coming in off the left, Tyrone Mears had to perfectly time his challenge inside the box.

But it was Kevin Phillips who came closest to opening the scoring in the first half when, after being fed by Zoltan Gera on the edge of the box, he curled his shot off the top of the crossbar.

Early in the second half Bywater grabbed a shot from Koumas, and Kiely saved at the feet of Peschisolido, before the introduction of teenager Giles Barnes – still not fully fit but hoping to make an impact as he had done in the second leg of the semi-final against Southampton.

Barnes wasn't involved in Derby's best move of the match so far, captain Matt Oakley seeing his powerful drive superbly saved by Kiely following a clever pass from Craig Fagan, but he most certainly was a central figure just after the hour.

Fagan and Oakley snapped in with challenges inside the Derby half and the ball came out to Howard, who drove forward before slipping it to Barnes.

Barnes immediately drove his cross low in front of goal where Stephen Pearson came in to score from close range for his first goal since his January arrival from Celtic.

That was that as far as Derby's goalscoring chances were concerned as they looked to hold on to what they had and there were scares at the other end as West Brom pushed on in search of an equaliser.

Mears again superbly challenged Koumas and Bywater saved from Jonathan Greening and Paul Robinson, though he was never seriously tested.

Tempers got a little frayed as time ticked down and the Baggies mounted one last threat when Robinson's free kick in stoppage time was deflected wide for a corner, which Pearson then headed clear as referee Graham Poll theatrically blew the final whistle – on his own career too, as it was his last match.

The celebrations began immediately as Derby's return to the Premier League was confirmed and the sight of team skipper Oakley lifting the trophy alongside injured club captain Michael Johnson will forever remain etched on the minds of the club's supporters.

Davies spoke in the immediate aftermath of leading a side to play-off glory, following his failures in 2005 and 2006 with Preston North End, and he said, 'It's not about the money but the success of this club – we are delighted.

'The players deserve it – they showed great courage. Now all we can do is go and enjoy it and give it our best.

'They were magnificent and they deserve all they get. We just wanted to get the first goal – it was important.

'It is great credit to everyone. We were very organised and prepared all week.'

But while that was a standard post-match manager offering, some of Davies's other comments quickly started to sour the occasion for Rams fans.

He spoke of how great the achievement was without his 'right arm', his former Preston assistant boss David Kelly who hadn't been able to join him in the move from Deepdale in 2006 due to contractual issues.

And he also offered thinly-veiled threats that, while Derby would be in the Premier League in 2007/08, he might not be the man managing them.

Citing people at the club who he said had criticised and in some cases 'abused' his players with their comments, along with what he felt was a lack of patience 'in and around the club', Davies was suggesting that he might walk away.

He said, 'There's lots of talking to be done. I'm very proud, I'm not saying I don't want to be manager of Derby County but I don't think anything's 100 per cent guaranteed.

'I'm not prepared to discuss it at the moment but I'll sit down with people at the club and then see what happens after that.

'I'm not saying I won't be Derby manager next season but it's always been my intention to get to the end of the season and then think about my future.

'I thank everyone at the club who supported us and others at the club who have criticised my players – even put the boot in at times – I thank them as well because they've been our inspiration at times.'

Davies's outburst was broadcast in the after-match media interviews and following the press conference with newspaper journalists and soon found its way to the attention of Derby's fans.

The players, however, were purely focused on their achievement, and match-winner Pearson said, 'It was a massive goal and I'm delighted for everyone connected with the club. It will live long in the memory.

'It's been remarkable, the turnaround. With the changes in personnel it normally takes time and it has been an amazing achievement.'

Striker Howard revealed, 'I can't describe it. I'm absolutely over the moon. What a day. It was tough, they are a good side and it was always going to be tough but we dug in deep.

'We deserved that and the manager deserved that.'

Chairman Peter Gadsby added, 'We were dead and buried a year ago and thought the chance had gone.

'We had a three-year plan and it has been accelerated – that is all down to Billy and his team.

'This is great credit to him and all the lads. It means a lot to us and the East Midlands and we will enjoy it.'

I experienced a decidedly odd moment in the mixed zone where post-match interviews take place as West Brom manager Tony Mowbray could clearly be heard humming the tune to the terrace chant 'da da da da Stevie Howard' as he made his way down the line.

The night after the victory, thousands of fans lined the streets of Derby to welcome their heroes home from Wembley and celebrate the victory.

Then it was a case of turning attentions fully towards preparing for life in the Premier League.

Davies would remain in charge after seemingly settling his differences and signing a one-year extension to his contract, while he got his wish with Kelly eventually joining him as assistant manager and former Scotland boss Craig Brown arrived as 'football consultant'.

Davies broke Derby's transfer record in the summer of 2007 with the signing of Robert Earnshaw from Norwich City for £3.5m and he also spent big on Claude Davis, £3m from Sheffield United, along with lower-key signings like Lewis Price, Andy Griffin and Benny Feilhaber before adding Eddie Lewis early in the following season.

But it did not take long for the glory to become a thing of the past, while the Wembley victory turned out to be the 147th and final appearance in a Rams shirt by Seth Johnson as the knee injury that forced him off late on would ultimately end his playing career.

And author Gareth ended up getting his hands on the play-off final trophy too – when he looked after it following the celebratory bus tour and ended up with it back in his flat, where it sat proudly on the mantelpiece until he went back to work at Pride Park the following morning!

45 v Newcastle United 1-0

17 September 2007. Attendance: 33,016
Pride Park Stadium. Premier League

DERBY COUNTY:	NEWCASTLE UNITED:
Bywater	Harper
Mears	Taylor (Beye 75)
Leacock	Cacapa
Davis	Rozenhal
Griffin	Smith
Teale	N'Zogbia
Oakley	Geremi (Faye 60)
Pearson	Milner
Lewis (McEveley 87)	Butt
Howard	Owen (Martins 55)
Miller (Feilhaber 80)	Viduka
Unused subs: Earnshaw, Todd, Jones	*Unused subs:* Given (GK), Pattison
Referee: Peter Walton	

BY everyone's admission the Premier League had been a real culture shock for the Rams when they went up via the play-offs under Billy Davies.

There were a number of reasons for this.

Promotion through a Wembley victory meant that the club was automatically three weeks behind every other outfit in the top flight with preparations; many of the players in your price zone would have already been snapped up, your current players have less relaxation and recuperation time during the close season and so on.

It should also be remembered that Davies and the board of directors had put together a three-year plan which incredibly took the club into the promised land at the first time of asking.

Inevitably this meant that some of the team building that had gone on during the previous summer included some players who were brought in to help on the journey but who would not be expected to be used at the final destination.

Added to the list of odds against was, of course, the fact that the top division had changed hugely in the time since Derby had gone down in 2002.

The Premier League was absolutely awash with money, meaning that even clubs with smaller fan bases, less tradition, and less impressive facilities were streets ahead of Derby when budgeting for the forthcoming season

The campaign had started brightly enough as the fixture compilers had given the Rams an opening day game against Portsmouth. It ended all square, but the 2-2 draw at least showed that Derby had the heart to fight back and gain something when defeat was looking likely. It also gave them their first point.

The second game was away at big-spending Manchester City, and although that ended in defeat by one goal at least the game being so tight suggested it was possible to run the big boys close.

Matters rather started to unravel after that. A trip to North London ended with a 4-0 defeat against Tottenham Hotspur, and further losses against Birmingham City, Blackpool on penalties in the League Cup at Pride Park Stadium, and an absolute mauling by Liverpool who scored six without reply at Anfield suggested that the wheels were coming off in spectacular fashion.

Davies's men, who had looked rock solid in defence and dangerous in attack only a few months earlier, were now leaking goals like there was no tomorrow while treating the opposing goal as foreign land never to be explored.

Davies turned to experienced Scottish international striker Kenny Miller to provide a potent goal threat, and circumstances dictated that the man signed from Celtic would make his debut in front of millions thanks to Sky on a Monday night at Pride Park against Newcastle United.

Miller had been captured at the end of the August transfer window but had to wait to make his bow because of the international break, during which time the Rams lost Craig Fagan to a suspension after he was found guilty by the FA of an off-the-ball incident at Liverpool. But this night was all about Miller and his spectacular introduction to life as Derby's new number 14.

Playing alongside target man Steve Howard, a lifelong Newcastle fan, Miller struck the crucial blow six minutes before half-time.

Stephen Bywater's clearance had gone long into the Newcastle half but was not dealt with by the visitors and dropped to Miller, some 30 yards from goal.

Miller took a touch to control the ball, set his sights and unleashed a curling shot with the outside of his right foot that looped up then dipped back under the bar and into the back of Steve Harper's net.

Miller had earlier failed to take a good opportunity after creating a chance for himself, as had full-back Tyrone Mears, and their nerves were perhaps indicative of Derby's troubled start to the season.

Newcastle had earlier had chances of their own, notably when James Milner broke free and found Michael Owen but the England striker went too far after rounding Bywater and David Rozenhal could not convert his pull-back.

The goal came after the visitors saw a strong penalty appeal turned down after they argued that Leacock had fouled Rozenhal, then the same pairing clashed again after the break but once more referee Peter Walton saw nothing wrong.

Derby were well worth the three points after putting in a performance of grit, determination and no shortage of good football that belied how badly they had started the season. They could, and perhaps should, have been further out of sight but Howard missed with two good headed chances to score against his favourite club, the sort of opportunity he had taken with clinical regularity during the promotion season.

But 1-0 was enough and it seemed that, after an uplifting night under the Pride Park floodlights, the two-week international break had been just what the doctor ordered.

Relief that the first Premier League win had been registered was clear on the faces of players, management and supporters alike after the game.

Newcastle may not have been a top four side but were at least of a standard to suggest that Derby could stand shoulder to shoulder with genuine Premier League clubs and match them blow for blow.

The points lifted the Rams off the foot of the table and everyone started optimistically looking upwards.

Whatever the season held, at least they were not going to take the record for the longest sequence of games since the start of a campaign before registering a win.

Interviewed after the game by the BBC, Davies was upbeat and bullish as he said, 'We're up and running.

'We have a lot of hard work ahead, but hopefully we can kick on. We controlled the game and the chances we created were first-class.

'I'm delighted with the players and they can take a lot of confidence from this victory.'

It proved to be no more than fighting talk. The following Saturday they travelled to the Emirates and conceded five without reply against an admittedly very good Arsenal side.

When they only managed a 1-1 draw at home to Bolton Wanderers – one of the sides that they needed to beat on their own patch if they were to have a realistic chance of survival – it became clear that Derby as a Premier League club were in big trouble, even though Miller netted his second goal in three games.

The season never did turn round. By late November Davies and his backroom staff were out to be replaced by Paul Jewell, who had enjoyed success in charge of Wigan Athletic and Bradford City previously.

Jewell had been appointed by Adam Pearson, the Rams' new chairman who had taken over from Peter Gadsby after buying a majority shareholding in the club.

And there were more changes off the field in January 2008 when a consortium managed by American company General Sports and Entertainment took over the club in a deal apparently worth £50m.

But on the field, despite wholesale changes of players during the January window that included the signing of Robbie Savage, never a popular figure at Pride Park, the season lurched from one nightmare to the next.

After the Bolton game Derby did not pick up another point until 20 October, a 0-0 draw at Fulham, then lost their next seven – though Howard did score their first away goal of the season on 8 December when losing 4-1 at Manchester United.

The run of defeats was ended, ironically, with a 2-2 draw away to Newcastle that saw the home side only escape with a point thanks to a late equaliser.

But it got no better. On only one occasion did Derby manage to go two games unbeaten, when they drew 1-1 at home to Manchester City on 30 January 2008 – two days after the GSE takeover – and 2-2 at Birmingham City the following Saturday.

A 0-0 draw at home to Sunderland on 1 March took the Rams to ten points for the season and they made it 11 with a 2-2 scoreline at Pride Park against Fulham at the end of the month.

That was as good as it got as, ironically after one of their better performances of the season, Derby were relegated that day – the top flight's lowest ever exit through the trapdoor. They lost all of their remaining six matches, including a final-day 4-0 drubbing at home to Reading who still joined them in going down.

Their 11 points is an English record in the era of three for a win; the single victory is a joint low alongside Loughborough's Second Division season of 1899/1900; the 20 goals scored is a low for English football's top flight in any of its guises – all of which it is hard to see ever being beaten.

The abysmal form stretched over into the 2008/09 season too as Derby did not win another league game until 13 September – almost an entire calendar year – when beating Sheffield United, ending a run of 38 games without a victory that is also a record.

46 v Forest Green Rovers 4-3

3 January 2009. Attendance: 4,836
The New Lawn. FA Cup Third Round

DERBY COUNTY:	FOREST GREEN ROVERS:
Carroll	Burton
Albrechtsen (Powell HT)	Gill
Beardsley	Jones
Nyatanga	Clist
Addison	Kempson
Camara	Stonehouse
Green	Rigoglioso
Commons	Fowler
Teale (Barazite 71)	Smith (Afful 64)
Varney (Davies 81)	Lawless
Hulse	Mangan (Mohamed 68)
Unused subs: Bywater (GK), Barnes, Savage, Villa	*Unused subs:* Robinson (GK), Preece, Thomas, McDonald, Platt
Referee: Paul Taylor	

DERBY COUNTY'S FA Cup history is not exactly littered with great games and memorable successes, so poor they have generally been in the world's greatest cup competition.

But when the draw for the 2008/09 third round was made and paired the Rams with Conference National side Forest Green Rovers there was a sense of stepping into the unknown.

Indeed, the first call one of your authors received after the news broke asked simply, 'Where the hell is Forest Green Rovers?'

As it happened, Gareth had prior experience of the club having visited them back in 2001 for an FA Trophy tie with Matlock Town – but this was to be something completely different altogether.

Forest Green Rovers are based in Nailsworth, a small town near Stroud in Gloucestershire, and have been in existence in various guises since 1890 but had only been in the Conference since 1998 and had not threatened to win promotion to the Football League.

They had reached the FA Trophy Final in 1999, losing to Kingstonian at Wembley, an occasion which saw them become the first side ever to reach the final of both the FA Trophy and the FA Vase, a competition they won back in 1982, then they reached the FA Trophy Final again in 2001 after eliminating Matlock in the last 32.

Known as 'The Little Club on the Hill' due to their ground – The Lawn – being situated on top of a hill, Forest Green enjoyed a couple of decent FA Cup runs and moved stadiums in 2006.

Not that they moved far as they relocated just a few hundred yards up the road to what became known as The New Lawn with their old venue replaced by housing.

Derby had actually played at The Lawn before under Jim Smith, having sent a team down for a testimonial match in the early part of the new millennium, but this was unsurprisingly the first competitive meeting between the two sides and therefore their first visit to the new stadium, in which Rovers were hosting their first ever match in the third round of the FA Cup having gone one round further than in the previous season.

Their path had been largely untroubled, though they needed a replay to beat Ashford (Middlesex) 4-0 in the fourth qualifying round then won 1-0 at Team Bath in the first round proper, before going on to cause a stir by beating Rochdale – then of League 2 – 2-0 at The New Lawn in the second round.

Their form going into the meeting with Derby had been poor as since beating Rochdale they had won just one Conference match, 2-1 at home to Barrow in their final outing before third round day, and in that time they had also lost 3-2 at home to Nigel Clough's Burton Albion.

But if Rovers were struggling, Derby were well and truly in trouble as they had won just once in the Championship since 15 November, a 1-0 victory at home to Watford in mid-December, and although they had also reached the semi-finals of the League Cup – with the first leg at home to Manchester United to come just four days after the visit to Gloucestershire – there was turmoil at Pride Park.

The year had ended with Paul Jewell's resignation following a home defeat by Ipswich Town so his former assistant boss Chris Hutchings had been tasked with leading the side at Forest Green.

Hutchings went into the match well aware of the potential for an upset if his players were not on their game.

He told the *Derby Telegraph*, 'They [the Forest Green players] will run that extra mile instead of that extra inch.

'It is all about attitude – we've got to make sure we have players out there who are willing to do the same. That's what I'll be looking for.

'It's a massive game for them and they want to try to show us what they can do.

'We have had them watched and got reports on them, so we have a good idea of what to expect. Jim Harvey's teams are renowned for trying to play football and that is all credit to him.

'We are looking forward to going down there and pitting our wits against them.'

Hutchings would be assisted at The New Lawn by Brian Borrows and David Lowe, two of the coaches from the Rams' Academy, following the departure of first-team coach Mark Seagraves.

And he praised how the players had dealt with the changes, adding, 'The players have responded very well in the circumstances, as I would expect them to.

'Its just a matter now of business as usual and getting down to preparing for the game.'

You had to go back to December 1985 for the last time Derby faced non-league opposition in the FA Cup, when they beat Telford United 6-1 at the Baseball Ground, though one of their darkest hours came in 1955 when Boston United – including six former Rams – beat them 6-1 at the BBG, a record victory for a non-league team against Football League opposition.

So everything was well and truly in place for a proper FA Cup shock – the non-league side at home to their illustrious opponents, who were in chaos at the time, a packed and raucous home crowd, a 3pm kick-off on third round day, bright sunshine and yet a frozen pitch.

There were concerns over whether the game would go ahead, such was the condition of the playing surface, but referee Paul Taylor deemed it fit enough even though one of the goal areas – which was blocked from receiving any sun by the stand behind the goal – was almost solid.

That was the end Derby defended in the first half so Roy Carroll opted for padded trousers rather than regular shorts and he lined up behind a much-changed defence that included a couple of unexpected faces in the full-back positions.

On the left was Mo Camara, who had not featured in a Derby squad since September 2007's 6-0 mauling at Liverpool in the Premier League. He had been on loan at Norwich City later that season then went to Blackpool for the first few months of 2008/09.

On the right was Jason Beardsley, who had at at least been involved in match squads as an unused substitute over the previous 16 months but was making only his second senior appearance with his debut having come against Blackpool in the League Cup in August 2007.

And the pair must have wondered what had hit them when Derby found themselves two down to their non-league challengers with just 20 minutes gone, a start that made a mockery of the 76 places between the two clubs on the league ladder.

The first goal arrived with 14 on the clock as Derby failed to deal with a long ball and Jonathan Smith let fly with a volley from outside the box that left Carroll with no chance.

Carroll was beaten at his near post six minutes later by an angled drive from Alex Lawless, who had been sent away down the right and left with plenty of space to run into – and all this after Carroll had prevented Adriano Rigoglioso from opening the scoring with just ten seconds played. Something had to change otherwise Derby were heading for humiliation and the first shoots of recovery arrived midway through the first half with Kris Commons switching from the left wing to a position behind lead striker Rob Hulse.

It was a move that immediately sparked new life into the Rams and with five minutes of the half left they were back in it through Hulse, who forced the rebound home after his first header from Commons's cross was saved by Terry Burton.

And before the break they were level with Martin Albrechtsen on the end of another teasing Commons delivery to nod in at the far post.

Derby might have gone in front in the second period through Luke Varney, who was denied by Burton, then Hulse missed the target with two good opportunities before later forcing Burton into a save only for Commons to put the rebound wide.

And with that Forest Green made them pay by taking the lead again with 18 minutes left through Paul Stonehouse, whose shot from just inside of the box squirmed past Carroll's dive and had the home fans anticipating an upset once more.

Their hopes were only raised for four minutes as Paul Green's crisp finish drove Derby level once more, then it appeared a replay at Pride Park would be necessary before late heartbreak for the home side.

Commons weaved his magic once again to get into the box where he was pulled down by Darren Jones who earned a straight red card for his troubles.

Up stepped Steven Davies, who had only been on the field for five minutes, to keep his head – and his balance on the now-icy surface – to hammer home the penalty and send Derby through.

Having come through a genuine FA Cup classic the over-riding feeling among those of a Derby persuasion was one of relief that they had avoided what would have been a serious embarrassment.

Hutchings admitted that his players were 'fortunate' to have got through.

He said, 'We were 2-0 down after 20 minutes and things were not looking too good. The game had gone away from us but all credit to the lads for coming back. They dug deep and that is all you can ask for.

'There are always upsets in the Cup and Forest Green is a place where you could get beaten and end up with egg on your face.

'We are fortunate to get through. I imagine Jim Harvey will feel a little bit aggrieved they haven't got at least a draw. But we are in the hat for the next round and that is the most important thing.

'I suppose we were in a no-win situation but, by hook or by crook, we've got through. Hopefully that will give us a bit of confidence.'

The tactical change of shifting Commons from a wider area to a more central position midway through the first half paid off for the Rams and Hutchings explained the thinking behind it.

'We had to change things because it was not working,' he said.

'We put Kris Commons in midfield to stop Lee Fowler picking the ball up for them.

'Kris can influence the game and we were on the back foot for the first 20 minutes. I thought when he went in there, it stopped them playing a bit and we were more of a threat.

'That worked quite well and equalising just before half-time was a big plus for us. We know Kris can play that role and he did well.

'Conceding to go 3-2 down didn't help but the lads came back and battled well. It wasn't a day for football, the conditions dictated that.'

And match-winner Davies revealed that, in the absence of regular penalty taker Nathan Ellington, it was between him and Green to take the crucial spot-kick.

He said, 'A few of the lads wanted it but me and Greenie stepped up. I asked him if I could have it and he didn't really want to give it to me.

'I said to him, "Come on lad, I haven't scored for a while. You've already scored today. Any chance?" Thankfully, he let me take it.'

Derby's FA Cup exploits continued in the next round while switching Commons to his position just off the striker paid dividends only four days later – you will read about both of those instances over the coming chapters.

The attendance of 4,836 remains at the time of writing a record for The New Lawn, while Forest Green repeated their feat of reaching the third round 12 months later but went down 2-1 away to Notts County.

Derby were not, however, so fortunate the next time they faced non-league opposition in the FA Cup – losing 2-1 away to Crawley Town in the 2010/11 third round thanks to a last-minute goal from the home side.

v Manchester United 1-0

7 January 2009. Attendance: 30,194
Pride Park Stadium. League Cup Semi-Final

DERBY COUNTY:	MANCHESTER UNITED:
Carroll	Kuszczak
Connolly	Rafael
Todd (Savage 87)	Vidic
Nyatanga	O'Shea
Camara	Evans
Sterjovski (Teale 58)	Anderson (Carrick 74)
Green	Scholes (Ronaldo 63)
Addison	Nani
Davies (Barazite 81)	Gibson
Commons	Tevez
Hulse	Welbeck (Rooney 63)
Unused subs: Bywater (GK), Powell, Hines, Dickinson	*Unused subs:* Amos (GK), Fletcher, Possebon, Giggs
Referee: Phil Dowd	

I T would be totally unjust to blame Paul Jewell for the continued decline of Derby County after the disastrous adventure that was the 2007/08 Premier League campaign. He inherited a squad that was ill-equipped for life in the top flight, and he was then given a considerable amount of money to use in the January transfer window in the vain hope that the club could survive in the Premier League.

Even at the time it seemed a bad idea, and Jewell and Adam Pearson – who had been part of the club's executive management when the decision to spend was made – admitted that it would have been a more sensible option to 'keep their powder dry' and spend big in the summer of 2008 in order to launch an assault on promotion back to the Prem.

It would be fair, however, to say that wins were initially as hard to come by under Jewell as they had been under Billy Davies.

In fact by the time that Jewell's Derby had registered their first victory in the league, a 2-1 win at home to Sheffield United on Saturday 13 September, almost an entire year had elapsed since the previous one at home to Newcastle United in the top flight.

There had been a success over Sheffield Wednesday in the previous season's FA Cup, but the game itself had ended all square with the Rams progressing via a successful penalty shoot-out following the replay at Hillsborough.

That said, there were genuine wins in the League Cup as in their second match of 2008/09 the Rams came from behind to beat League 2 side Lincoln City at Pride Park Stadium – though they needed extra time to see off the Imps 3-1 thanks to Nathan Ellington's hat-trick.

A victory inside 90 minutes arrived later in August as in the second round they triumphed 1-0 away to Preston North End thanks to Paul Green's header on a night that saw Paul Connolly take the captain's armband for the first time and teenager Miles Addison make his presence felt in midfield.

It seemed of little significance at the time as the League Cup in its various names was not a competition that particularly troubled Derby, who usually fell at the first or second hurdle.

This time was to prove different however. Circumstances dictated that it would not be until 4 November that Jewell's men travelled to the Withdean Stadium where they trounced Brighton & Hove Albion 4-1, with Ellington netting again and Tito Villa bagging a hat-trick.

Because of the delay to the Brighton tie the winners knew they would be at home in the fourth round just seven days later and waiting there were one of Derby's old enemies – Leeds United.

By now the Rams were finding the winning habit in the league, and with the confidence that created put Leeds away thanks to a 2-1 scoreline against their League 1 opponents with Villa and Ellington on target once more.

That was enough to put the club into the quarter-finals for the first time since 1990, when they were eliminated by West Ham United, and they were given a tough task with an away trip to Stoke City, promoted to the Premier League at the end of the previous season.

The Potters, in front of their vociferous Britannia Stadium fans, were expected to end any Pride Park interest in the competition for another year.

It is always cold at Stoke, even in the middle of a heatwave, but on a freezing Tuesday night in December there was little to warm the hardy bunch of Rams fans who had made the short journey down the A50.

There was not much good football being played by either team but Derby did have their moments to break down a typically dogged Stoke line-up.

And then, in stoppage time, came the incident that turned the game in the Rams' favour. Andy Griffin, a summer 2007 signing ahead of the Premier League season and now back at Stoke, was harshly adjudged to have handled Gary Teale's cross.

Ellington was the calmest man in the stadium as he casually rolled in his penalty and with no time for the home side to come back, the Rams were in the last four of the League Cup for the first time since 1968 when they were eliminated by Leeds.

They had last reached the semi-finals of a major competition in 1976 when they were beaten in the FA Cup by Manchester United – who would be their opponents this time around.

United were the defending Premier League and European champions, and after the draw was made they added the World Club Championship to their trophy cabinet.

And between the Stoke game and the first leg against United an awful lot happened for Derby.

Jewell had been taking stock of his ability to take the club forward, and resigned after a home defeat to Ipswich Town on 28 December 2008.

His assistant Chris Hutchings took charge for the next game, the FA Cup tie against non-league Forest Green Rovers. Derby's board then acted quickly to secure a full-time replacement for Jewell and chose the man with a magical name as far as Rams fans were concerned – Clough. Nigel, the son of Brian, to be precise.

Clough was scheduled to take over as manager the day after the first leg of the Manchester United game but was officially introduced to the press immediately before the match, making for the unusual situation of more journalists attending to speak to the new manager than to cover the game.

With Clough not taking over until the following day the Rams would be led by Academy coaches David Lowe and Brian Borrows, as Hutchings – who was scheduled to take charge – decided to leave once the announcement was made, though the pair largely stayed out of the pre-match spotlight and let the players do the talking.

Striker Rob Hulse, who had put Manchester United out of the competition during his days with West Bromwich Albion in 2003, said, 'As long as we put in a good performance and defend well as a team, then hopefully we can get something out the game and go to Old Trafford with it all to play for.

'We are going to need a massive performance. Everyone is going to need to be at their best to match Manchester United and, hopefully, some of their players won't be at their top level.

'That is how you get results against the best teams in the world. We need to all pull together and hope they have an off-day.'

Off the field, meanwhile, the club announced some special offers for supporters – a free black and white scarf would be given to every Rams fan, along with a free copy of the match programme, which had been increased in size to 100 pages to mark the special occasion.

One unfortunate omission from the programme was Andy Todd on the Rams' squad list at the back with the experienced defender having just returned from his loan spell at Northampton Town.

Todd was given a surprise recall to Derby's starting line-up, as was Mile Sterjovski for his first appearance since the win over Leeds, while Mo Camara kept his place at left-back.

Robbie Savage was among the substitutes and there were some big names on the United bench too with Ryan Giggs, Michael Carrick, Wayne Rooney and Cristiano Ronaldo all in reserve should they be required.

Derby made a bright opening with Sterjovski going close and Steven Davies twice being denied, once by goalkeeper Tomasz Kuszczak and once by Nemanja Vidic, and on 30 minutes they were deservedly in front.

Commons had started in behind striker Rob Hulse, following his successful switch there in the FA Cup tie at Forest Green, and he collected a pass inside from Sterjovski before steadying himself and rifling in an unstoppable shot well beyond the dive of Kuszczak. It seemed to take a split-second for the realisation to dawn that Derby were actually in front, so used to failure the fans had become over recent months.

Derby couldn't add to their advantage before half-time but they were rarely threatened and former United goalkeeper Roy Carroll was enjoying a quiet evening against his old club.

The visitors waited until just after the hour to bring on the big guns as Ronaldo and Rooney were introduced for Danny Welbeck and Paul Scholes, who had both found it tough going in the face of Derby's powerful performance.

Ronaldo's only real threat came with a dipping free kick within his usually deadly range but as Pride Park held its collective breath, the ball dropped just wide of the post.

And with ten minutes remaining the Rams might have gone 2-0 up. Commons beat John O'Shea before seeing Kuszczak parry his shot and Hulse, running in, could do nothing but make contact and hope – and unfortunately his shot went just over.

Paul Green also fired one just over the top and Carrick headed straight at Carroll but there was no doubting that Derby were good value for their victory.

And, given everything that was happening in the build-up to this clash, it was an outcome that surely nobody could have predicted.

It was a result that left everybody connected with Derby absolutely thrilled and put the club 90 minutes away from a first major final since 1946.

Match-winner Commons said, 'I'm delighted. I couldn't have caught it any sweeter and it flew in the bottom corner.

'To win 1-0 against the World Club champions – and to score the winning goal – is a dream come true.

'Everyone played their part. It was just one of those performances that you are going to remember for the rest of your life – to say that you performed against the best and came out on top. Defensively, I think that's the best we've played all season. Andy Todd came in and he was awesome.

'We definitely gave it to them from the first whistle and [Manchester United manager] Alex Ferguson said we could have won by more, which you don't usually hear.

'We played with confidence and no fear. We knocked it about a bit and, at times, we really did cause them problems.

'The fact they couldn't break us down and had to resort to the likes of Rooney, Ronaldo and Carrick – world-class players – is great credit to the lads.

'Hopefully, we can keep them at bay for another 90 minutes but, whatever happens in the second leg, this is a great achievement.'

Ferguson had indeed admitted his side had deserved their loss, and he said, 'I think we are lucky. We could have lost by more.

'In any semi-final you hope to give yourself breathing space and you hope to win the game.

'But we expect to recover from a 1-0 deficit against anyone at Old Trafford and I am sure we will.

'We were so bad and Derby will rue the fact they didn't score more.'

With Clough taking over the following day, the result meant that Lowe ended his caretaker spell in charge with a win in his single match, as Hutchings had done previously, so Clough's first game leading the Rams would mean a third different manager in as many matches.

Due to bad weather Clough's Derby managerial debut was delayed for ten days as a frozen pitch at Cardiff City denied him the chance to build on the feel good factor.

His first game in charge was a defeat at home to Queens Park Rangers, followed by the second leg of the League Cup semi-final at Old Trafford.

Nani, O'Shea and Tevez scored before half-time but a Giles Barnes penalty with ten minutes of the 90 remaining meant the Rams were a goal away from extra time.

Ronaldo added his own spot-kick on 89 though the last word was Derby's as Barnes curled home a superb free kick to leave it 4-3 on aggregate and give the Rams pride in their defeat.

For Derby fans it had been a real adventure – but no one was too worried as there was an FA Cup battle against the old enemy Nottingham Forest just around the corner too, and eventually another crack at United.

Their bench contained two interesting twists too as striker Liam Dickinson was among the substitutes for his sole involvement in a match squad after arriving from

Stockport County the previous summer then departing on various loans, while defender Seb Hines had joined on loan from Middlesbrough.

He sat on the bench for both legs without getting on and was not involved in another squad before returning to Boro at the end of his loan.

As for the League Cup, the Rams did not win another game in the competition until August 2013 when they were 1-0 victors at Oldham Athletic.

Prior to that they were eliminated in 2009, 2010, 2011 and 2012 at the first round stage by lower division opposition.

48 v Nottingham Forest 3-2

4 February 2009. Attendance: 29,001
The City Ground. FA Cup Fourth Round Replay

DERBY COUNTY:
Bywater
Connolly
McEveley
Green
Commons
Savage
Hulse (Ellington 82)
Nyatanga
Teale
Barazite
Albrechtsen
Unused subs: Carroll (GK), Stewart, Villa,
Sterjovski, Todd, Pearson

Referee: Chris Foy

NOTTINGHAM FOREST:
Smith
Wilson
Chambers
Morgan
Breckin
Perch (Byrne 70)
McGugan
Tyson (Newbold 86)
McCleary (Heath 81)
Cohen
Thornhill
Unused subs: Darlow (GK), Bencherif, Reid,
Whitehurst

HECTIC fixture schedules meant that neither side would have wanted this game – and it's rare to say that when you're talking about a Derby County v Nottingham Forest fixture.

However, a 1-1 draw in the initial match at Pride Park Stadium thanks to Robert Earnshaw equalising for the visitors against his old club, who had been in front thanks to Rob Hulse's first-half goal, ensured that the two old rivals would have to try again.

And any game between Derby and Forest always has plenty of intrigue to it but this time that had gone up a fair bit because of both clubs' respective managerial situations.

The Forest hot-seat had been filled by Colin Calderwood in May 2006 and the Scot led the Reds to promotion in 2008 but, having returned to the Championship, they had won just four times by Christmas and the final straw came on Boxing Day as they went down 4-2 to Doncaster Rovers at the City Ground.

Calderwood's time in charge was up and two days later a 1-0 defeat at home to Ipswich Town, Derby's sixth defeat in the last nine games, meant it was all change at Pride Park and Paul Jewell resigned after just over a year in the job. This all happened before the third round of the FA Cup had even taken place and the speculation was flying about who would be taking charge at both clubs – only for both vacancies to be filled by men whose careers had been notable for their time with the opposition.

The first announcement came from the City Ground as Calderwood was replaced by Billy Davies, his fellow Scot, who hadn't worked since being sacked as Derby's manager in November 2007 after a rift opened between himself and Adam Pearson, at the time the Rams' new chairman.

Davies had guided Derby to the Premier League via that play-off final win at Wembley but took just minutes to seriously sour his relationship with the supporters and he was replaced by Jewell with relegation almost certain, even at a relatively early stage of the season.

The draw for the third round had already been made and sent Forest to Manchester City, though Davies didn't take charge of that match and left duties to caretaker John Pemberton, who oversaw a remarkable 3-0 win away to the newly-rich Premier League outfit.

Derby's challenge and subsequent route into round four was far more of a banana skin and their managerial situation had not been resolved by the time Chris Hutchings, Jewell's former assistant, led the side away to Conference National club Forest Green Rovers and they came through a 4-3 thriller.

You will have read about that match in an earlier chapter but it wasn't long before the hot-seat was filled as Derby went down the A38 to Burton Albion for their boss Nigel Clough, son of Brian, and the second-highest goalscorer in Forest's history.

The draw for the fourth round was made the day after the Forest Green match and two days before Clough was announced as Derby's new manager so as soon as he started his job he knew that he would soon be facing his old club in the dug-out of the Rams, while it also meant a quick return to his former home for Davies.

A serious family illness meant that, in the end, Davies was not present for the 1-1 draw and left his duties to his coaching staff, who had all been with him at Derby, but the need for a replay meant that Clough would be returning to the City Ground – where he had spent so many years as a player and where there was a stand named after his late father.

And looking ahead to the replay, Clough admitted, 'It will be somewhat emotional and a little bit strange with it being such a big game.

'But the main thing will be what happens on the pitch and about the supporters and atmosphere they generate.

'Having played there for a few years, it will certainly be familiar. Some things have changed there over the years, a couple of stands are different now, but the atmosphere that we used to get over the years when we did play Derby will be just the same.'

Davies was also looking forward to the occasion and said that he was only focused on success with his current employers, rather than thinking back to his time at Derby.

He said, 'I've got nothing to prove to Derby County, their fans or anybody else. I'm very satisfied with what was achieved during the period I was with them – I've moved on and don't have any bitter vendetta against the fans or the club.

'It's now time for me to look to the future and not the past and it's all about keeping Forest in the Championship and then looking beyond that.'

And just for good measure, as if a midweek FA Cup replay under the floodlights between Derby and Forest didn't have enough to get the juices flowing, the incentive was there to get through.

The draw for the fifth round had been made and the winners knew they would be rewarded with a home fixture against Manchester United – the defending Premier League, Champions League and Club World Cup winners, who had recently beaten Derby over two legs in the semi-final of the League Cup.

And like all local derby matches this one reached a fast pace right from the kick-off but unfortunately from the Rams' perspective, they did not get into their stride particularly quickly and they were punished after only two minutes.

Forest won a corner on their right and the Rams could only clear the ball out as far as Chris Cohen, who fired in a shot from the edge of the box that might have glanced off another player on the way through but soon nestled in the back of the net with Stephen Bywater beaten.

Kris Commons, back on his old ground for the first time since his controversial move along the A52 to Derby the previous summer, nearly got his new club back on level terms only for the home side to see good opportunities for a second wasted by Lewis McGugan and Nathan Tyson.

But with 14 minutes on the clock they were two clear as Tyson ran clear of the visiting defence and was taken down by Bywater, who was yellow-carded for his troubles, before the Forest man stepped up and emphatically fired in the resulting penalty.

The Forest faithful were in dreamland and expecting a cruise into the fifth round for their side but these matches are nothing if not topsy-turvy and the Rams were back in it on 27 minutes through leading scorer Rob Hulse, who was found delightfully by Gary Teale's cross for a neat header into the corner past Paul Smith.

Derby had looked likely to score before Hulse's goal and they continued to push for an equaliser before the break, though patience was a virtue and they were rewarded on the hour when they did level things up.

Teale was once again the creator from his left-wing position as he whipped in another inviting cross but this time the welcome recipient was central midfielder Paul Green, who timed his run perfectly to nod it home and spark off wild celebrations from the Derby supporters behind that goal in the lower tier of the Bridgford End.

Fans of both clubs might have been forgiven for settling for extra time at that point but neither set of players thought that way as the match moved from one end to the other with Green threatening for Derby and Garath McCleary forcing a save from Bywater.

Then came the crucial moment in the 74th minute. Commons, becoming ever more dangerous, cracked a shot against the post from distance and with Forest failing to clear properly, the former Red punished his old mates by creating space just outside the box and looping his shot beyond Smith, via a slight deflection off Wes Morgan, and into the back of the net. If the celebrations for the equaliser were wild, this time they were positively euphoric with Commons the centre of attention, both from players and supporters.

From there it was a case of seeing the job through for Derby and that they did with no real scares as Forest, stunned by the scale of the turnaround, failed to lift themselves for another push.

The post-match image of Derby captain Robbie Savage celebrating on the pitch, waving a black and white scarf above his head towards the ecstatic fans behind the goal, has become an iconic reminder of one of the club's most remarkable FA Cup ties.

If you are going to win a game away to your local rivals then coming from 2-0 down after a quarter of an hour or so to take it 3-2 has to be up there with the best.

And when that winning goal comes from a player who moved from one club to the other the previous summer, causing controversy in the process, the night is even sweeter.

Commons had, not surprisingly, been the recipient of constant stick and howls of abuse from his old fans but he answered them in the perfect way, though he declined the opportunity to speak to the media after the match.

As did Derby boss Clough, despite leading the Rams to their first win at the City Ground since 1971 when Brian was in charge, so it was left to coach Andy Garner to do the rounds of interviews and his use of the word 'unbelievable' was a perfect choice.

He said, 'That was an unbelievable night. We had a terrible start, but we felt that to get the goal back before half-time would put us in with a chance.

'We said that to the lads at half-time, that it was good for them to get back in the game, we said it was there if they wanted it and the second half was unbelievable.

'We were disappointed with the start to the game but the way we played after that, the commitment we showed, we're getting there.

'The players have shown a lot of character. You're maybe thinking at two down the game is over but tonight we have seen great character in all of the players.

'When you work as hard as they have done tonight you know you have got a chance.

'Kris can do things like that, he's a good player, and I'm sure he will enjoy that goal for a long time.'

In the home dressing room the mood was not so buoyant but Davies still found positives to take despite his side letting slip their commanding position.

He said, 'I'm disappointed at losing a two-goal lead. We scored a fantastic first goal from a well-worked corner kick but once we had a two-goal lead inexperience kicked in.

'We dropped off the game, we sat off them and allowed them to put crosses into the box and when it went to 2-1 I felt that was a big turning point.

'Derby showed more experience and more know-how at the start of the second half, they moved the ball around much better and then came back into the game with a similar goal – we didn't stop the cross, we didn't pick up in the box and they had a free header.

'My words to the players were clear: be very proud of what you have achieved in the sense of who you competed against, a side that's not long out of the Premier League that has spent their parachute payment and built up a massive squad.'

The result sent Forest spinning out of the FA Cup but for Derby it earned them a place in the last 16 of the competition for the second time in three years and that earlier-mentioned encounter with Manchester United.

That would be the third meeting of the year between United and Derby following the League Cup exploits in January and, mindful of his side's beating in the first leg of the semi-final, Sir Alex Ferguson took no chances and sent a stronger side down for the FA Cup match.

Their second visit to Pride Park in a matter of weeks might have resulted in a comfortable-looking 4-1 win but they needed to show all their mettle as Derby pushed them all the way.

Ryan Giggs was in sublime form and a joy to watch but the goals in the first half came from Nani and Darron Gibson, then Cristiano Ronaldo made it three early in the second period.

Derby had something to cheer when Miles Addison got one back but the final word was United's thanks to Danny Welbeck's curling late finish.

But before February was out, Clough's men had another memorable City Ground occasion to savour as they cruised to a 3-1 Championship win against Forest on their way to finishing 18th in the table, a place and a point above their red rivals.

v Leeds United 2-1

7 August 2010. Attendance: 26,761
Elland Road. Football League Championship

DERBY COUNTY:	LEEDS UNITED:
Bywater	Schmeichel
Brayford	Connolly
Roberts	Collins
Leacock	Naylor
Anderson (Barker HT)	Bessone
Bailey	Kilkenny (Clayton 77)
Savage	Sam (White 70)
Cywka (Pringle 74)	Howson (Grella 86)
Green	Johnson
Commons (Porter 84)	Becchio
Hulse	Watt
Unused subs: Deeney (GK), Buxton, Moxey, Doyle	*Unused subs:* Higgs (GK), Bruce, Bromby, Hughes

Referee: Neil Swarbrick

I
T doesn't matter how well you have fared in the campaign gone by – the opening day of the season is always an occasion to look forward to. And when that opening day sends Derby County away to Leeds United the interest levels go up by several notches.

As you will have read elsewhere in this book the rivalry between the two clubs goes back to the days of Brian Clough's Derby taking on Don Revie's Leeds in some titanic battles, followed by Clough's infamous 44 days in charge at Elland Road.

Even in more recent years the two clubs had faced off in some controversial matches but hadn't met in the Championship since the final day of the 2006/07 season when the Rams were 2-0 victors as they built towards their successful play-off campaign under Billy Davies, while the Whites arrived at Pride Park that May afternoon already relegated to League 1 with the final nail in their coffin a points deduction for going into administration days before. It would be their first spell ever below the top two tiers of English football.

Derby's stay in the top flight was famously short while Leeds were deducted further points for the 2007/08 season but they made a good fist of attempting to get back up at the first attempt, only losing out by a single goal to Doncaster Rovers in the play-off final at Wembley.

Rivalries were renewed in November 2008 when the draw for the fourth round of the League Cup paired the two at Pride Park, Derby going through 2-1 against their lower division opponents thanks to early goals from Tito Villa and Nathan Ellington to earn themselves a quarter-final place in the competition for the first time since 1990.

Leeds reached the play-offs again in 2008/09 but this time failed to reach Wembley as they went down 2-1 on aggregate to Millwall, who included former Derby midfielder Adam Bolder in their side for both legs – Bolder had previously scored for Derby in a 2-0 win at home to Leeds in January 2005. January 2009 had seen Nigel Clough take over as the Rams' manager and he did well to keep the side in the Championship before, in his first full campaign in charge, guiding his dad's old club to 14th in the table and nine points above the relegation zone.

But events in Yorkshire were to set this particular match up as Leeds, at the third time of asking, finally on promotion from League 1, although they did it the hard way by only clinching second spot on the final day of the season by coming from behind – with only ten men – to beat Bristol Rovers 2-1 at Elland Road.

They had also caused a stir in the FA Cup in January by winning 1-0 at Manchester United in one of the competition's biggest shocks of recent times.

And in a nice twist the fixture calendar gave them a home game against Derby for their first match back in the second tier, just as it had done in 2004 when they hosted the Rams on the opening day after relegation from the Premier League.

They won that one 1-0 then claimed a 3-1 success in the following season's Elland Road encounter thanks to a hat-trick from future Ram Rob Hulse but Derby had exacted a measure of revenge on their last visit in December 2006 when Giles Barnes headed the only goal in a 1-0 success, the Rams' first victory at the ground since November 1974.

The summer of 2010 had seen Derby busy in the transfer market, bringing in midfielder James Bailey and defender John Brayford in a double deal from Crewe Alexandra, along with turning the loans of Millwall winger David Martin – who had played for the Lions in both legs of their play-off semi-final against Leeds in 2009 – and Wigan Athletic forward Tomasz Cywka into permanent deals, and bringing in experienced Doncaster Rovers left-back Gareth Roberts on a free. Teenage American forward Conor Doyle signed in the days leading up to the game.

Notable departures were winger Gary Teale to Sheffield Wednesday, defender Jay McEveley to Barnsley, and his fellow stopper Paul Connolly, who had been Clough's first Derby captain in 2009 but had been allowed to leave – and joined Leeds.

Connolly was destined to make his Leeds debut against his old club and behind him was goalkeeper Kasper Schmeichel, son of the Manchester United great Peter, who had appeared against the Rams in the Premier League during the 1990s.

So with the scene well and truly set for a memorable opening day attentions turned to the televised Saturday evening encounter.

For Derby, facing a newly-promoted side for the third successive opening day having vanquished Peterborough United in 2009 and lost to Doncaster in 2008, the message was simple: lay down a marker.

Speaking to the *Derby Telegraph*, boss Clough said, 'It is another promoted side on the opening day and they will naturally be on a high but what a great fixture, and that is how we felt when it first came out.

'We are going to play and not be intimidated by anyone this season. And if you are going to play with no fear, which we are asking the players to do, let's show it at Elland Road because there will be no more intimidating place in the Championship.

'The confidence of the lads will grow if we can get off to a good start. That's why going to Leeds on the first day is brilliant and then we've got Cardiff at home.

'Let's see if we can get good results against two of the best teams in the division.'

In his bid to get the season off to the ideal start, Clough opted to continue with the 4-2-3-1 formation that he had been employing throughout the pre-season campaign.

Debuts were given to Brayford and Roberts, on the right and left of the back four respectively, as they flanked central defenders Russell Anderson and Dean Leacock.

James Bailey also lined up from the off in one of the two holding midfield positions, alongside skipper Robbie Savage, leaving a fluid-looking three of Cywka, Paul Green and Kris Commons in behind line-leader Hulse, back on his old ground.

The big surprise on the bench was the presence of Shaun Barker, the 2009/10 Player of the Year, having not kicked a ball at all during pre-season because of an ongoing thigh problem and having only spent an hour the previous day training with the squad.

Derby were right at it from the first whistle and Commons went close before a minute had passed following good work from Bailey, who settled in quickly to his new surroundings.

And it was no surprise when the scoring was opened with 13 minutes on the clock as Derby's football continued to bamboozle Leeds.

This time Green was the architect, driving forward with a surging run before feeding Hulse who, from a tight angle to the right of goal, hammered his shot in at Schmeichel's near post before declining to celebrate against his old club.

The lead lasted for just three minutes as some slack defensive work let the home side in for an equaliser.

Leacock's loose pass was seized upon by Jonny Howson ahead of Savage and the Leeds youngster then pulled the ball back for Luciano Becchio to tap in from close range.

Leeds stepped it up and Richard Naylor hit the bar but they were behind again before the half-hour and once more it was down to some excellent football from Derby.

Bailey and Green combined to find Commons, who had the Leeds defence going backwards before slipping his pass to Cywka, who was fouled inside the box by Lloyd Sam.

Commons stepped up to calmly roll the spot-kick past Schmeichel, who spectacularly stopped the Scottish international putting Derby 3-1 up before the break.

Derby were less fluent after half-time but their display was no less pleasing as they dug in with great determination, typified by Barker who came on at half-time to replace the injured Anderson and looked as if he had never been away.

His combination with Leacock meant Stephen Bywater had very little to do in a second period that was notable for some remarkable saves by his opposite number.

Schmeichel, signed during the summer from Notts County, blocked one point-blank effort from Green but saved his best for a double effort that denied Hulse and then Barker. The save from Hulse, low down to a powerful shot, was brilliant enough but Schmeichel then got up to somehow divert Barker's effort from the rebound away to safety.

It was as good a save as you will see anywhere but his outfield colleagues did not show the same form as they struggled to mount a serious threat on Derby's goal, only going close with eight minutes left as Roberts headed Neill Collins's effort off the line.

So for the second season in succession Derby had beaten a newly-promoted side 2-1 – and they had laid down the marker that Clough was looking for.

It wasn't just the result that was eye-opening, though that was good enough, as the Rams' performance was a seriously impressive way to start the campaign.

To send a young team with several debutants into the hostile environment of Elland Road and see them come back with a victory was a fine achievement by Clough – who had taken his players through a somewhat interesting pre-match routine on their arrival.

In what could be perceived as a move straight out of his dad's play book, Clough and his players got off their team coach early and walked the last few hundred yards to the stadium.

Mobile phone video footage later surfaced on YouTube of the last stretch as the squad walked through the route reserved for the bus and were flanked by fans either side of them.

The welcome from the Leeds followers was not as lively as it could have been but it was noticeable that the players barely batted an eyelid, so focused were they on the task in hand.

But was it a psychological move from Clough, sending out a message that his players had no fear?

The answer, he revealed, was far more simple. 'We were early,' Clough said when speaking to the press after the match.

He continued, 'We did not park the bus, it just dropped us off because we were early and the changing room is pretty small here and warm, so we didn't want to be in it too long before the game.

'So we just had a last five-minute stroll and soaked up the atmosphere. I don't think many of the locals recognised us. If they did, they didn't say anything.'

The move was also well received by goalscorer Commons, who said in the *Derby Telegraph*, 'The gaffer mentioned it was a beautiful day and said it would be a nice walk for us. With the timing of the kick-off I think he was keen to have a walk and loosen our legs.

'It was a chance for us to have a look and see what the stadium's about. We've signed a few young lads who have played lower-league football and a walk to the stadium opened their eyes to what sort of occasion it was.

'There were plenty of fans about but we didn't get any stick – they just asked if the coach had broken down!'

The result was certainly a pleasing one for everyone connected with Derby and it was their fourth win in succession against Leeds.

Rams fans always feel something of a sense of triumph whenever the Yorkshire side are beaten and Clough was asked, given the clubs' previous history and his father's part in that, if this one was even more satisfying.

'No, not at all,' he replied. 'I feel more pleasure because they would not let my little lad, William, walk on the pitch an hour and a quarter before the game. Under-16s are not allowed on the pitch. It's a club rule, apparently.

'So I get more pleasure winning after that than something that happened 36 years ago.'

But if Clough was hoping that the win would indeed give Derby the chance of a flying start to the season, his players let him down.

The Rams were knocked out of the League Cup three days later at League 2 side Crewe and didn't pick up a second Championship victory until 25 September, by which time they had signed Spanish former Real Madrid forward Alberto Bueno on loan from Real Valladolid.

Beating Palace 5-0 sparked a purple patch that left Derby fourth in the table by the end of November but the downfall from there was startling as they won just four more games all season, a run that also included an FA Cup exit away to non-league Crawley Town, and finished 19th, seven points above the bottom three.

The campaign's final victory came in April as Leeds were beaten for a fifth time in succession, 2-1 at Pride Park, and doubles over them in 2011/12 and 2012/13 meant that by the summer of 2013 Derby had recorded an amazing NINE straight victories against the Yorkshire club!

50 v Nottingham Forest 2-1

17 September 2011. Attendance: 27,536
The City Ground. Football League Championship

DERBY COUNTY:	NOTTINGHAM FOREST:
Fielding	Camp
Brayford	Gunter
O'Brien	Morgan
Shackell	Chambers
Roberts	Cohen (Lynch 32)
B Davies	Reid (McGugan 68)
Bryson	Moussi
Hendrick	Greening (Findley 61)
Ward (Tyson 66)	Majewski
Cywka (Legzdins 2)	Derbyshire
Robinson (Anderson 87)	Miller
Unused subs: S Davies, Croft	*Unused subs:* Smith (GK), Moloney
Referee: Scott Mathieson	

NO matter how exciting the fixtures may be, there is never really a good time to play a local derby. It is definitely rare to find both clubs in fine form or going through a slump at the same time – usually it is one doing better than the other.

That was not quite the case this time around although Derby had won their first four league matches for the first time in 105 years, while Forest had only won one of their first seven.

The point about stability was also a key one as Nigel Clough had just started his third full season in charge of Derby and although his contract was due to expire at the end of the 2011/12 season, the noises coming out of the boardroom suggested his stay would be extended.

Forest had been through managerial turmoil over recent months with Billy Davies departing in typically turbulent style, despite having guided the club to a second successive play-off semi-final.

He was replaced by another man with strong Derby connections, former Rams player and coach Steve McClaren, who was back in English football after spells in Holland with FC Twente and Germany with VfL Wolfsburg following his disastrous reign as England boss.

Both teams went into the autumn afternoon fixture having lost their previous two matches and were looking for a good result to get their season going again.

And from Derby's perspective there was an element of restoring some pride against the old enemy after the previous season's meetings, which had seen Forest do the double and rack up a 5-2 win at the City Ground.

That match was in December 2010 but there had been such a turnaround at Pride Park in the months afterwards that only one Ram, John Brayford, would be playing this time around having also lined up in that post-Christmas disaster.

'Is that a plus or a minus? I'm not sure,' Clough said of whether that would make any difference to his side's mentality.

'I think a plus in terms of they will not have any baggage associated with the fixture over the years but a minus is that it might take them a little bit by surprise in the first ten or 15 minutes. But it took the senior pros by surprise last season.

'We think we know what we are going to get from the players now, even the youngsters. When you put Mark O'Brien and Jeff Hendrick on the pitch, as with the majority of players we are putting on the pitch at the moment, I think we get a consistent level of performance. That has been seen in the first six games, certainly.

'We know we haven't played brilliantly at times, but we have been hard to beat, hard to score against and that is what we want to take to Nottingham tomorrow.

'We know what the game means to the fans, it means the same to us. Don't forget, underneath it all we are all supporters.'

Clough had appeared in the fixture for Forest during his own playing days, as had Jonny Metgod and Gary Crosby, two members of his coaching staff at Derby. Their colleagues Andy Garner and Martin Taylor had also lined up for the Rams against Forest.

'It has been part of their lives as well and the things that we did then we think some of them are just as relevant today as they were 20-odd years ago,' said Clough.

'People talk about the Merseyside and Manchester derbies. We think this derby is more akin to Manchester and Liverpool. It is not in the same city.

'We are half an hour apart, or something like that, and I think the dislike is intensified because of that distance. Everton and Liverpool don't like each other but they are still together a bit more, the same with Manchester United and Manchester City.

'But the rivalry tends to be a bit more intense with that 20- or 30-mile gap between the two, like Manchester United and Leeds.

'Whether it was because we were playing, I don't know, but the derbies didn't seem as hyped up as the Derby and Forest game has been in the last few years.'

Derby were backed by 4,000 fans in the Bridgford End stand but the travelling supporters were horrified by what unfolded right in front of them just a minute into the game. Goalkeeper Frank Fielding tangled with Forest's Ishmael Miller on the edge of the six-yard box and was given a red card by referee Scott Mathieson for denying what was deemed to be a clear goalscoring opportunity.

Forest fans were in total agreement with the decision but those of a black and white persuasion were not, and argued that Miller had got his shot away before the unavoidable collision happened while Gareth Roberts had also cleared the ball to safety.

Their pleas fell on deaf ears so Fielding walked and on came Adam Legzdins for his first appearance since signing in the summer from Burton Albion and Tomasz Cywka was the unlucky man to make way.

Legzdins had barely taken his position on the goal line before he was picking the ball out of the back of the net following Andy Reid's emphatic penalty.

But what goes around often comes around and on 29 minutes Derby found themselves level after a goal that the home fans felt should not have stood.

Jeff Hendrick picked up the ball in midfield and drove away from Forest's Chris Cohen, who went down having seemingly fallen awkwardly.

It was apparent early on that the player was seriously injured but stopping play is the referee's decision and Mathieson waved for the action to continue so Derby's players were well within their rights not to kick the ball out, despite Forest's complaints.

The ball eventually found its way to Jamie Ward out on the left wing. Ward skipped past two defenders and got to the goal line before getting inside the Forest box and somehow squeezing his shot in the narrowest of gaps at the near post past Lee Camp, the former Derby goalkeeper and Ward's Northern Ireland international colleague.

With the game level at half-time the home fans were calling for their players to raise their game, which they did early in the second period.

Reid went close twice and Matt Derbyshire almost got a toe to a cross that any contact whatsoever would have diverted in.

But Derby were not prepared to lie down and protected Legzdins well, then could have gone 2-1 up themselves through Hendrick.

The young Irishman was picked out delightfully by a Ben Davies cross but somehow Hendrick managed to place his header wide of the post when it seemed simpler to score.

Such moments can destroy a young player but with 72 minutes gone Hendrick came up with the game's crucial moment.

Derby won a rare corner on the right and Forest failed to clear their lines, only succeeding in finding Davies just outside the box. Davies rolled the ball sideways to Hendrick, whose curling low right-footed shot smacked of composure belying his young age and nestled neatly in the bottom-left corner to leave Camp helpless.

Hendrick immediately ran to the edge of the turf and celebrated right in front of the massed ranks of Derby fans before being joined by his fellow players.

The home supporters, and the players themselves for that matter, could see what appeared as if it would be a straightforward home win against their biggest rivals drifting away. Forest fans also had something else to grumble about in the 66th minute when Nathan Tyson arrived for his Derby debut.

Tyson had been at Forest since January 2006 but opted for a summer 2011 move to Pride Park at the end of his contract, echoing what Kris Commons had done in 2011, and injury had prevented him from appearing for his new employers until the return to his old home.

The home faithful also directed their anger towards chief executive Mark Arthur who they seemingly blamed for a lack of investment in new players over the previous summer.

Their current crop did mount something of a late charge in their bid to rescue something from the game but Derby's defence, with Jason Shackell and Mark O'Brien outstanding in the centre, were in no mood to give anything away and Legzdins dealt with everything that came his way.

Clough chose the word 'staggering' as a perfect way of summing up his side's performance when talking to the media after the match.

He said, 'In the context of the moment, and coming off the back of consecutive defeats and against the adversity of the opening two minutes, I thought it was an absolutely remarkable performance – staggering.

'It was beyond what we could have expected. I would have taken a draw at any point during the game. It is about honesty, hard work and spirit. We have got that in abundance in the dressing room.'

Match-winner Hendrick added, 'Jamie Ward and Theo Robinson were straight over to me to tell me to keep my head up [after his missed header] – and that helped me a lot.

'Sometimes, people can hammer you for missing a chance like that but they kept my spirits up and made sure I kept going. The whole squad is very close at the moment and we are all working hard for each other.

'Winning against our local rivals makes it even better and it will bring us closer. The team spirit is unreal.

'Morale had maybe gone down a bit after the last couple of games, although we felt we played well in those matches. Those results didn't go our way but we made amends against Forest.'

Derby went on to beat Millwall 3-0 in their next match, and had they have beaten Barnsley at Pride Park a few days later they would have gone top of the table for the first time since 2007.

That game was a 1-1 draw and they only then picked up two more three-pointers before Christmas, when they started a run of four successive victories to end 2011 and start 2012.

Momentum stalled with a 0-0 draw at Burnley and a 3-2 defeat at Barnsley which should have sent them into the return against Forest.

That was scheduled for Sunday 5 February but was called off on the morning of the match due to the heavy snowfall that had swept across the country, leading to many of the roads in and around Derby being dangerous to travel on.

Forest had lost nine of their previous 11 in the Championship prior to 5 February but they had bigger issues to deal with as the night before the originally-scheduled date, owner and former chairman Nigel Doughty died suddenly at the age of just 54.

Doughty had stood down from the chair in October 2011, just a couple of weeks after the defeat to Derby, in a period of turmoil at the City Ground.

Forest had been beaten 3-1 at home to Birmingham City and McClaren resigned as manager afterwards so Doughty, accepting responsibility for appointing McClaren in the first place, also stepped back.

Former Forest boss Frank Clark replaced Doughty at the top and the manager's job went to Steve Cotterill.

The return against Forest was re-arranged for Tuesday 13 March with Derby 16th in the table and Forest below them.

It was a typically closely-fought affair at Pride Park on a night that saw the atmosphere at times turn nasty with a small section of Derby fans singing unpleasant songs about Doughty, and some Forest followers responding in kind when Rams skipper Shaun Barker was prone in front of them with the most serious of knee injuries.

But once again it all went Derby's way though they had to wait until the 94th minute before securing the 1-0 win thanks to Jake Buxton's effort, which confirmed a Rams double over the Reds for the first time since the 1971/72 season under Brian Clough.

Rather unsurprisingly, this particular win behind enemy lines has gone down in legend as far as Derby fans are concerned.

A group of supporters raised funds to have a plane fly a banner reading 'WE ONLY HAD 10 MEN – NEVER FORGOTTEN' over the City Ground and Pride Park on 19 November, when Forest beat Ipswich Town 3-2 before going SEVEN games without scoring in front of their own fans.

And the Tuesday after the September success, one Rams fan had an advertisement placed in the Pets, Lost and Found section of the *Nottingham Post*. It read:

'Lead belonging to dog (red). Lost in the West Bridgford area about 14.30pm, Saturday, September 17. Priceless sentimental value. Tel: 01332 121212 or 01332 121212.'